The Modern Arabic Bible

Edinburgh Studies in Modern Arabic Literature
Series Editor: Rasheed El-Enany

edinburghuniversitypress.com/series/small

The Modern Arabic Bible

Translation, Dissemination and Literary Impact

Rana Issa

EDINBURGH
University Press

Edinburgh University Press is one of the leading university presses in the UK. We publish academic books and journals in our selected subject areas across the humanities and social sciences, combining cutting-edge scholarship with high editorial and production values to produce academic works of lasting importance. For more information visit our website: edinburghuniversitypress.com

Edinburgh University Press Ltd
The Tun – Holyrood Road
12 (2f) Jackson's Entry
Edinburgh EH8 8PJ

Typeset in 11/15 Times New Roman by
Cheshire Typesetting Ltd, Cuddington, Cheshire, and
printed and bound by CPI Group (UK) Ltd,
Croydon, CR0 4YY

A CIP record for this book is available from the British Library

ISBN 978 1 4744 6715 5 (hardback)
ISBN 978 1 4744 6717 9 (webready PDF)
ISBN 978 1 4744 6718 6 (epub)

Contents

Figures

Series Editor's Foreword

Edinburgh Studies in Modern Arabic Literature is a unique series that aims to fill a glaring gap in scholarship in the field of modern Arabic literature. Its dedication to Arabic literature in the modern period (that is, from the nineteenth century onwards) is what makes it unique among series undertaken by academic publishers in the English-speaking world. Individual books on modern Arabic literature in general or aspects of it have been and continue to be published sporadically. Series on Islamic studies and Arab/ Islamic thought and civilisation are not in short supply either in the academic world, but these are far removed from the study of Arabic literature qua literature, that is, imaginative, creative literature as we understand the term when, for instance, we speak of English literature or French literature. Even series labelled 'Arabic/Middle Eastern Literature' make no period distinction, extending their purview from the sixth century to the present, and often including non-Arabic literatures of the region. This series aims to redress the situation by focusing on the Arabic literature and criticism of today, stretching its interest to the earliest beginnings of Arab modernity in the nineteenth century. The need for such a dedicated series, and generally for the redoubling of scholarly endeavour in researching and introducing modern Arabic literature to the Western reader, has never been stronger. Among activities and events heightening public, let alone academic, interest in all things Arab, and not least Arabic literature, are the significant growth in the last decades of the translation of contemporary Arab authors from all genres, especially fiction, into English; the higher profile of Arabic literature internationally since the award of the Nobel Prize in Literature to Naguib Mahfouz in 1988; the growing number of Arab authors living in the Western diaspora and writing both in English and Arabic; the adoption of such authors and others by mainstream, high-circulation publishers, as opposed to the academic publishers of the past; and the establishment of prestigious prizes, such as the International Prize for Arabic Fiction, popularly referred to in the Arab world as the Arabic Booker, run by the Man Booker Foundation, which brings huge publicity to the shortlist and winner every year, as well as translation contracts into English and other languages. It is therefore part of the ambition of this series that it will increasingly address a wider reading public beyond its natural territory of students and researchers in Arabic and world literature. Nor indeed is the academic readership of the series expected to be confined to specialists in literature in the light of the growing trend for interdisciplinarity, which increasingly sees scholars crossing field boundaries in their research tools and coming up with findings that equally cross discipline borders in their appeal.

This latest addition to nineteenth-century studies of Arabic thought and literature in this series, will pair fittingly with one of its earlier titles, namely Abdulrazzak Patel's *The Arab* Nahda: *the Making of the Intellectual and Humanist Movement* (2013) and not just because both books are studies of the nineteenth century. For while Abdulrazzak Patel focuses on significant Muslim figures of the Nahda, Rana Issa studies some of their Christian partners in the making of the Arab *nahda* with particular reference to translators of the Bible. This however is a study that goes beyond an examination of translations of the Bible into modern Arabic. This is because the two authors Rana Issa focuses on, i.e., Ahmad Faris Al-Shidyaq and Butrus al-Bustani, are colossal figures in the history of the evolution of modern Arabic language and literature, the translation of the Bible being just one element of their huge modernising endeavours. Focusing on their biblical translations will serve as key to their wider efforts to take Arabic language and literature into realms of modernity, where it had yet to venture. The book engages with its material in its historical context while benefiting from perspectives of translation studies, postcolonial studies and world literature.

Professor Rasheed El-Enany,
Series Editor,
Emeritus Professor of Modern Arabic Literature,
University of Exeter

Acknowledgements

This book is the direct outcome of a decade of labour, of agitated nights staring into empty space in different rooms, of travels to new and old cities, of visiting magnificent libraries, and libraries whose present poverty cannot beat their past ambitions, of random meetings with generous people, of times of longing for a clear mind and a shorter sojourn away from home. In those years I have been grateful for and profoundly moved by the spiritedness and kindness that good people everywhere share.

Gratitude, says the master Arab lexicographer, Ibn Manzūr, is like thankfulness; yet thankfulness is only for a deed performed, while gratitude is more general; you are grateful to a person for his beautiful character, for who he is, and not only his deeds. It is in this sense that I am grateful to Helge Jordheim, whose solid charm and fearsome intelligence has been transformative in every way, from the moment he agreed to become my supervisor during my doctoral years, to the friendship that I have come to rely on and trust many years after. Tarek el-Ariss has been a friend and mentor whose passion for the literary and whose impeccable sensitivity in describing our darkest moments, coupled with his forgiving relations to people, have pushed me to find my own voice, and nurtured me through long discussions and gestures of care. Sonja Mejcher Atassi must be thanked for facilitating my transition from a young scholar to an assistant professor grappling with writing my first book while balancing between teaching and service. Hala Auji and Teresa Pepe have been there along the way as friends and peers, we have shared chapters, proposals, versions and drinks, and I am deeply grateful for their scholarly solidarity and candid empathy. To Jorunn Økland and Ragnhild Zorgati I owe a feminist encouragement from more senior scholars who were conversation partners as well as political allies, and who spoke to me about what being a woman in academia sometimes entails.

I am grateful for the grants and scholarships that made my research possible. The Kultrans project at UiO financed the doctoral work that started this book and allowed me to visit archives in Cambridge, Oxford and Beirut. With Helge Jordheim, I received several grants from the Norwegian Research Council that facilitated my post-doctoral research phase in Paris and elsewhere. With a Houghton Library fellowship and a grant from the Faculty of Arts and Sciences at the American University of Beirut, I was able to spend a month rummaging through the archives of the American Board of Commissioners for Foreign Missions in 2017. I was also able to spend two months developing the outline for this book at the Center of Advanced Studies in Oslo in 2019. I received a generous private donation to support my research on Butrus al-Bustani from the Bustani family and have been deeply grateful to Samir Bustani and Kamran Rastegar for their faith in my work. I would also like to thank the journals and the editors that have sent my work to rigorous peer review and contributed to making this book particularly gratifying to work on. A small section of Chapter Four occurred in a longer form in the *Journal of Semitic Studies*, and a section of Chapter Five is more expanded in the *Journal of Arabic Literature*.

Many colleagues and friends have been instrumental in providing me with feedback for this book. Humphrey Davies was a good friend and mentor and his feedback on this book is invaluable. He will always be remembered with fondness and love; his passing away is a great loss for me personally and for the discipline. Chapters received feedback from Hilary Kilpatrick, he died since I wrote this and I want to pay a better tribute to him a little earlier. Tarif Khalidi, Anna Ziajka Stanton, Zeina Halabi, Marwa Elshakrey, Heather Sharkey, Elias Khoury, Fawwaz Traboulsi and Peter Hill. I am indebted to their collegiality and effort. Orit Bashkin read my dissertation and left me with feedback that I had to battle with for many years and Ilham Khuri-Makdisi's support for me from the early beginnings of this project has been so heartwarming. Michael Allan's sunny support and Stephen Sheehi's militant solidarity were necessary for my growing belief in my own abilities to work through the Bible. George Sabra, the late Rev. Ghassan Khalaf, Elie Dennaoui and Miriam Lindgren Hjälm have been most welcoming to my efforts to write about a book dear to their hearts and have been crucial for my growing sensitivity to the Bible. My students who read the Bible alongside me, and who challenged me to reformulate certain positions through the questions they brought with them to the classroom, allowed me to understand the relevance this story has to present times. I especially would like to thank the brilliant Rita Raad, for being a dependable and smart research assistant, whose eye for detail, and dedication to scholarship was the touch of grace I needed to finish this book. Randa Azkul's assistance with cataloguing my archival collection was much appreciated.

To Nada Akkaoui, Olfa Saadaoui and Samia my mother, I owe the time I actually wrote the book. These tender women provided me with the quietude and care needed to pursue my writing schedule and were happy to see me work and enjoy myself. Line Khateeb took me in at my most traumatised moments following the explosion in Beirut in August 2020, providing her home, care and support as I tried to battle PTSD and finish writing this manuscript, and I am most grateful for her friendship and the generosity of her family. Jumana Manna and Zeina Bali have been regular interlocutors, friends whose intelligence and love I have depended upon for strength all those years. I am thankful for the continuous friendship and support of Izzat Darwaze who always opens his home to me in London, his advice and connections are always so welcome and so valuable. My ex-husband Bendik Sørvig continues to remain a friend and a facilitator of my work-life balance.

Suneela Mubayi's support cannot be overstated, with the labour she exerted reading through the manuscript. Her loving support includes hours and days of bantering about Arabic culture across time and genre, and her knowledge of Arabic was in many instances instructive to this book. Ben Koerber's friendship and solidarity was manifested in his reading through the entire manuscript and encouraging me to submit it. Amal, Nour, Hakim and Issa_with_kidz, so special, so special to me, thank you for being so proud of me. The book must thank all these people for coming into the world. It has been an exhilarating experience that has taught me that I can depend on people, and build community, sutured around a book, bringing unlikely groups of people together, all of them nourishing me and allowing me to cultivate my writing and the daily resolve it takes to see a book like this one into publication.

Note on Transliteration and Abbreviations

Following house style, Arabic names and terms have not been transliterated in the main text. You can find the transliterated forms of these words in the index. When transcription is applied to articulate the phonetic value of the word, I have depended on the *IJMIS* transcription style as my guide.

Dedicated to my students at the American University of Beirut, whose curiosity vitalises and gives hope. To students who cannot afford private education, to those who wanted to be students but were too poor to afford it – in praise of your talents and the nurture you deserve.

Introduction

This book examines the history of modern Arabic Bible's translation as one of the key discursive spaces that shaped our inquiries into the problem of modernity. As this book argues, the Bible provides an ideal example for the study of translation *temporally*. Through a comparison of Western missionary protagonists, and the local translators Butrus al-Bustani (1819–83) and Ahmad Faris al-Shidyaq (1804–87), I explore translation through its temporal dimensions in order to illuminate the earliest beginnings of some of the ideas about the past that we carry today. I claim that translation's temporalities entangle the Bible with modernity and set standards for how to write, transfer, publish and read books. I further propose that translation's temporalities are not just located in Walter's Benjamin's definition of translation as the 'afterlife' of a particular text, but also include larger temporal processes that are mediated in how the Bible came to be perceived as a quintessentially modern text in the nineteenth century. By turning to the Bible to explore the changes in the perception of Arabic language and literature in modernity, I suggest that a literary history from a translational perspective cannot be subordinated to the linguistic – as is often proposed in translation studies and its current deployments of the concept of 'untranslatability'. I turn to conceptual history and its temporal focus and borrow the theory of 'multiple temporalities'[1] into translation studies in order to suggest that the discourse of modernity is a linguistic response to, and intervention into, the transformations in the political economy of globalisation that can be exemplified in many objects, including the Bible and its transformation into an exchange commodity. In the *Modern Arabic Bible*, I argue that translation performed a synchronistic labour and that this labour resulted in identifying these practices with modernity. Through this book, I aim to pursue this claim about modernity's synchronising work towards the entanglements that reveal the negotiation of a common modernity that is nevertheless incommensurable with itself, with only relative standards of measurement.

The task of studying translation thus becomes the key to unlocking how ideologies of language and literature responded to as well as shaped the historical context. In this sense, I select details that reveal how the Bible was produced as an exchange commodity. I show that translation is not just a technical activity nor is it solely an occasion for the circulation of texts across linguistic borders, but it is a contingent event that is shaped by intention and mediates the historical dynamics of its context; translation continues and prolongs a tradition, turns a text into tradition, as well as facilitates the continued relevance of a past text for a new time.

The nineteenth century was punctuated by a series of major Bible publishing events around the world. Translated into more than eighty languages in the nineteenth century, the Bible became, in the space of a few decades, the most widely translated and distributed text, a position that it has not relinquished since then, resulting today in a multilingual library of Bible versions comprising more than a thousand languages, and in many competing versions for the large languages.[2] Some of those languages already had Bibles published in their vernaculars. Such is the case with Arabic. It boasts of a Bible tradition that goes as far back as the seventh century, and possibly even earlier. In the nineteenth century, at least six different translations were undertaken and more than two dozen more were reinvented by the movable type of the modern printing presses. These Bible translations are considered important literary events that helped shape the intellectual innovations of Arab modernity, provoking new attitudes towards language and literature in the wake of renewed contact between Europe and the Ottoman Empire. Unlike other Western textual commodities that either preceded or followed these translations, the Bible was not an importation of a Western text. Yet in the nineteenth century, it became associated with Western missionaries whose sense of identity was integrally linked to thinking of the Bible as a foundational

text. Equipped to produce cheap Bibles, American and British persever-
ance transformed scripture into an exchange commodity and contributed
to shaping the book market that characterised the so-called 'period of
awakening and renaissance', the *nahda*, as a modern textual era.

For the translation of the Arabic Bible in the nineteenth century, the
death of the foreign evangelists meant that local helpers were released
from their contractual obligations. Upon the death of British missionary
Samuel Lee and American missionary Eli Smith, the young local helpers, Ahmad Faris al-Shidyaq and Butrus al-Bustani, chose to terminate
their employment with the missionary institutions. They left the Bible
translation project unfinished and went on to become foundational figures
of Arabic modernity. Despite the trajectories that death would interrupt,
the relationships these local translators cultivated with the missionaries
were crucial for encouraging these men to walk out on a secretarial fate as
scribes in the employ of the church or the local emir, and into a capitalist
economy of book markets and lucrative authorship. By comparing their
divergent conceptions of the past, this book explores how their employment as Bible translators working for American, British and Jesuit missionaries worlded their perceptions of their native language and expanded
their literary sources of reference. Through the Bible, they acquired access
to a burgeoning field of world literary production that relied on translation
and shipping to disseminate a select number of books around the globe.
They were in other words at the beginning of a wave that culminates today
in the discipline of World Literature. This newly worlded consciousness
connected them far beyond the neighbouring languages and regions that
encircled them. Their thinking around Arabic as a global language and
literature took shape. The Bible occasioned a literary transformation that
broke with centuries of Arabic Bible translation, which had typically been
produced by the scribal Christian communities that bred these translators
and provided them with an education.

Literary historiography has been too quick to draw conclusions
about the symbolic role of the Bible translations and their Syro-Lebanese
Christian translators in propagating a celebratory discourse of modernity.
In Anglophone scholarship, George Antonius was quick to proclaim
the American missionaries as 'pioneers' that instigated 'the intellectual

effervescence which marked the first stirrings of the Arab revival'.[3] For Albert Hourani, meanwhile, Christian Arab writers, unlike their Muslim counterparts, were quick to convert their attention to the missionaries and '[break] away from their communities into the comparative freedom of the new Protestant community created by American and British missionaries', and were emboldened to imbue their writing with 'an "anti-clerical" element absent from that of their Muslim contemporaries'.[4] The same views are also propagated by a wide range of scholars. From the intellectual history of Hisham Sharabi where Christians are dubbed as 'Westernisers', to the chronology of Arab literary modernity presented by Sabry Hafez that despite its analytical merits, boxes the foundational figures of the *nahda* along sectarian lines, to Shmuel Moreh's Eurocentric vision of Arabic literature, the Christian Arabs of the Levant and the translations of the Bible that they worked on are too often credited with offering 'modern solutions to linguistic problems', 'reviving' the Arabic language from its 'fastidious inertia' and even in 'rooting modern literary form in the Bible'.[5] Despite the divergent political positions of those scholars, they seem nevertheless to be in agreement that the Bible was a successful tool (albeit not the only tool) that 'liberated' the Arabic language 'from the shackles of tradition'. The problem with these proclamations rests in their essentialist understanding of Christianity as an identity that defines those who carry it, particularly in how this identity becomes loaded with paradoxical modernistic values about secularism's break with tradition on the path to progress. Thinking about translation Pierre Cachia writes,

> Christian Arabs – mainly Syrians – were in fact to make disproportionately large contributions to several aspects of the Nahdah in its early stages, if only because (at a time when group loyalties were formed on religious rather than national or ethnic axes) they found it easier than did the Muslims to accept ideas originating in, or transmitted by, Christian Europe.[6]

Those Christians, as Cachia argues, were quick to redirect 'their [literary] energies towards far-reaching reforms for which acquaintance with the achievements of "the west" has been and to a large extent remains essential'.[7] They had in common with the 'west' the Bible, which as Moreh argued was the basis of modern poetic technique for both 'western' authors as well as the 'Christian Arab' authors associated with modernisa-tion.[8] Even when scholars have been careful not to bind the *nahda* writers to their religious identities, they displaced the question of identity onto the Bible as one of the primary vessels for modernisation. We encounter such quick leaps of faith in Samir Kassir's historiography of Beirut, where he writes that these Bible translations left 'a profound mark on the moderni-zation of Arabic',[9] without considering what this modernisation entailed for the language. In an otherwise economic history of modern Lebanon by the Marxist scholar Fawwaz Traboulsi, the nineteenth century translations are recollected as 'landmark[s] in [the effort] to liberate Arabic writing from its torpor and conventional styles . . . as the process of translation contributed to the innovation of Arabic prose'.[10] Traboulsi repeats a view on the pre-nineteenth century as widespread as it is erroneous. For the so-called period of *inhitat* or 'decay' was far from being unproductive but has suffered from a narrow understanding of the function of language and literature in the service of national causes. In all these histories, and despite the placement of the Bible at the centre of a narrative of modernity, it remains scantily mentioned or analysed, with at best a cursory explora-tion of any concrete influences that the Bible had on Arabic language and literature in the nineteenth century. An important exception remains the late Sasson Somekh's brief article about the influence of the modern translations of the Bible on subsequent works of Arabic literature. As he concludes in a study on the history of the Bible translations and their inter-textual traces on modern Arabic literature, 'it is obvious that these features were in large measure generated by the incursion of Western culture into the modern Arab works'.[11] Somekh also credits these Bibles with major contributions to the *nahda*. This book departs from the master narrative of the *nahda*, by attending to one of its most famous literary landmarks through a framework that analyses, rather than takes for granted, how Christian literary identity was constructed, and how it became imbued with the temporal values of modernity.

The *nahda* acquired literary value not only as an emblem for a period, but also as a set of salubrious literary practices associated with the task of enlightening the nation and rescuing Arabic from the stronghold of tradi-tion and Islam. This master narrative of the *nahda* begins with Napoleon's invasion of Egypt in 1798 and with the arrival of Western missionaries in Syro-Lebanon in the early 1800s. In the Levant, local Christian authors were its main catalysts, but it also included some Muslim authors who identified the need to modernise, secularise, and emulate European mores and attitudes to knowledge and society. In those narratives the Bible is written into a historical tale of modernity that has endured since Jurji Zaydan's *History of Arabic Literature*, which proclaimed that this modernity, which he also referred to as the *nahda*, was an 'external development', brought about by colonial and missionary interests, and introduced through translation to Syria, Egypt and other Arab regions.[12] Its external weight is what distinguishes it from earlier moments of *nahda* that Arabic culture experienced across time, from the pre-Islamic period until the Abbasid era, when the *nahdas* suddenly stopped, until the final awakening of the nineteenth century. In this master narrative, the *nahda* is constructed as a debt to the West, stripping local actors of their agency in the historical shape that it came to take. In his gratitude to the West, Zaydan constructed continuities that were based on translation, and produced ruptures with a long tradition of Arabic writing that he relegated to irrelevance and untranslatability. This book instead argues that attention to Zaydan's predecessors reveals how this master narrative came to be, and what consequences it has had on the development of Arabic language and literature.

The *nahda* is a periodising label that groups together a collection of texts produced at the same time. It is a synchronistic label that has kept a long line of scholars busy with unpacking and learning about a period that witnessed increased cultural iterations. The metaphor of 'awakening' suggests a shared temporal starting point that separates the time of stupor from the time of *nahda*. As a metaphor, George Antonius claimed in 1938 that it came from Ibrahim al-Yaziji's famous anti-Turkish poem from 1871. But there were other precedents. In *Nafir Suriyya,* Butrus al-Bustani deploys the metaphor to demand a unified national front that ruptures with the bloody 1860 war between the Maronites and Druze of Mount Lebanon and Christians and Muslims in Aleppo and Damascus, and which arises from barbarism. *Nuhud* is also what he expected from his society in his 'Khutba fi Adab al-'arab', (Speech on the Culture of the Arabs). In the deployment of this metaphor, al-Bustani ruptures from the immediate past, with the dominance of Ottoman rule, and Muslim hegemony over language and literature. Instead, he recovers the history of Abbasid glory and rewrites it by shining a light on the central role Christian translators played in the development of Arabic letters. Locating Arab excellence with the Islamicate Abbasids and their Christian scholars, al-Bustani constructs a past of glory that he contrasts with a present of torpor and decay. This narrative dominated how Arabic literary history was written and how the *nahda* was defined.

The men who make up the *nahda*, the *nahdawis*, built their reputation as renaissance men, who authored what came to be associated with the Arab awakening. As harbingers of modernity, these men constructed relations to the past that presented a rupture with how the past had been handled prior to the *nahda*. This book compares al-Bustani's conception of the past with that of al-Shidyaq's, in order to illuminate the earliest beginnings of some of the ideas about the past that we carry today. In al-Bustani's encyclopaedia for example, the past was packaged and hermetically sealed to be preserved as books in a library. It was not engaged with or learned from, and it was certainly not part of a transhistorical literary conversation. Meanwhile al-Shidyaq's engagement distinguished itself by how his writings let themselves be haunted by the past through citations and intertextual digestion of books the author had read, had opinions about and which nourished his own writing. Haunted as he was, al-Shidyaq never brandished the need for temporal rupture that was so characteristic of the period. There was no *nahda* for al-Shidyaq beyond the one that makes him rise from bed, often insomniac, a trope that he persistently produced in relation to *adab*, or literature. Translations of the Bible mediated these contrasting perceptions and approaches to the past particularly in how the translation strategies were injected with a modern afterlife.

The Bible and its production present us with a narrative that entangles conceptions of translation, literature and language in a period that promoted itself as modernising, secularising and progressive. As Western missionaries teamed up with local (mostly Christian), Syro-Lebanese scholars to produce a new Arabic Bible, translation emerged as one of the *nahda*'s primary literary and intellectual jousting grounds for the articulation of conflicting intentions and negotiations.[13] I suggest that Bible translation is what David Scott conceives of as a 'problem-space', a discursive context that intervenes in the 'ensemble of questions and answers' we can pose to explore the problem of modernity,

> What defines this discursive context are not only the particular problems that get posed as problems as such . . . but the particular questions that seem worth asking and the kinds of answers that seem worth having.[14]

These problem-spaces are concepts, texts, processes and objects that have absorbed much of their context. They are sites of dispute and conflict; linguistically they are untranslatables, sedimenting so much meaning that critique can begin by identifying the residues that do not make the transfer into another language and by questioning the process that produced such a meaning as an untransferable excess.

As a problem-space, Bible translation has produced a 'context of dispute' that had *historical consequences* for Arabic literature and language in ways that were non-existent for prior translations, and the strategies that governed them. Today, the Bible no longer dwells in a problem-space, and its translation does not have the same overdetermined value that it once had in the nineteenth century. Today, a Bible translation may create a slight tremor that may rattle a few people,[15] but it remains a far cry from how the Bible became meaningful for thinking about Arabic language and literature in the nineteenth century.

Despite its diminished role today, some of the problematics of the Bible's earlier life in global modernity have sedimented in the present, particularly in Anglophone theories about textual transfers across languages. The overwhelming interest in theorising translation has been more focused on geographical transfers and has deployed spatial metaphors in the thinking of translation. Such concepts as 'translation zone',[16] 'domestication and foreignisation',[17] 'ecosystem'[18] and 'circulation'[19] have generalised translation as a movement in space. The Bible invites a different reflection, as a repeatedly translated text, to examine translation's *temporal* dimension. The questions that the Bible compels examine how translation mediates rupture over continuity and modernity over tradition: thereby focusing on temporalities as frameworks for our apprehension of space. Homi Bhabha captures the tempo-spatial relationship well when he defines the function of translation as one that inculcates feelings of 'belat-edness' and 'catching-up'.[20] The emergence of these temporal anxieties is relevant for the stories we tell ourselves about modernity.

Historians of literature and culture, unlike these theoreticians of trans-lation, have had to contend with translation's entangled temporalities as conduits of historical and aesthetic processes. These scholars contributed in crucial ways to a translational turn in literary studies by making legible the impact of the movement of ideas and discourses on local cultures and on a world republic of letters. I build on their work and contribute a long reflection about translation as a movement through time that undergoes temporal adjustments with the changing political economy of capital-ism. Many existing narratives tell how local writers since the nineteenth century have either collaborated or subverted the colonial model. Samah Selim, Ussama Makdisi, Timothy Mitchel, Shaden Tageldin, Richard Jacquemond and others have shown how local writers and cultural actors appropriated Western knowledge in order to rechannel the colonial influ-ence towards a more liberatory national politics.[21] As they liberate their narratives from essentialist proclamations of what constitutes the field of Arabic culture and history, these scholars have not reexamined the 'West' as a coherent label for a site of cultural production. Despite the nuance with which they describe how local translators appropriated western texts to intervene in the horizon of expectations of local readers, the West is reduced to its colonial identity and spatial triumph.

Despite the dedication to dismantling colonial discursive strong-holds outside the West, the postcolonial model persists in assumptions of literature as representative of collective identities. Some literature is indeed that, but the 'literary' as I unpack it throughout this book goes beyond its capacity to mediate sociological processes and power differ-entials between groups. When one focuses on how 'the experience of colonialism translates native time', as Shaden Tageldin does,[22] literature's representational attention to what constitutes the native and the coloniser can blot out the extent to which literature is polyphonic and is forged through disagreement about its social function in sites dubbed 'native'. Maintaining the representational focus, the question of modernity does not move beyond the anxieties of 'time lag', that forces the colonised into a perpetual effort to 'catch up with Europe' that Bhabha identified. A focus on time in its multiple temporalities widens the analytical lens to account for the relationships that were forged between foreigners and locals, where sometimes the Westerners were the foreigners and sometimes the Arab scholar. These relationships were forged in the shadow of the colonial but cannot be reduced to this context.

The postcolonial framing of the *nahda* history within spatial divisions does not account for how identity divides have been overcome and successful mediations between unlikely protagonists took place. The postcolonial paradigm that thinks of literature as a window to the nation misses the extent to which authors write to lay claims to a problem-space, as they dispute and align themselves with other authors around them. In recent years, more scholars have begun to attend to the problems of the literary beyond the postcolonial paradigm. In the work of Tarek el-Ariss, Peter Hill, Hanssen-Weiss, Michael Allan, Marwa Elshakry and others, we encounter the literary as a conflicted site for the articulation of authorial identity that is not representational but derives the power of its mimetic function through other means. These scholars have destabilised the geographic labels through examining how Arab modernity was conceived to serve the dynamic relations between the political and cultural elite.[23] For el-Ariss, the literary is the site for the staging and performance of the modern self, Hill discovers in it a site for reflection on social class and future societies, Hanssen and Weiss reveal its stubbornly individual, anti-representational and yet insistently political articulations in the works of public intellectuals, while Allan refocuses the exploration of the mimetics on the ethics of reading, and Elshakry reveals the literary as a paradoxical space, subversive of its own proclaimed ideological paradigms. These scholars effectively deconstruct the narrative of progress that underlies normative conceptions of the *nahda*, which 'casts modernization as a passage from ignorance to enlightenment [and] becomes integral to the redefinition of literature and the semiotic ideology it comes to delimit'.[24]

Thinking through the problem-space, the authors of the *nahda* are read in their altercations with fellow authors (both foreign and local) about what constitutes modernity. Through exploring modernity as a temporal ideology, this book proposes a relativisation of colonial relations historically, as they are negotiated by various actors, both local and foreign, to widen or foreclose the scope of certain opportunities and constraints brought about by the colonial encounter. This relativisation allows for multiple narratives to emerge that have thought of political, social and literary problems without direct reliance on the colonial dichotomies of Eurocentrism.

For nineteenth-century Protestants, the Bible was an occasion to rearrange temporal relations. The new *nahda* Bible was proclaimed to be a rupture with repetitive practices of translating Bibles, and challenged how these Bibles were consequently read, against a millennium-long canon of Biblia Arabica. While in earlier times the Bible was hardly ever exchanged for money, in this era it became an exchange commodity, sold to anonymous buyers. Before the nineteenth century, and for most of those who could read it, the Bible came from the church. It was a symbol of its treasure troves, which church wardens and popes gifted in celebrations of new local patriarchs and clergymen. When it circulated, it did so in a gift economy, as well as in elementary level literacy education, administered by the church. The transformation of the Bible into a commodity facilitated its temporal alignment with modernity by dressing it in newness through a process of translation and publication that depended on industrial technologies and on an economic sphere that was being globalised and made fit for the circulation of capital. These processes were concretely rooted in ideologies of time and language and are clearly manifest in the new Arabic Bible.

Whilst the origin of the Bible had not even been a question in the past, with the Protestants the question of its origins became salient. Attending to its historical materiality, the Protestants imbued its philological history with symbolic value. No regard was to be paid anymore to the patriarchs of the church and their handling of scripture, as the source that bestows Bible sacredness on their clergy and parishes. Rather, in the nineteenth century origins became an important value, and the Hebrew and Greek linguistic origins of the Bible became an aspect of its sacredness. The philological angle gave the Protestants their competitive edge over the Oriental churches. Philology for them was based on a conception of truth that was entangled with human error. The philological history of the Bible allowed them to circumvent human error by going directly to the Greek and Hebrew sources. The Catholics by contrast had doctrinal stakes in erasing error and in upholding the *infallibility* of the Pope and all his pronouncements, including those that pertained to the place of the Bible in religious life. By turning the Bible into an exchange commodity, the Protestants defined their influence through peddling the Bible, and trusted that solitary reading, and what it cultivates in the individual sovereignty of interpretation would ultimately lead to widening the Christian community. Unlike the Catholic and the Orthodox churches, the Protestants posited the Bible to be the '*sole* [and not] the *supplementary* guide to truth and life'.[25] The relationship the Protestants cultivated with the population was one of exchange, where a Bible translated from original languages was the avenue to branch out into educational projects that also provided the truths of knowledge and science, for a fee, monetising truth and labouring to make it 'affordable'.

Like the early Reformers, the missionaries of the nineteenth century left the Levant with a vital educational legacy that originated from the Protestant commitment to mass education.[26] The Bible may have been the initial project undertaken by the American missionaries, but their legacy today lives on in the history of the Syrian Protestant College, today's American University of Beirut (AUB), which was founded in 1866, one year after the continuous text of the Smith Bustani Van Dyck (SBV) version was published. In its 160-so years of existence, AUB has been the leading academic institution in the region that facilitated the translation, adaptation and mastery of knowledge made in Western locales and in modern Arab society as well as facilitating the travel of texts and academics from Arab cultures to Western centres of knowledge. The Bible constituted the genesis of this legacy and is relevant for questions that seek to describe what was new about Protestant reading practices, and how translation, as a total textual practice of exchanging and reading texts, became the pedagogical model for thinking liberal arts education since the nineteenth century.[27]

As I write this introduction in September 2020, AUB is undergoing one of its most severe crises in its 160-year history, following the spiralling collapse of the Lebanese economy and the mass protests that ensued in October 2019, which has swiftly thrown everything and everyone in freefall. In the international and media hype about the crisis in the university, the missionaries are sometimes quoted, and their legacy continues to revolve around a story of benevolence and a commitment to enlightenment. In an article by David Ignatius in the *Washington Post*, the early Protestants are credited with spreading 'values that might empower the people of the Middle East', that grew into AUB, being perceived as a seat for the 'benign "soft power"' of the United States.[28] In this narrative favouring the American story, the overwhelming local investments in AUB as a private university by students as well as faculty and staff get erased. Even now, when repeating this story of enlightenment, the local participants and their stories are not reported on or quoted. Local scholars and students then as now, are at best depicted as recipients of charity, in similar ways to how historians have written about modernity as a gift for the people of the East. By attending to the Bible, this book hopes to dislodge some of the chronic assumptions about the place of Americans, and the Bible, in the canon of modern Arabic. I do so by maintaining the tension between the missionaries and the local helpers they employed. I explore the stories written by the 'local helpers' who chose to navigate the American master narrative of benevolence.

As I show, the local scholars sometimes subverted this narrative, but at other times, they displayed an alternative set of interests that cannot be summarised by the missionary tale. Organising this book in two parts reflects this tension and demonstrates how, when the missionaries released the local translators from their service, the consequences were not causal, but variegated, fractured and unpredictable. The first part of this book focuses on the missionary tales, while the second part demonstrates the unpredictability of the local scholars and their understanding of their positionality as Arabic writers. As I contend, local literary concerns made use of certain possibilities that the missionaries opened to devise new literary trajectories that were sometimes in opposition to the missionaries, and at other times in opposition to other groups and narratives in circulation around them.

Missionary Style Reformation

The Bible became modern when its production mediated the discourse of rupture that was to demarcate the nineteenth century as an era so different from what had preceded it that it was labelled the *nahda*, the awakening that came after a period of *inhitat*, or decay. Taking seriously the temporal dynamics of continuity and interruption, *The Modern Arabic Bible* examines how these temporalities came to shape the precarities of translation as a profession considered marginal to literary pursuit, and its impact on an emergent world of letters. It examines the transformations in attitudes and deployments of translation as a modernising literary practice capable of defining the position of a local language in a world republic of letters. This book has implications for how we imagine the global pull of the literary market and questions some of the assumptions about translation and its dynamics since the nineteenth century.

Protestant theologies of translatability coincided with modernity's reliance on translation as a mode for cultural expansion under conditions of national awakening and colonialism. As disciples of Calvinist and Lutheran approaches to the Bible, the Protestant missionaries reinvented the task of translation through exploiting the opportunities made possible by industrial capital. From their mastery of new printing technologies and modern transportation possibilities, and armed with lessons from a flourishing New England academia in a variety of fields, the Protestants considered themselves agents of civilisation, leading the world to a better future. Harking from the Dutch Reformed Churches, the Americans retained from Calvin his view about the relationship between the divine and human authorships of the Bible. In his commentary to the Gospel of John, Calvin wrote that

> whatever might be [John's] motive for writing at that time, there can be no doubt whatever that God intended a far higher benefit for his Church. He therefore dictated to the Four Evangelists what they should write, in such a manner that, while each had his own part assigned to him, the whole might be collected into one body; and it is now our duty to blend the Four by a mutual relation, so that we may permit ourselves to be taught of them, as by one mouth.[29]

Translating into the vernacular, and advocating for unmediated access to the text by ordinary people, Calvin spoke about this relationship in terms of a concept of 'accommodation', a concept that defines God's word as it embodies the constraining dictions of human speech because God in his grace cultivates a relationship with the faithful and forges channels of communication[30] between Himself and his trusting human subjects.[31]

According to both Luther and Calvin, the Bible was itself the word of God, taking on human form just as God's word, Jesus Christ, took on human flesh.[32] The paradox was that the inerrancy of the original scripture in Hebrew and Greek did not 'contravene human authorship' for it was the Holy Spirit that dictated to the apostles and prophets the words of the text.[33] The original text was thus a translation of God's word into human speech, and likewise in their translation labour, Luther and other reformers modelled their enterprise on the apostles' relationship with the divine. Like the apostles and prophets, they too were scribes[34] translating the Hebrew and Greek scriptures that were considered inerrant and divine into an accessible language.

For the early Reformers and the missionary institutions that inherited them in the nineteenth century, the authorship of the Holy Spirit generated confidence in translatability as a stability paradigm for the reproduction of meaning in a polyglot Bible project. For the local Arab churches, which already possessed Bibles in vernacular languages and which were forced to contend with the arrival of American missionaries in the Levant, the newness of the Protestant approach to the Bible was in its commoditisation as an object of exchange. The translational difference was minor and was concentrated on negotiating the declarations of the Protestant Bible that it was translated from original languages. This declaration and the methodologies that it shored up in the minds of readers cast doubt over the legitimacy of their own heritage of Arabic translations of the Bible, a heritage that was hardly interested in garnering legitimacy for a version based on a valorisation of the original language as source text. The emphasis on the original language of the Bible introduced a new approach to religion and to language. Arabic's origins and its entanglement with Christianity and with Islam became foregrounded.

The Bible was crucial for certain strands of Arab thought that were being authored at the time regarding the politics of language and religion. Those who considered translation as an enactment of *translation studii* that returned to the East the power of knowledge that the West had taken from it, also deployed the Bible in the origin stories that they constructed about Arabic's etymological history against a historical backdrop of civil war and sectarian division.[35] *Translatio studii*, originally a

Renaissance term that captures the flight of knowledge accompanying the change in Imperial rule from the East to the West, began to structure Arab stories of modernity and the dependence of these stories on translation as an activity that generates modern, local knowledge. As al-Bustani would put it, knowledge had first been translated Westwards from the Arabs and now it was coming back.[36] Through glossing the eschatological dreams of Messianic time with modernist notions of progress, the Protestants who translated the modern Arabic Bible succeeded in localising the text linguistically so that it could circulate as if *native* to the readers who were to receive it. Translating to convert, the Protestants created measures of progress that encompassed everything from their own efficiency in producing cheap Bibles in huge quantities (and producing the school systems that would circulate them) all the way to the evaluation of their converts' sincerity in faith. Bringing together Messianic eschatology with modernity's narratives of progress, the Protestants reinvented the Bible as a modern scripture relevant for the moral purchase of the new era.

Throughout this book, I focus on how a practice of translation based on continuity, repetition and dependency was replaced by another practice based on rupture, philology, and competition. As this latter practice dominates how translation is conceived and practiced in the modern *nahda*, I further consider how this conjuncture revives an Arabic standard that conjures the Abbasid era in the historical narratives that were propagated about Arabic language and literature. In the case of Arabic, and through the emergent modern concept of *fusha* (Modern Standard Arabic), classical Arabic was revived, but its lexicon was cleaned of archaisms. The decision to translate the Bible in *fusha* went against an entire tradition of Arabic Bible translation that generally preferred dialects of Arabic in their versions. When the Arabic Bible is studied at all, it is usually these versions that interest scholars and many volumes of works have been produced to explore their linguistic varieties.[37] Scholars seem to find in the dialectical varieties a good tool for the cataloguing of the various manuscript families, as we find in the works of Hikamt Kachouh, Joshau Blau and others. The deployment of sociolinguistic methods may have been useful for the historicising of manuscripts and the discovery of kinship relationships between various families. However, for our purposes these studies show the extent to which the classical methods of translating the Bible to Arabic were unconcerned with conforming to the rules of standard Arabic. In the nineteenth century, it was no longer possible to translate such verses with colloquial word choice and grammar, such as we find in the following two verses that combine standard and Levantine colloquial Arabic:

لذلك أقول لكم ان كل خطيه وافترى يغفر للناس بعد توبتهم فاما الافترى على روح القدس
لا يغفر للناس ابد الدهر

Wherefore I say unto you, All manner of sin and blasphemy shall be forgiven unto men: but the blasphemy against the Holy Ghost shall not be forgiven unto men. (Matthew 12:31).

انه اتخذ تلاميذ كثيرة ويعمد ازيد من يوحنا

Jesus made and baptised more disciples than John, (John 4:1)[38]

This tradition, which commenced the translation into Arabic in the seventh century in South Palestine, is overwhelmingly variegated in its treatment of Arabic writing style and included some lone instance of a *fusha* translation in rhymed prose, emulating the style of the Quran, but there had never been an attempt to standardise the Bible into a high register of Arabic that nevertheless brandishes a new writing style that would ultimately become the standard. One could for example encounter such lines that start with the Islamic basmallah incipit as: بسم الله الرحمن الرحيم هذي نبوة دانيل المبارك in Ms Sinai Arabic 2 of the Book of Daniel: 1:1.[39] The Protestant innovation by contrast standardised the language of the Bible, rid it of any Quran'ic phrasings or concepts, and facilitated its circulation outside the confines of Beirut, where American missionaries laboured.

For the missionaries as well as for Butrus al-Bustani, who worked on the American sponsored SBV version, classical Arabic was to be distinguished from *fusha*. Even if the latter was modelled on the classical register, it was distinguished from it in the rejection of classical Arabic as archaic, with too copious a lexicon that nevertheless lacked enough vocabulary to refer to the modern era. *Fusha*, by contrast, was the modern standard, and distinguished itself lexically but not morphologically or grammatically from the classical register. Through the syntactical stability classical Arabic afforded, the missionaries and the local translators-cum-writers that were employed by them reinvented the written standard with a simplified lexicon that sported new concepts. The innovation was thus paradoxical. On the one hand the grammar of high literature was applied to the translation with exceptional precision, while the variegated dialects of earlier translations were abandoned. Also abandoned were the motley concepts typical of the older versions, in favor of a standaridised glossary that can be termed as a unified Christian theological vocabulary, when in earlier translations such conceptual unification was lacking and no serious qualms about borrowing from the language of the Qur'an was displayed. The paradox came in how the new Bible was perceived as modern and in how it was proclaimed to have impacted modern Arabic, when in fact it was redeploying a classical anxiety about correct grammar so typical of centuries of Arabic writing. For al-Bustani, this alignment of the Bible with the high registers of Arabic literary conventions presented it as a circular return of the energies of the Renaissance back to the East. For the Protestants, this new Bible was finally severed from what they perceived as a corrupt tradition of Biblia Arabica that had uprooted it from its continuities in place and location and instead anchored it temporally in philological origins, which the obsession with grammar nicely mediated. Al-Bustani appropriated this Protestant desire, and built upon it a discourse around *adab* and *lugha* (language and literature), and the methods of generating civilising forms of knowledge.

Translation's Temporal Task

Translation in the nineteenth century became temporally meaningful not only as a method of conducting philology, but also in the synchronistic narrative of modernity that it helped to shape. As a historiographical practice integral to the production of world literature, translation participated in synchronising the problem-spaces of modernity. It aligned the temporalities that produced modernity as an epoch that, as Reinhardt Koselleck observes, is characterised by no other historical content than that of newness in contrast with 'the preceding "old" time [and] preceding epochs', which had more historical content in their label than a concept of temporality (compare 'modernity' to the labelling of the Bronze Age, or the Abbasid age).[40] Newness described all these Protestant translations across the globe. Their newness consisted in the global translation activity that was managed from new locations and new metropoles. Missionary institutions had headquarters in Cambridge, Boston and some other supporting cities, wholly new locations for the Arab Christians who were traditionally more familiar with places closer to home like Antioch, Rome, or Jerusalem. Directives and instructions on how to embark on the project of Biblical translation were distributed via post to missionaries worldwide. These directives set in place a framework that aligned the Bible in dozens of languages, translating from source texts that Anglophone Protestants deemed to be authoritative versions of the Bible. In Arabic the source texts were Hebrew and Greek, but in other locations the King James Bible sufficed.

The Bible synchronised languages and created what Emily Apter has characterised as 'the filiation of nonsynchronic nation forms and far-flung philology'.[41] The excessive translation of the Bible in the nineteenth century made conspicuous the paradox of 'translatability and untranslatability of genre and poetic form'[42] as global questions of how to negotiate a convincing Bible translation that is fit for proselytisation. I propose that the question was a temporal one and that it helps us make generalisable remarks about the temporal purchase of translation as a practice. This mediation of a new temporality can be discerned in the concepts of translation that came into vogue in the nineteenth century. After centuries of referring to translation as *naql*, the nineteenth century translators began to refer to their labour as one of *tarjama*.[43] Whereas *naql* literally means *copy*, *transport* and *carry over*, the new word *tarjama* recollected translation's connection to the biblical Targums as well as to the Abbassid movement of translation that was spearheaded by Christians and Jews for the benefit of Islamicate Arab thought. This conceptual shift in the nineteenth century was triggered by the Bible, and captures the new attention translation came to enjoy with its new nomenclature.

From the Abbassid era to the nineteenth century, *tarjama* had been a term that was generally used to refer to a genre of historiography associated with biographical writing. It replaced *naql*, the most popular Arabic synonym for translation for the same period.[44] It is known that classical Arabic lexicographers connect *tarjama* to another lexeme *rajama* in the Qur'an that derives from the root word *r-j-m*. *Rajama* describes the devil as a subject to be stoned, *rajim*. This is the only association for the word *tarjama* that survived in the classical dictionaries, but this meaning had more to do with dominant theologies of lexicography and translation than with the historical life of the term. According to al-Shidyaq, *tarjama* is a word that the Arabic dictionaries like to associate with the devil merely because of their dogmatic attachment to a three-letter root system, but the term itself is of foreign etymon.[45] New research on historical semantics finds that the root, *r-g-m* is common to Semitic languages and spans meanings that include 'to yell and to judge', 'to announce', 'to respond', 'to express', 'to cover', 'to accuse', 'to curse' and indeed also 'to throw stones'.[46] If we are to accept al-Shidyaq's judgement that *tarjama* is a four-letter root, then it is an Arabic calque from the biblical Targums, which are a genre of Bible that conflated the books together, and was translated from Hebrew to Aramaic when the Jews were still in Babylon.[47] As a calque, *tarjama* attests to an awareness of translation as a mediating activity that can take myriad forms, just as in the activity that surrounded Bible iteration in Arabic and other languages across time. Its re-emergence in the *nahda* as the most common term to designate 'translation' signifies the shift towards the Bible as a competing foundational text that could, in adjacency to the Qur'an, become a legitimate source for Arabic concepts and semantics in the modern era. Replacing *naql* with *tarjama* emphasises a historical genealogy that retains the Bible as the origin story for thinking about translation. It foregrounds translation as a movement through time. Whilst *naql*'s sense of motion does have a temporal dimension, it is one that can be measured through technical efficiency and speed. What *tarjama* offsets, however, is a temporalisation that roots itself historically, within a translational genealogy that has an epistemic impact on the chain of literacy from writing and reading to the pedagogies of dissemination and the technologies of publishing across time.

Beyond historicising the concept of translation, what concept of time attaches to its operation? Does the temporality of translation consist of a text's literary history, its 'afterlife' as Walter Benjamin proclaimed?[48] Or is it in the text's own organising temporality, its own constructions and grapplings with time? For scholars of translation that have reflected on translation's temporal dimensions, the seeming opposition between these questions is resolved through exploring the entanglements between various temporalities from the very rudiments of the text at the level of the word, to its reception in the target language as a translated text. When analysing translation, we are often drawn to the intersections between word histories, which map linguistic selections across a historical continuum. These words become our signposts, directing our research beyond the narrow confines of linguistic and literary disciplines. I follow this methodology in my explorations of some of the conceptual innovations that resulted in a Christian glossary of religious terms particularly in chapters 3 and 4.

The emergence of translation as a mode for the production of modernity marked a shift from earlier epochs. It became a tool for synchronisation that produced newness and gave value to this newness that ultimately translated into exchange commodities on the market of books. In earlier times, translation was tasked with the transmission of antediluvian wisdom, say in the translation of Greek texts to Arabic in the Abbasid era,[49] or the European translations of Greek, via Arabic and Latin following the fall of Andalusia. In those times, the economy around the production of knowledge did not depend on a text's commoditisation for securing the livelihoods of authors and translators. Rather, systems of patronage maintained the scribal class as vassals to the political leaders of emirates and fiefdoms, and regions that orbited around either the church or the bureaucratic government in Istanbul. In translation studies, such *longue durée* awareness remains largely absent from the field.

In an early book theorising translation through a postcolonial lens, Apter advocates for an approach to the study of literature away from the comparative model,[50] but she also expresses dissatisfaction with a model of 'world literature' that remains immune to reflections about how translatability and untranslatability are paradigms entrenched in political economy and its subversions. In both these paradigms, the movement of translation across spaces is monitored and mapped. She proposes to replace the comparative lens with the 'warp' of trans*national* explorations of literature and with the 'woof' of trans*lational* demarcations across language lines,[51] retaining an interest in the geographical complexities that translation triggers. Apter 'suggest[s] a formal homology between the global cartography of epic literary world systems and the nanoscale nexus of word exchanges in a single translated text'.[52] She would later correct this view, and self-critique her earlier work for how it continues with spatial analysis in translation. In her own words, 'border-crossing has become such an all-purpose, ubiquitous way of talking about translation that its purchase on the politics of actual borders – whether linguistic or territorial-has been attenuated'.[53] But what one must retain from her earlier work is its attention to the relationship between translation and literary history. For her, as a method of literary history, translation 'introduced synchrony into the heavily diachronic tradition of literary history'.[54] Her interest in this synchrony translates into 'diasporic language communities, print and media public spheres, institutions of governmentality and language policy-making, theatres of war, and literary theories with particular relevance to the history and future of comparative literature'.[55] In *Against World Literature*, Apter retains her temporal interests as the method for unpacking these synchronies. Deferring to Benjamin's scattered work on language and translation, she finds in the notion of contemporaneity, the now-time, the *Jetztzeit*, historical compressions as translation's intention and its most politically motivated function.

In this book, Apter suggests a temporal lens that seeks in untranslatability an alternate mode of literary history that does not conform to Eurocentric periodisations. She solicits a focus on 'minorities' defined as living under 'temporal units' and for these units to become contemporaneous in the writing of literary history. Seen as time units, minorities are inscribed in a representational rubric that frames them with the logic of time-lag as the primary temporality worth writing about. 'Minorities' as a conceptual construct is itself Eurocentric in its persistent reduction of the world to those locations in the West that these 'minorities' inhabit and whose languages they must learn. Apter argues that the focus should instead be on narratives 'that untime Eurocentric historicist frames and allow anachronic aesthetic phenomena to "compear"',[56] to appear together, synchronistically. Translation can shape the methodology of this approach, she argues, because it departs from literary periodisation by conjoining different temporalities. For Apter, periodisation can as much orbit around a text, or a concept, as it does upon the conditions of transformation that history seeks to address. She advocates for a search among the concepts being un/translated for what could capture meaningful time units and proliferate 'new names for periods as yet unnamed, or which become discernible only as Untranslatables of periodicity'.[57] Through treating periodisation as untranslatable, she argues, and by focusing on the name of a period, one can unhinge Eurochronology. But what does one achieve when her theorisation is applied to the *nahda*, a period that has unstable cognates in English that equate it with the Renaissance, the enlightenment, modernity, a problem that we often resolve by calquing the word into English in Latin letters?

If the *nahda* is indeed an untranslatable period, why then does it also translate some of its oppressions and policing of state and language (as well as the subversions of such oppressions) so well into English? And is there an alternate way to introduce the translatability of Arabic history beyond Apter's thesis that 'contrary to what U.S. military strategy would suggest, Arabic is translatable?'[58] Can the comparison shift to a translatability based on synchronisation that nevertheless labels as asynchronous and untranslatable the excesses that could not be aligned and standardised but that do not necessarily fit an East/West discourse? I am thinking here of the concept of *Allah* as it is standardised in all the major Bible translations of the nineteenth century. The word itself did not enjoy such unrivalled stability in earlier translations, and often its orthography was far from uniform.[59] Compare with the concept of *Suriyya*, that was introduced in the Bible for the first time in the *nahda*, and that was to distinguish a biblical concept of Syria from the Muslim *Sham* that had typically been deployed in previous Bible translations. In the filiative asynchronicities that helped promote the American Bible as a pioneering version, reference to a Eurochronology may obscure the loaded diachronic ruptures that the Protestants and their helpers introduced in the language policies that shaped Arabic since the *nahda*.

Following Apter, one can point to how the *nahda* is indeed an untranslatable, like other names of periods such as modernity or contemporaneity. However, rather than focusing on the linguistic purchase of the untranslatable, this book presents a literary history of translation that insists on the primacy of the historical in shaping the linguistic. Through inverting the typical approach to translation to explore the temporal dimensions of translation, I analyse how language *responds* to temporal dynamics and historical relations. Thus, rather than universalising modernity as a European temporal ideology of synchronisation, and consequently relegating the non-European to anachrony, this book demonstrates how the discourse of modernity emerged from historical transformations that ushered in a new and globalised political economy. These transformations as I suggest can be analysed in the translation processes that produced the Bible as a new commodity that contributed to how modernity was conceived and how it shaped approaches to Arabic language and literature since the nineteenth century. So, rather than the commitment a close reading of the biblical text which typifies how the Arabic Bible is generally studied, this book presents a historical reading of the Bible as a commodity and thus connects the historical developments that can be recuperated from the archives to the linguistic choices taken in the text in order to evolve an analysis of translation as a labour of synchronising the non-synchronous.

The analytical frame is provided by a geological metaphor of time as sedimentation rather than by framing the analysis through periodisation, epoch-analysis and its geographical translation of contemporaneity. Thus, the Bible is explored through its base multiplicities and its synchronicities in flux. The job then becomes to identify the problem-spaces. One such example that I discuss is the accusations of mistranslation that Jesuit and Protestant missionaries hurled at one another, the dissolution of untranslatable layers of meaning within intentional manipulations and deliberate semantic adjustments inserted by the translators for political and ideological ends. In this example, the accusations, rather than the biblical text comprise the object of study. Another example is al-Bustani's ideological deployment of untranslatability as an anachrony that confines the reach of the canon of Arabic literature to local relevance. Here the object of study is some of modernity's key concepts, where I analyse how they relate to and make use of the Bible. A third example is the insomniac temporality that al-Shidyaq inhabits in order to critique the *nahda* paradigm of awakening, that I discuss in the last chapter of this book, where the Bible is referenced as a way to mount a critique of a dominant discourse about what modernity entails. Those examples show that 'history is never identical with its linguistic registration and formulated experience, whether this is expressed orally or in writing, but at the same time, it is not independent of these linguistic articulations'.[60]

Bible Sediments in the *Nahda*

Narrating history through the untranslatables of periodicity, as seen through Apter's translational lens, gives priority to language, to the name of the period as an object of investigation. The risk in such an approach is that it neglects the diachronic and suppresses the very cultural history that it sought to 'compear', in order to subvert the Eurochronology that dominates world literature. The geographical identification of a certain time with Europe persists in exploring translation strictly within a postcolonial paradigm that attaches to the idea of Europe a synchronic state-time as well as a colonial-time that is nevertheless far from stable and far from being an object of scholarly control.

I write about historical entanglements to tell a story that embraces 'a multiplicity of possible viewpoints and the divergences resulting from languages, terminologies, categorizations and conceptualizations, traditions, and disciplinary usages, [adding] another dimension to the inquiry'. Through thinking of this narrative within a methodology of *histoire croisée*, or entangled history, I emphasise nodes and connections that were important for the generation of meaning.[61] In a methodology of entangled history, the very problem of how to periodise is irrelevant if we are to take history and language as mutually constitutive. Critiquing the work of periodisation, and building on Reinhard Koselleck's observations on 'multiple temporalities', Helge Jerdheim writes that 'periods in chronological succession take shape when history is brought to a standstill by means of representation and turned into what Foucault refers to as "the restrictive figure of a synchronic system".'[62] Instead of periodisation, a geological metaphor of sedimentation conjoins the figures of language and history and turns to language as a comprehensive semantic reservoir of historical reality. Language shifts at a different speed from history and is asynchronous with it even if it sometimes captures some of its fluctuations. When it captures the movement of time, language accumulates into its lexical vastness the meanings and experiences of this reality. Some words are more capable than others at fitting the historical meanings generated into their usage. These words, as Koselleck defines them, are concepts, and like untranslatables, they are 'ambiguous'. Unlike ordinary words, concepts do the work of assembling 'the plurality of historical experiences as well as a series of theoretical and historical issues in one whole, which is only given in the concept itself and can only be experienced there',[63] making concepts sites for conflicting meanings and asynchronous experiences. Rather than periodisation, which the Bible as a text eschews because it derives its authenticity from its antiquity as well as its continued relevance to so many people, I borrow from the theoretical insights of conceptual history, particularly the theory of multiple temporalities that for Jordheim encompasses 'entire texts that can be read and interpreted in terms of how they refer to or point at the past, the present and the future'.[64]

Jordheim brings attention to how words and texts have multitemporal vectors. As he writes, 'conceptual meanings [and like them texts] do not only succeed each other chronologically but co-exist, overlap, or come into conflict with one another and thus enter into a synchronic, multi-layered structure'.[65] Through this gathering force of synchronicity, meanings are formed in ways that denaturalise the sprawling non-synchronic temporalities of universes, worlds and microcosms. What Jordheim teases out of Koselleck is how within this gathering force of synchronicity, time gets 'out of joint' and sometimes leads to new conceptual possibilities while foreclosing others. As Jordheim writes in a more recent essay

> Synchronicity is never a given, but always the product of work, of a complex set of linguistic, conceptual and technological practices of synchronization, which are found in every culture and at every time, but which have become especially dominant in that period of western history that we often call modernity.[66]

In *The Modern Arabic Bible*, I claim that translation was deployed as a tool of synchronisation and that it succeeded in becoming concomitant with practices we associate with modernity. Is this modernity, clothed in Arabic as the *nahda*, incommensurable with western modernity? I contend that the synchronistic practices of modernity entangled Arabic and Arabic speakers with a common and incommensurable modernity that was never-theless articulated and measured relatively, through standardising tempo-ral values in a world that continued to experience temporalities differently.

The Bible is a shared text that belongs to churches organised between Eastern and Western communities, traversing a geography and a long history of religious, commercial and political exchange. It embodies the synchronistic forces that tie those communities together. As scripture, it is worshipped differently by the different churches, and it is subject to diverging calendars and liturgical practices. The temporalities to which it belongs are variegated and interlaced, conflicting as well as synchronis-ing. Within the context of its global translations, the Arabic Bible, along with other Bibles that were produced at the time, became what Walter Benjamin refers to as a 'fragment of a vessel'; vernacular slivers of 'a greater language', a language that makes the world's different vernaculars into next of kin, deriving as they all do from a pure source.[67] This meta-phor of the vessel as pure source grapples with the synchronicities of the non-synchronous through the image of the sliver, with its particular and unrepeatable shape that nevertheless shares with other irregular slivers the position of being part of a whole. For Benjamin, these fragments are bound by ties of kinship that precede the historical and are folded into 'pure language'. Benjamin theorises the origins of language outside of time, and suggests that the task of translation is to synchronise between languages and to reveal 'this special kinship [which] holds because languages are no strangers to one another, but are, a priori and apart from all historical relationships, interrelated in what they want to express'.[68] I claim that this view of translation and of world languages is historical, contrary to Benjamin's poetic valorisation of language over history. As this book will show, this kinship is a consequence of fraught historical processes and of individual intentions and ambitions that culminate in synching languages and origin stories together and thereby making it possible to think with some coherence about the world's languages – what can be referred to as a discourse of translatability.

The Modern Arabic Bible claims that thinking of Arabic as a frag-ment that has kinship ties with other languages is a historical development that emerged out of the evangelical missionary efforts to make the Bible available in more than eighty languages, in mostly colonial locations, around the world. This polylingual project and its highly regulated strategies of translation synchronised the world's languages through connecting them all to the same predetermined source texts that are pure in as much as they are God's word, the filiative source, its fragments revealing an asynchronous kinship of Babylonian dispersions. Seen through language's tensions with history, the task of a literary history of translation is to make legible how linguistic ideologies and literary practices were responding to as well as intervening in the historical context. I suggest that a literary history of translation is written at the intersection between the text's diachronic life and its synchronic adjacency to other texts. Through such a relativised notion of what remains stable and what changes in the life of a book, I introduce the political economy of the Bible as the main transformation that offset a discourse on modernity that revolved around Bible translation. I argue that this political economy can be told through a textual focus on the changing materiality of the Bible across time, in multiple locations and languages, and through the modes of exchange by which it circulated. I suggest that concepts like commoditisation, competition and standardisation have temporal purchases that feed the synchronistic efforts that the Bible mediated. Rather than study these concepts within economic history, I argue that attending to their temporal principle reveals their historical continuities with earlier political economies. As I argue, under captialism commoditisation, competition and standardisation mediate the temporalities associated with modernity such as synchronisation, acceleration and progress. Throughout this book, I illuminate various other temporalities as they come into direct tension with the synchronistic temporalities of the Protestants. I thus explore how concepts like origins, tradition and newness defined the more successful versions of the modern Arabic Bible.

I propose a series of readings that unpack the processes that led to Arabic becoming a global vernacular that orbits around the Bible as the foundational text for modernity. I do so by considering the imaginative relations that the protagonists constructed between words and meanings, between texts and other texts, and between texts and their contexts. In this sense, I work philologically, following a definition of the enterprise that

Sheldon Pollock proposed when he wrote that 'philology is, or should be, the discipline of making sense of texts. It is not a theory of language – that's linguistics – or theory of meaning or truth – that's philosophy – but a theory of textuality as well as the history of textualized meaning'.[69] I attend to the materiality of the process of translation, question the choices that were taken in the text to examine, and interpret, details as minute as the font used, to the rhetorical tools, the price of a copy of the Bible, and the value that certain words acquire in the effort to distinguish one's labours from the work of competitors. These are focal points that present alternatives to the classical understanding of the philological as merely a close reading of a text. It follows Gerard Genette's argumentation that the paratextual is to be as much a part of the philological reading exercise as the text itself.[70] In this sense, I unpack the transformations that beset the Bible and its impact on Arabic when it became an exchange commodity. I argue that this re-production of the Bible within the political economy of capitalism turns the Bible into a device of synchronisation that foreclosed certain modes of continuity with a millennium-long tradition of Biblia Arabica; while simultaneously configuring new modes of vernacularising Arabic in a network of other global vernaculars that orbit around the Bible.

My philological engagement in this book weaves together a praxis of reading that identifies its primary sources not only in the texts of the Bible versions, but also includes archival sources in the form of other books, newspapers, letters, minutes of meetings, announcements and some rare and out of print texts as equally worthy of being read closely for outlining the traces the translation of the modern Arabic Bible left of the language and the literature. I parse these texts and the concepts that are entangled with them with the aid of lexicons, grammars and digital corpora, as well as other writings by the protagonists. I couple this materialist reading practice with scholarly reflections on theories of literature, translation, history and linguistics. I cover the early *nahda* period and end my narrative with the death of the main protagonists in the story, around the 1870s. I present five chapters that are structured around two enmeshed and convergent narratives: translation is not simply a derivative literary practice that occasions the travel of texts across languages, but a historical event that mediates the dynamics of its context. Secondly, translation shapes traveling traditions by continuing with a tradition, canonising certain texts, and by appropriating a past text to service contingent intentions and ambitions.

I admit the pragmatics of my selections – writing about how translation enacts continuities and ruptures, by selecting four Bible versions, two local translators and their writings, and three missionary institutions, can offer only partial solutions to the large claims I make about translation in the nineteenth century. I think of pragmatics as the horizon for translation practices, that captures the level of ambition of translators, as they navigate a landscape of possibilities as well as constraints, working within a framework that deems their labour ancillary to the venerable position of the original, as the supreme reference point and fountain of originality. Translators, then as now, find themselves within a system of limited resources, when time and funding are predetermined by the institutions that employ them. As we see when death interrupts the biblical projects, the relationships that bind the translation teams prove precarious and the choices that the protagonists make vis-à-vis the Bible were taken pragmatically.

We can find pragmatism as a practice that drives the field of translation studies from its inception in the modern university, as it became pedagogically systematised by Bible scholar and a founding father of the discipline, Eugene Nida. Producing mostly textbooks for university students, Nida set the standard that treated translation as a wordsmith vocation, cobbling between languages according to a prescribed format, something paramount to a translation grammar, laying the ground rules for transfers between languages. In his autobiographical account of his vocation as a translation scholar, and distinguished member of the United Bible society, Nida recounts a series of anecdotes from the hundreds of travels he undertook on behalf of the Bible society to doctor Bible translations undertaken in hundreds of languages and to lecture about the profession in leading universities. In *Fascinated by Languages*, the reader encounters a man who viewed translation within a discourse of translatability first expressed by Benjamin, and whose job was to ensure that new versions of the Bible indeed became the fragments of one biblical vessel, to carry the divine word and disseminate the idea that all those Bible versions were equally sacred and worthy of veneration. Yet Nida was a translator, and he never let his faith in the Good Book get in the way of his vocation.

Pragmatic as a translator must be, Nida was sometimes called upon to accept translations that did not fulfil the expectations for the Holy Book. In one of his stories from South America, he speaks about a nurse who translated the New Testament to an obscure language of one of the tribes. He was asked to review the translation and approve it for publication by the local Bible Society there. He deemed the translation of poor quality, rendered word for word. He nevertheless approved the work because,

> several hundred people had become Christians and had learned to read painstakingly some mimeographed copies of the translation . . . In such circumstances need outweighs quality, especially when one realizes that in so many cases the lives of people have been singularly blessed by translations that have also been far from intelligible. And so, I urged the publication.[71]

Forgiving error to satisfy contextual needs over theological ideals, Nida, like the other translators we encounter in this book, relied on a typical trope in the translator's profession. As the translator of the Latin Vulgate Bible, St Jerome, would write when defending himself against the charges of heresy 'since to err is human and to admit error is prudent, I beg you, my critic, whoever you are, to amend the error'.[72] Error is part of a translator's labour, like any other human labour, but the translator's error seems doubly compounded when the original is assumed to be perfect. Error shunts subsequent translation practices and motivates a new reader to retranslate and amend a fault in a favourite text. Nida makes room for error in the concepts he coined within this discourse of translatability. These 'errors' will be highlighted and explored for the temporal dissonance they introduce to the synchronisation process and will function as points of entry for a materialist reading of the Bible as literature. Attending to the protagonists that produced new Bibles and examining their labour, this book signals the rupture in how Bibles came to be handled in the nineteenth century by proclaiming the Bible to be a commodity.

The concept of commodity captures the Bible's trajectory from a text produced under specific institutional conditions of knowledge dissemination, in which conceptions of reader expectations and market preferences were negotiated through the production process, to the Bible as an object of exchange destined for a consumer.[73] The transformation of the Bible into a commodity expanded its use value as an article of faith, and brought it into contact with the complexities of the global political economy. Unlike some of the hermetic practices of translating Bibles in monasteries for the immediate benefit of the community, the commoditised Bible must negotiate for itself a place in the market, and risk judgement on its value by potential buyers.

The story unfolds around the emergence of translation as the domain for the cultivation of a shared world view, and a mode of being, that rests on assumptions about the power of certain books to transform people and the relations between them. I address how an emergent culture of translation redefines those relations of power competitively, through certain linguistic and literary practices that are adopted to increase the dissemination and readership of a text. I also examine the emergence of translation through the Bible for what it mediates of modern temporalities that elevate newness to a value to be pursued and celebrated. I do so in two parts. In the first three chapters, I focus on the emergence of the Bible as an exchange commodity and the rivalries that erupted between British, American and Jesuit missionaries. In these chapters I explore the temporalities of acceleration, rupture, tradition and origin as they legitimated certain practices of translation and circulation that become salient in the nineteenth century. In the last two chapters I explore the work of the local helpers, al-Bustani and al-Shidyaq, in the aftermath of their release from their employment with the missionaries.

In the first part of the book, I organise the chapters around the prism of the Bible to present a storyline that embeds my theoretical interests in concrete historical details of the Bible's translation. The first chapter questions what is so new about the modern translation of the Arab Bible. By comparing the American venture to its British counterpart, I answer this question by exploring the shift from gift to commodity exchange. In this chapter I argue that the synchronisations necessary for commodity exchange transformed Arabic into a global vernacular that reproduces the publishing tastes and literary ideology of a transnational American missionary organisation. The second chapter examines how the rivalry between Catholics and Protestants changed in kind when the Bible became

an exchange commodity. As I argue, the Catholics were forced to synchronise with the Americans and reproduce important attributes of their Bible,
but they staked their competitive advantage by brandishing a concept
of tradition against the valorisation of origins typical of the philological methods of the Protestants. The third chapter asks what exactly was
synchronic in the new Bible and what was relegated to the excesses of
asynchrony. Through exploring how the missionary's effort to translate
the Bible into Arabic rivalled the Qur'an's claims to exclusivity in this
language, I show how standardising Arabic and producing a seeming
continuity with its classical register in fact enacted a rupture, not only
with older translations of the Bible, but also reduced the variety of writing
registers in order to construct a vehicular language that departs from the
lexicon of the classical register and favours more quotidian words while
rejecting the non-normative grammar of the colloquial styles.

In the second part of the book, I explore 'release' as a concept that
depends on some level of normalisation of the synchronistic force of the
missionary intervention. In Chapter Four, I turn to the literary legacy of
Butrus al-Bustani, one of the translators that worked with the American
missionaries, and a key figure in the inauguration of the *nahda* as a period
of progress and civilisation. This chapter connects his translation of the
Bible with his work on a simplified Arabic dictionary, a six-volume
encyclopaedia as well as other shorter texts, to show how al-Bustani was
preoccupied with the construction of parity between his own local culture and the Western culture in which he had studied and from which he
translated. As I show, al-Bustani capitalised on the legitimacy that being a
Bible translator afforded him, and he deployed it to readjust the historical
narratives about the past of the Arabs, from the origins of their language
to the quality of their literature. In Chapter Five, I turn to Ahmad Faris
al-Shidyaq as one of the rare critics of the *nahda* and its temporalities of
modernity, progress and rupture. Unlike al-Bustani, al-Shidyaq viewed the
Bible as just another job. So, while he submitted himself to the experience
of becoming a Bible translator, he cultivated an irreverent literary persona.
Through tracing his rejection of translation as a mere subordinate of writing, I frame al-Shidyaq's criticality through the temporality of insomnia as
the most enduring trope for his writing time. As I argue, insomnia enabled

al-Shidyaq to conceive of literature outside the project of modernisation and its derivative temporalities of progress and civilisation.

Taken together the five chapters of this book can be read as a long tale about the Bible and its aftermath in Arabic language and literature. It starts with the moment that the Bible became a problem-space and traces the tale through its conceptual history as well as through biographical accounts of the protagonists and the Bible versions on which they worked. When I release the local scholars from the master narrative of the Bible, I continue to trace the Bible as an intertextual presence in their writings. But these chapters also function as independent essays, each charting a particular set of questions about the temporalities of translation.

If one finds truth by the Book alone, as the Protestants preached, our protagonists and their inheritors accepted this paradigm but replaced the Bible with other books, more amenable for the truths they sought.

Notes

1. Helge Jordheim, 'Against Periodization (Koselleck's Theory of Multiple Temporalities)', *History and Theory* 51 (May 2012): 151–71.
2. 'Key Facts about Bible Access', *United Bible Societies* (blog). https://www.unitedbiblesocieties.org/key-facts-bible-access/. Accessed 20 May 2020.
3. George Antonius, *The Arab Awakening: The Story of the Arab National Movement* (Beirut: Librairie du Liban, 1969), 43.
4. Albert Hourani, *Arabic Thought in the Liberal Age, 1798–1939* (Cambridge: Cambridge University Press, 1984), 96.
5. Sabry Hafez, *The Genesis of Arabic Narrative Discourse: A Study in the Sociology of Modern Arab Literature* (London: Saqi Books, 1993), 47; Hisham Sharabi, *Al-Muthaqqafun al-'arab wa al-Gharb* (Beirut: Dar Nilson, 1970); Shmuel Moreh, *Studies in Modern Arabic Prose and Poetry* (Leiden: Brill, 1988).
6. Pierre Cachia, 'Translations and Adaptations 1834–1914', in *Modern Arabic Literature*, ed. M. M. Badawi (Cambridge: Cambridge University Press, 1992), 23–35, 26.
7. Ibid., 23.
8. Moreh, *Studies in Modern Arabic Prose and Poetry*, 10.
9. Samir Kassir, *Beirut,* trans. M. B. DeBevoise (Berkeley: University of California Press, 2010), 170.

10. Fawwaz Traboulsi, *A History of Modern Lebanon* (London: Pluto Press, 2012), 65.

11. Sasson Somekh, 'Biblical Echoes in Modern Arabic Literature', *Journal of Arabic Literature* 26, nos. 1/2 (June 1995): 186–200, 200. See also his later essay on the history of these translations, Sasson Somekh, 'Arabic Bibles in the Modern Age: Linguistic and Stylistic Issues', in *The Professorship of Semitic Languages at Uppsala University 400 Years*, ed. Bo Isaksson, Mats Eskhult, and Gail Ramsay (Uppsala: Uppsala Universitet, 2005), 191–98.

12. Jurji Zaydan, *Tarikh Adab al-Lugha al-'Arabiyyah*. (Cairo: Al-Hindawi, 2012), 1181.

13. Binay shows how the SBV is a version that was produced by a multi-confessional group of translators and copy editors. See Sara Binay, 'Revision of the Manuscripts of the "so-Called Smith-Van Dyck Bible." Some Remarks on the Making of the Bible Translation', in *Translating the Bible into Arabic: Historical, Text-Critical, and Literary Aspects*, ed. Sara Binay and Stefan Leder, Beiruter Texte Und Studien 131 (Beirut: Ergon Verlag, 2012), 75–84.

14. David Scott, *Conscripts of Modernity: The Tragedy of Colonial Enlightenment* (Durham, NC: Duke University Press, 2004), 4.

15. See for example the furore around the Wycliffe translation of the Arabic Bible that was published in 2012 by the Summer Institute of Linguistics. Even as it made the news, it cannot be said to have become a major concern for the Arabic writing cultural elite as the nineteenth century translations would become. See Nina Shea, 'Bibles That Translate "The Father" as "Allah"', *Hudson Institute*. (February 14, 2012). https://www.hudson.org/research/8737-bibles-that-translate-the-father-as-allah-. Hala Homsi, 'Translations that Islamicize the Bible and is Being Disseminated Regionally . . . and the Lebanese who is on the Lookout', *Lebanese Forces*. https://www.lebanese-forces.com/2012/05/30/216691/. Accessed 17 October 2019.

16. Emily S. Apter, *The Translation Zone: A New Comparative Literature* (Princeton: Princeton University Press, 2006).

17. Lawrence Venuti, *The Translator's Invisibility: A History of Translation* (London: Routledge, 1995).

18. Franco Moretti, *Atlas of the European Novel, 1800–1900* (London: Verso, 1999).

19. David Damrosch, *What Is World Literature?* (Princeton: Princeton University Press, 2003).

20. Homi K. Bhabha, 'Race Time and the Location of Culture', in *The Location of Culture* (London: Routledge, 1994).

21. Samah Selim. *Popular Fiction, Translation and the Nahda in Egypt* (Cham: Springer International Publishing, 2019); Ussama Makdisi, *Artillery of Heaven: American Missionaries and the Failed Conversion of the Middle East* (Ithaca: Cornell University Press, 2008); Timothy Mitchell, *Colonising Egypt* (Berkeley: University of California Press, 1988); Shaden. M. Tageldin, *Disarming Words: Empire and the Seductions of Translation in Egypt* (Berkeley: University of California Press, 2011); Richard Jacquemond, 'Towards an Economy and Poetics of Translation From and Into Arabic', in *Cultural Encounters in Translation from Arabic*, ed. Said Faiq (Clevedon: Multilingual Matters, 2004), 117–27.

22. Tageldin, *Disarming Words*, 26.

23. Tarek El-Ariss, *The Arab Renaissance: A Bilingual Anthology of the Nahda* (New York: The Modern Language Association of America, 2018); Tarek El-Ariss, *Trials of Arab Modernity: Literary Affect and the New Political.* (New York: Fordham Press, 2013); Marwa Elshakry, *Reading Darwin in Arabic, 1860–1950* (Chicago: University of Chicago Press, 2013); Peter Hill, *Utopia and Civilisation in the Arab Nahda* (Cambridge: Cambridge University Press, 2020); Michael Allan, *In the Shadow of World Literature: Sites of Reading in Colonial Egypt* (Princeton: Princeton University Press, 2016); Jens Hanssen and Max Weiss, *Arabic Thought beyond the Liberal Age: Towards an Intellectual History of the Nahda* (Cambridge: Cambridge University Press, 2016).

24. Allan, *In the Shadow of World Literature*, 6.

25. Paul Lehmann, 'The Reformers' Use of the Bible', *Theology Today* 3, no. 3 (1946–47): 328–44, 332.

26. The exclusivity of the Bible in matters of faith was responsible for the pioneering theories and practices of education that the Reformers advanced as far back as the sixteenth century. As Ilona Rashkow observes, in that century, 'Renaissance philosophy had attempted to highlight the importance of Hebrew and Greek for the humanist scholar, and the Reformation, with its emphasis on the two founts of religion, sola fide, sola scriptura, emphasized it still further. If Scripture was the key to faith, as the reformers maintained, then it was necessary that an accurate Bible be in the keeping of all Christians. The humanists were able to show that some of the difficulties of the Vulgate were due to mistakes in the Latin translation. With *ad fontes*

as the battle-cry of Renaissance humanism, it was necessary for biblical translators to return to the original texts and although Hebrew and Greek were not studied easily in Renaissance England, biblical translation was an important aspect of humanism'. See Ilona N. Rashkow, 'The Renaissance', in *The Blackwell Companion to the Bible and Culture*, ed. John F. A. Sawyer (Oxford: Blackwell Publishing, 2012), 54–68, 55.

27. Nadia Maria El-Cheikh, Bilāl Urfah'lī, and Lina Choueiri, *One Hundred and Fifty* (Beirut: AUB Press, 2016).

28. David Ignatius, 'The American University of Beirut Deserves Our Help', *The Washington Post*, 11 June 2020, https://www.washingtonpost.com/opin ions/2020/06/10/american-university-beirut-deserves-our-aid/. Accessed 17 March 2021.

29. Quoted in Lehmann. 'The Reformers' Use of the Bible', 339.

30. These channels, as Calvin understood them, came in two main forms: through a dedicated and daily biblical reading practice and through rituals of prayer that combined the individual's own wishes from God with a standard and predetermined set of utterances that derive the authority of their content from 'the standard of the gospel', without reference to the Pope, saints, or the Virgin Mary. Elsie McKee, 'Praying for the Dead or for the King? Prayers of Intercession in the Roman Catholic and Reformed Traditions', *International Congress for Calvin Research* (Philadelphia: Westminster Theological Seminary, 2018).

31. As theologian Edward Dowey defines it 'the term accommodation refers to the process by which God reduces or adjusts to human capacities what he wills to reveal of the infinite mysteries of his being, which by their very nature are beyond the powers of the mind of man to grasp'. Quoted in Jon Balserak, *Divinity Compromised: A Study of Divine Accommodation in the Thought of John Calvin* (Dordrecht: Springer, 2006), 2.

32. Lehmann, 'The Reformers' Use of the Bible', 340.

33. Ibid., 339.

34. That the apostles were scribes was an enabling historical backdrop for translators in general. In Arabic, the translators came from scribal educa- tion, which they then reformulated into a translational vocation. I speak about how *turjuman* (Arabic: translator) coincided with *katib* (premodern Arabic: scribe, modern Arabic: author) in Rana Issa, 'Genealogies and Kinships: Biblia Arabica and Translation in the Nahda', in *In the Shoes of the Other: Interdisciplinary Essays in Translation Studies from Cairo*, ed.

Samia Mehrez (Cairo: Al Kotob Khan, 2019). 201–10. In this article I argue that 'The change in concepts [of translation] went beyond the introduction of new concepts into Arabic, and the signifiers used for the vocation itself were changed, so that we no longer consider translation as one of the tasks of a scribal worker', 203.

35. This argument is made by Elshakry to describe the translation of Darwin. With the Bible it was even more the case, because of its oriental origins. See Elshakry, *Reading Darwin in Arabic*. On the actual history of the concept, see Karlheinz Stierle, 'Translatio Studii and Renaissance: From Vertical to Horizontal Translation', in *The Translatability of Cultures: Figurations of the Space Between*, ed. Sanford Budick and Wolfgang Iser (Stanford: Stanford University Press, 1996), 55–67.

36. Butrus al-Bustani, *Khutba Fi Adab al-'arab* (Beirut: AUB Archives and Special Collections, 1859).

37. Joshua Blau, *A Grammar of Christian Arabic: Based Mainly on South-Palestinian Texts from the First Millennium* (Louvain: Secretariat du Corpus SCO, 1966); Kees Versteegh, *The Arabic Language* (Edinburgh: Edinburgh University Press, 1997); Sidney Griffith, *The Bible in Arabic: The Scriptures of the "People of the Book" in the Language of Islam* (Princeton: Princeton University Press, 2013); Isaac Hall, 'The Arabic Bible of Drs. Eli Smith and Cornelius V. A. Van Dyck', *Journal of the American Oriental Society* 11 (1885): 276–86; Cornelius Van Dyck and Eli Smith, *Brief Documentary History of the Translations of the Scriptures into the Arabic Language* (Beirut: Syria Mission Press, 1900).

38. Hikmat Kachouh, *The Arabic Versions of the Gospels: The Manuscripts and their Families* (Berlin: De Greuyter, 2012), 171, 186.

39. Miriam L Hjälm, *Christian Arabic Versions of Daniel: A Comparative Study of Early MSS and Translation Techniques in MSS Sinai Ar. 1 and 2* (Leiden: Brill, 2016).

40. Modernity's difference from such other epochs as the Abbasids, or the Bronze Age, is precisely in how it raises temporality into a value, contrast to the Abbasids who are valorised as rulers, or the Bronze Age where the metal, a concrete object was defining of an epoch. Reinhart Koselleck, 'Neuzeit: Remarks on the Semantics of Modern Concepts of Movement'. *Futures Past: On the Semantics of Historical Time* (Cambridge, MA: MIT Press, 1985), 245–76, 246.

41. Emily Apter, 'Taskography: Translation as Genre of Literary Labor', *PMLA* 122, no. 5 (October 2007): 1403–15, 1404.

42. Ibid.
43. M. Copperson and S. Somekh, 'Translation', in *Encyclopaedia of Arabic Literature*, ed. Julie Scott Miesami and Paul Starkey (New York: Routledge, 1998).
44. Dana Sajdi, *The Barber of Damascus: Nouveau Literacy in the Eighteenth-Century Ottoman Levant* (Stanford: Stanford University Press, 2013).
45. Ahmad Faris al-Shidyaq, *Al-Jasus 'ala l-qamus* (Qustantiniyah: al-Jawa'ib, 1882).
46. See *The Doha Historical Dictionary of the Arabic Language*. https://www.dohadictionary.org/dictionary/%D8%B1%D8%AC%D9%85. Accessed 9 August 2020.
47. George H. Schodde, 'The Targums', *The Old Testament Student* 8, no. 7 (1889): 262–6.
48. Walter Benjamin, 'The Task of the Translator: An Introduction to the Translation of Baudelaire's Tableaux Parisiens', in *Illuminations* (London: Pimlico, 1999), 70–82.
49. Hayrettin Yucesoy, 'Translation as Self-Consciousness: Ancient Sciences, Antediluvian Wisdom, and the Abbasid Translation Movement', *Journal of World History* 20, no.4 (December 2009): 523–57, https://doi.org/10.1353/jwh.0.0084. Accessed 5 November 2020.
50. Apter, *The Translation Zone*.
51. Apter, 'Taskography'.
52. Ibid., 1404.
53. Emily Apter, *Against World Literature: On the Politics of Untranslatability* (New York: Verso, 2013), 211.
54. Apter, *The Translation Zone*, 179.
55. Ibid., 6.
56. Apter borrows from Jean Luc Nancy 'compear': co-appear. See Apter, *Against World Literature*, 146.
57. Ibid., 138.
58. Apter, *The Translation Zone,* xi.
59. Hikmat Kachouh, 'The Arabic Versions of the Gospels: A Case Study of John 1.1 and 1.18', in *The Bible in Arab Christianity*, ed. David Thomas (Leiden: Brill, 2007), 9–36.
60. Koselleck, *Futures Past*, 159.
61. Michael Werner and Benedeicte Zimmermann, 'Beyond: Comparison: Histoire Croisée and the Challenge of Reflexivity', *History and Theory* 45, no.1 (February 2006): 30–50, 32.

62. Helge Jordheim, 'Against Periodization (Koselleck's Theory of Multiple Temporalities)', *History and Theory* 51 (May 2012): 151–71, 161.

63. Koselleck quoted in Jordheim, 'Against Periodization', 163.

64. Jordheim, 'Against Periodization', 166.

65. Ibid., 169.

66. Helge Jordheim, 'Introduction: Multiple Times and the Work of Synchronization', *History and Theory* 53, no. 4 (2014): 498–518, 505–6.

67. Benjamin, 'The Task of the Translator'.

68. Ibid.

69. Sheldon Pollock, 'Future Philology? The Fate of a Soft Science in a Hard Word', *Critical Inquiry* 35 (Summer 2009): 931–61, 934.

70. Gerard Genette, *Paratexts: Thresholds of Interpretation*, trans. Jane E. Lewin (Cambridge: Cambridge University Press, 1997).

71. Eugene A. Nida, *Fascinated by Languages* (Amsterdam: J. Benjamins, 2003), 80.

72. St Jerome, 'Letter to Pammachius', in *The Translation Studies Reader*, ed. Lawrence Venuti (London: Routledge, 2012), 21–30, 24.

73. Appadurai defines commodities as products that are in and out of acquisition. Commodities represent 'very complex social forms and distributions of knowledge. In the first place, such knowledge can be two sorts: the knowledge (technical, social, aesthetic, and so forth) that goes into the production of the commodity; and the knowledge that goes into appropriately consuming the commodity. The production knowledge that is read into a commodity is quite different from the consumption knowledge that is read from the commodity . . . knowledge at both poles has technical, mythological, and evaluative components, and the two poles are susceptible to mutual and dialectical interaction'. See Arjun Appadurai, *The Social Life of Things: Commodities in Cultural Perspective* (Cambridge: Cambridge University Press, 1986), 41.

I

The Missionary Bible

A Global Perspective on the Commoditisation of the Arabic Bible

The nineteenth century marked the commoditisation of the Bible around the world. Protestant missionaries circulated the Bible and negotiated its value in various locations and across disparate cultures and religions through an unprecedented process of exchange. Choosing to travel the world to translate the Bible, they defined 'the first object of a Protestant mission ... to give the word of God to a people in their own tongue, wherein they were born, and in which the family converses at home'.[1] This object was dependent on turning the Bible into a cheap commodity, within financial reach of most local consumers. Its economic status was steered towards a 'situation in which its exchangeability (past, present, or future) for some other thing [became] its socially relevant feature'.[2] American and British missionaries proselytised, translated and disseminated Bibles in a multitude of vernaculars.[3] When these regions did not possess Bibles written in their languages (or even written languages as such), such as in New Zealand, parts of Latin America or Africa, the missionaries worked well in advance to supply those communities, sometimes with a written language and then with Bibles in local tongues.[4] In earlier centuries, the Bible had been available in the vernaculars of European and Levantine societies. In the nineteenth century, the Bible was translated into more than ninety languages, becoming the most translated book in the world,[5] running into several million print editions.[6] Translating to convert, the missionaries equated the act of reading with conversion, and laboured to proliferate

literacy amongst the locals. The exponential growth of Bible dissemination and publishing 'helped seed different forms of nationalism'.[7] In the
Levant, as elsewhere, these nationalisms were fomented with feelings of
sectarian exceptionalism that characterise the labour of conversion.

Languages such as Arabic, which already had a tradition of vernacular
Bible translation, exhibit the historically contingent dynamics of this commoditisation. It thus becomes possible to explore precisely what changed
in the nineteenth century through a diachronic comparison with versions of
the Bible from earlier epochs. This chapter charts the changes in the relations of exchange that the Bible mediates (as well as occludes) when commoditisation becomes its most salient feature. In Beirut, where the Smith
al-Bustani Van Dyck Bible was translated and sold, the American missionaries who supervised and financed the labour were executing instructions
from their superiors in Boston that broke with centuries of Arabic Bible
translation efforts in the West. The most conspicuous of those ruptures is
the shift in origins of biblical translation from the scholarly and religious
capitals of Europe, like Rome (London, Paris, Leiden or Cambridge, to
the hometowns of its intended readers: Beirut, Smyrna, Greece, Malta
or Armenia. The American and British evangelical intervention forged a
multinational market for Bible trade that had headquarters in New York
and London under the care of their respective Bible Societies – publishing
houses that traded multilingual translations of the Bible, Christian tracts
and other useful texts for missionary labour.

The intention to produce homegrown Bible versions disrupted a
practice that had been underway at least since the seventeenth century,
when churches (especially Rome and the various Protestant Churches that
emerged after the Reformation) disseminated translations of the Bible in
vernacular languages following the old ties with the Catholic Church since
medieval times, or made use of the newly established mercantile trade
routes to acquire adherents to the new Protestant Church that was spreading throughout Europe. In this era, Bible versions were treated as gifts
presented to the local churches or to the native population directly, without
the expectation of accumulation or profit that was to accompany the nineteenth century translations. While the British evangelists were the first to
struggle with the negotiation of new exchange relations with the natives,

the full commoditisation of the Bible was undertaken by the American missionaries, who decisively shifted away from the gift economy that had hitherto been predominant in Bible exchange.

In this chapter, I explore the political economy of the Bible. What I mean by that is the way in which the Bible market was conceived and Bible translation efforts were globally synchronised through recourse to two methodologies: the concept of population and the practice of commoditisation. I deal with these concepts in the first part of this chapter. As I show, commoditisation was built on temporalities of acceleration and newness that were deemed feasible after a thorough demographic study of the population had been conducted that spanned a region as far as Armenia and Persia, going to Turkey and Greece, and southwards all the way to Egypt. I explore the transformation to commodity exchange from gift exchange and link its accumulationist intent to the totalising desires that culminate in demographic surveys. I show how, through a scientific approach that combined mathematics and philology, the American missionaries treated the Levant as the seat of biblical ancientness and they hoped to revive its memory and example amongst the Levantines of the nineteenth century. In the second part I contrast their labour with the history of proselytisation which the British missionaries had first attempted in the seventeenth century, and why they failed once more in the nineteenth century. As I argue, the Americans combined commoditisation with proselytisation. Armed with demographic data, and studies that they began publishing as early as the beginning of the 1830s, the Americans had a concrete imagination of a market. Hoping for as many converts as possible, the Americans adjusted their translation strategies to target Muslims as the ultimate audience for their Bible version.

The Americans forged a market for the Bible and sought to accumulate profit from its sales. They used this profit to entirely feed their organisation, and augment its operations beyond a few project – adopting what we know today as a 'non-profit model'. In this way they departed from the economic model of the family with all its slippages into tribe, clan, church or phratry, which Marcel Mauss so thoroughly analysed in his classic study of 'gift-exchange'. Initially, they defined their relationship to the people they encountered through thinking of them as a statistically concievable population. This new model would ultimately replace the family structure of Ottoman governance, which depended for its power on rule by a class of notables.[8]

Michel Foucault contends that without a demographic perspective coalescing around the concept of a 'population', 'it was impossible to conceive the art of government except on the model of the family'.[9] This concept of family did not fit with the missionary dreams to convert the people of the East. For conversion, as the missionaries understood it, required the severance of such familial ties. This had its theological basis in the gospel of Luke 14:16, when Jesus addressed his followers that, 'if any man come to Me and hate not his father and mother, and wife and children, and brethren and sisters, yea, and his own life also, he cannot be My disciple'. Conversion is here imagined as an affiliative model, a wilful rejection of the family model through synchronistic determinants that are concretely embedded in thinking of the natives one encounters as a population that can be counted and measured and communicated to through a predetermined standard. Justified in their quest by the Bible, the missionaries were unapologetically contemptuous of the sovereign authorities in the Levant and were determined to exercise their power within a model of governmentality that, as Foucault notes, equates the interest of each individual consciousness with the interest of the population, 'regardless of what the particular interests and aspirations may be of the individuals who compose it'.[10]

The American Missionary Surveyors

The missionaries produced demographic catalogues on the populations, village by village, of Armenia, Eastern Europe, Greece, Turkey and Central Asia, all the way to the Levantine shores of Palestine and Syria. This aggregated data provided the missionaries with clear statistics of sectarian distribution, the price of commodities, salaries of government officials, geographical distances between routes and communications networks, literacy levels, climate measurements, architectural history, sacred history, key families and many other such inventories that together formed the basis for their interactions with the local populations.[11] Some of these statistics were published in books, while others are in the archives of

Eli Smith and other missionary figures who preserved their correspondence: 'anyone who has worked closely with Christian missionary reports or with travel accounts more broadly knows that such sources can be hit-or- miss in their details'.[12] Yet, despite their inaccuracy, and varying degrees of thoroughness in the missionary numbers, statistical *savoir* structured the relation between the missionaries and the natives in terms of governmentality and the instrumentalisation of economics for the politics of conversion. Their commoditised model of exchange derived from a demographic paradigm of soft governmentality. This paradigm affected the exchange of the Bible, but it was also the basis for missionary efforts in education and health. These basic and necessary services allowed the Americans to exercise a soft form of power that threatened Ottoman rule and its governmental parrying from such responsibilities.

The evangelical missionaries that were connected to the American Board of Commissioners for Foreign Missions (ABCFM) were reminded, before they took the journey away from home, of the evangelical vision and its statistical methodology. Learning languages, translation and press operations were all identified as the main labour of missionaries. As noted in a letter that Eli Smith received from Rufus Anderson, Vice President of the ABCFM, before he embarked on the *Brig Dove* headed for Malta, 'the large field lying open to the American missionaries on the shores and islands of the Mediterranean' required that missionaries concentrate their efforts on comparing works, translating, and printing 'in diverse languages', but also instructed that 'Christian researches are to be made in nearly a dozen different countries . . . else how will you know in what manner to use the press, so as to act most powerfully on their regions?'[13] This letter was standard correspondence, communicating what many missionaries worldwide received from ABCFM and then spent many years implementing. This research filtrated into various species of knowledge including statistics and demographic analyses, travelogues, histories, anthropologies, dictionaries, topologies and other such thorough fields of research that cultivated the missionary institution as a superbly learned body unrivalled in the Mediterranean and elsewhere.[14]

In another letter that Smith received shortly after his arrival in Malta in 1830, Andersen instructed him to provide predictions of the needs of the population, particularly in relation to a new translation of the Bible. For this first task, Armenia was identified as a key location, and Smith was expected to commence his labours by becoming acquainted with the Armenians, a devout group of Christians that were subordinate to Turkish rule. Smith was expected to study whether it is possible 'to furnish . . . a number of the Armenian people with the New Testament in their vernacular tongue'.[15] In order to predict whether such a Bible would find readers, Andersen expected Smith to 'make the Armenians the primary object of inquiry, [and] endeavour to gain information respecting all the Caucasians and other nations, in that part of Asia'.[16] The quest was for historical and demographic information that the traveller was expected to 'make distinct and full memorandums of facts relating to the objects of your tour, and you will not neglect any probable means of informing us of your progress'.[17] Smith would eventually publish his Armenian research with his companion Harrison Gray Otis Dwight under the thoroughly encompassing title *Missionary Researches in Armenia: Including a Journey through Asia Minor, and into Georgia and Persia, with a visit to the Nestorian and Chaldean Christians of Oormiah and Salmas* (1834). In the preface to the *Researches*, Smith reports that compared to the other churches in the region the Armenian Churches are accessible: 'the importance of evangelical labour among them, therefore, has been naturally regarded as enhanced, not only by the prospect of effecting their own improvement, but by the very inaccessibleness in other ways of the regions they inhabit'.[18]

The possibility for success among the Armenians was first identified, as Mehmet Ali Dogan observes, by the early missionaries Pliny Fisk and Levi Parson who wrote to their Boston headquarters that they 'are anxious to see something done, as soon as possible, for the Armenians. The readiness with which they purchase the Scriptures, encourages us'.[19] The leaders of the American mission in the United States responded with questions about the conditions of the Bible, and instructed the travellers to survey all Bible commodities then available on the market. In a letter entitled 'Instructions from the Prudential Committee of ABCFM', by Samuel Worcester, Fisk and Pliny were advised to supply data about Bible circulation, covering:

whether copies of it exist and are read – of what kind, and to what extent? Whether the circulation of it might be increased? – In what versions, by what means and in what amplitude? It will be an object also to ascertain what other books are in use or are held in esteem; and what useful books or tracts might be circulated, and in what languages.[20]

The existent possibilities identified among the Armenians were corroborated by the statistical data gathered by Smith and Dwight. Strategies for translating the Bible evolved from these aggregates. And for Arabic, a similar process began to take shape even if in the Arabic parts of the Levant, the arrival of the Protestants was not as welcome as amongst the Armenians. The Levantine reception of the Bible shares one similarity with the Armenian case, however, in that the political economy of biblical translation began to consolidate into a new market not previously available for the Bible. This market required a boldness that was bolstered by the weakening political position of the Ottomans in relation to the West. Following the Greek War of Independence, and the costly Crimean War, the Ottomans were forced to reorganise their government structures. After they issued the reform decrees of the *Tanzimat*, and loosened control over religious life, the missionaries took heart and became convinced that this new era was conducive for the consequences of the sales of a new Bible that would convert its readers to the new religion. For the Americans, the change in the political climate, and the improved clout of the British with the Ottoman authorities, increased their fortunes. As Heather Sharkey notes, the Americans began to depend on 'foreign advocates [who could] stand up for them: consuls on the ground, and political leaders from afar, who were ready to entreat, persuade, protest, or threaten on their behalf'.[21] The Protestants were backed by strong financial and moral support from their home constituencies, and were expanding across the world in this period. Constituted as voluntary societies that often represented multiple churches, the Protestant missions were diplomatically well-supported internationally. This welcoming political climate impacted how the Bible was commoditised and made into a handsome product. Ideas for a new Arabic Bible for a language that had had its own versions of the Bible since the seventh century, began to ferment. All the external conditions were becoming increasingly amiable.

As a commodity, the SBV version was cost-effective in both production and marketing. It advanced new economic conditions for the Bible that departed from the model typical of Rome's authority over its churches. Rome functioned on a patriarchal model derived from the family, and where commodities such as the Bible were almost exclusively given as gifts. The Protestants by contrast proposed to enter a relation of exchange with local communities based on Bible sales. The projects in education and health that would follow the Bible were subordinated to it, even if today these are the two most enduring aspects of the missionary legacy. The American conduct fostered a competitive climate amongst the Eastern churches, who recollected the rife history of the Reformation and Counter-Reformation, and its problematics relating to the vernacularisation of the Bible, its position in the rituals of faith and the traditions of interpretation that tore the Catholic modes of reading from their Protestant contenders.

In earlier times the Protestants were forbidden from proselytising in the Levantine domains. Then, the religio-political Ottoman system of rule was dependent on the clerics and notables of minorities for its administrative habits. In the nineteenth century, however, the Americans arrived with technologies that industrialised the production of books and school systems. With technologies that could disseminate the Bible cheaply, translation no longer operated within the centralisations of Bible production that were monopolised by powerful church authorities in Rome or Antioch. In the industrial market of cheap printing, the Bible entered the market of symbolic goods, and in this market, room for competition was large enough to be filled not only by the churches, but by anyone who had access to a printing press and was ambitious enough to produce a new version of the Bible. More than two dozen different Arabic translations of the Bible, or portions, were in circulation in the nineteenth century, not all of them officiated by a church, nor were they all fresh translations. In this market, a Bible translation acquired a readership through the ability of its producers to display what Pierre Bourdieu calls symbolic capital, 'a form of prestige and a name . . . readily convertible to economic capital',[22] whereby the exchange between the potential readers and producers of new translations depended on undeclared calculations that could be revealed in how the translators marketed their translations to their constituencies.

The Levant as Bibleland

What distinguished the Levantine market was its historical importance as the original location of Christianity. It is where Jesus was born and crucified, where miracles were performed, where Paul was blinded and saw once again, and where multitudes of Christians have continuously been present. It was also where St Jerome spent years working on the Latin Vulgate, as well as the location of the fall of the Byzantine Empire, the Islamic conquest and its dynasties, the Crusades, a backwater of Ottoman domains and, more recently, has been renewed as the central location for the discourses of the clash of civilisations. Proselytising in the Levant in the nineteenth century, the American missionaries were acutely aware of the historical layers that complicated their own historical narrative about the Levant. Their millenialist imagination fed on their dreams of bibleland, which was 'in significant ways more important than colonizing the American West', as Heather Sharkey observes.[23] The Levant was in the sermons everywhere they preached. As Rev. Heman Humphrey, pastor of the Congregational Church in Pittsfield wrote in his 1819 ordination sermon, entitled 'The Promised Land', delivered for Hiram Bingham and Asa Thurston, the leaders of the first mission to Sandwich Islands:

> As the nation of Israel was *militant*, so is the church now. As the land of Canaan belonged to Israel, in virtue of a divine grant, so does the world belong to the Church; and as God's chosen people still had much to do, before they could come into full and quiet possession of the land, so has the church a great work to accomplish, in subduing the world to the obedience of Christ.[24]

Working in the Levant was thus a privilege few missionaries came to enjoy, but it also carried a responsibility to transform the entire world about which they proselytised into ancient Levantines, whereby contemporary Levantines were expected to become a more authentic version of biblical communities. The route to this objective was a new and fine translation of the Bible that could effectively compete with the Qur'an.

The early missionaries stocked up on copies of Arabic Bibles and Christian tracts through the British evangelists who ran a depository in Malta, established in 1816, which had dominated the global production and distribution of multilingual Bible versions in the early decades of the nineteenth century.[25] The Bibles were popular with the local communities of the Levant despite their diverse confessional identities and linguistic practices, and even Muslims were eager to acquire them. These Bibles were cheaper than most of the books that could be purchased in a predominantly manuscript-based Arabic book market. The distribution of these books went in tandem with 'the spread of education, which in turn depended on the supply of suitable books to help diffuse both literacy and enlightened knowledge'.[26] So central was the Bible to their initiation with the local communities that they soon earned the title of *biblishiyin*, or Biblemen, foreigners who peddled in Arabic Bibles and who spoke broken Arabic.

In response to the increased sales of Bibles in its domains, the Maronite Church issued a decree directly forbidding any dealing with the *biblishiyin* at risk of excommunication. Copies of the Bible were rounded off and burned in town squares all over Mount Lebanon, and collaborators with the missionaries were harassed or imprisoned, like As'ad al-Shidyaq, who eventually perished in incarceration.[27] However, the zeal of the missionaries remained undeterred and crates of Bibles continued to arrive from Malta. The books themselves were mainly printed at the press of Richard Watts, a specialist of Oriental printing in London.[28] They came from a variety of sources including the famous Roman translation of the Bible known as the Biblia Sacra Arabica (BSA, 1671), which Arabic readers were most inclined to acquire either in print or in hand copies. In this climate, the missionaries publicly embarrassed the Maronite Church by complaining that the Bibles burned actually carried the seal of Rome.[29] Until they began producing their own Bible translations, Anglophone missionaries mainly relied on the BSA for the production of cheap Bible copies that they then sold and distributed in the Levant and other Arabic speaking countries.

Inheriting the British Missionaries in the Levant

Established in 1698, the British Society for the Propagation of Christian Knowledge (BSPCK) was the main institution that oversaw Bible translation and its global dissemination amongst Protestant missionaries. Despite their depository in Malta, that William Jowett established in 1815, and their solid presence in the Levant, the British interest in Arabic Bibles was articulated as a contribution to proselytisation efforts in Africa, Persia and India. Such is the case with the Newcastle Bible that was worked on by Professor of Arabic at Cambridge Rev. Joseph Dacre Carlyle (d.1804). The missionary historian John Owen notes that this translation was to aid colonial efforts in Africa.[30]

With the establishment of the Asiatic Society of Calcutta in 1784 by William Jones, Arabic publishing was introduced, and some key books of symbolic importance for the modern literary tastes in Arabic classics saw their first printing there.[31] In the catalogue of the Asiatic Society, one finds the earliest printed editions of *al-Mu'allaqat*, *The Arabian Nights* and al-Hamadhani's *Maqamat*. With support from the East India Company, and under the auspices of the Asiatic Society, the reputable missionary, Henry Martyn, recruited Nathaniel (Jawad bin) Sabat of Arabia, an Indian who converted to Protestantism and published 800 copies of the so-called Calcutta version, a New Testament translation into Arabic (1810) that was primarily sold in Bengal.[32] The translations identified 'Mohammadans' as primary readers, and from the outset presented the Bible in competition with the Qur'an. Martyn, who died six years after he travelled from Cambridge to become the Chaplain of the East India Company, and supervised the work of Sabat, had also supervised the production of a Bible in Persian (1816) and Urdu (the continuous text appeared in stages in the 1820s) before he died at the age of thirty-one. Quick to respond to the rivalry, Muslim scholars prepared Qur'an translations in Urdu that entered the market in the 1820s. As a response, Martyn wrote a tract that refuted the theological soundness of the Qur'an. This tract, entitled *Controversial Tracts on Christianity and Mohammedanism*, was published after his death by Carlyle's successor at Cambridge, Prof. Samuel Lee.[33] Lee was the secretary of the

Foreign Translation Office which reported to the British and Foreign Bible Society that was founded in 1804.

Lee began his tenure as a missionary scholar when evangelical Bible publishing was becoming most energetic. His first task for the Foreign Bible Society was the invention of Maori script in 1816, supervising the preparation of its grammar book, without ever learning the language, but as a fulfilment of his role of occupying the chair of Arabic and Hebrew languages at Cambridge.[34] Lee would eventually also translate *The Travels of Ibn Battuta* (1829) to English and supervise the translation of the Bible that was prepared by Ahmad Faris al-Shidyaq, which was published in 1857, five years after Lee's death and two years after the publication of al-Shidyaq's magnum opus *al-Saq ala al-Saq* (Paris, 1855).

The early presence of the British missionaries in Malta and the Mediterranean basin forged the first contours of the evangelical Bible market in the nineteenth century. Through their labours, the Bible was transformed into a commodity, and the success of its sales were measured and recorded. As Geoffrey Roper notes, by 1845, 'the Scriptures might be purchased in a dozen bookshops in Constantinople; without molestation'.[35] The pricing of those Bibles was a vexed issue for the British missionaries. The market they entered was not accustomed to Bible trading but generally received its Bibles through gifts and donations. And in the past, when they tried to proselytise through Bible distribution, they gave away their copies *en acte gratuit*.[36] Hoping to reach as many people as possible, the Society had to navigate a custom of gifting the Bible to a conspicuously poor population, and also their need to 'recoup at least some of its high printing and production costs, and ensure as far as possible that copies went only to genuine readers and not to the merely acquisitive or to those who aimed to resell at a profit'.[37]

The British missionaries welcomed the arrival of American missionaries to the Levant, particularly because they began to trade in new regions that had previously been neglected by the British, in the Eastern Mediterranean and in Armenia and Iraq. Speaking on behalf of the British missionaries, the historian William Canton considered the Americans 'very essential and valuable helpers to us; without them we should do little'.[38] Nevertheless they were also rivals who threatened to usurp the place of the British Empire in the hearts and souls of potential converts.

The Americans, who had counted the British among their partners at least since the eighteenth century, decided to intensify their activity in the Levant, since the region was not adequately covered by British missionaries.[39] They followed the British model in all their undertakings and even decided to produce an Arabic Bible that could supersede all versions sold by the British. The American missionaries took the decision to produce the SBV in 1832, and by 1834, the Arabic printing press had arrived in Beirut. Faris al-Shidyaq had already been in Malta since 1826, having left with the Americans after the incarceration of his brother As'ad. There he secured employment with the British and began to work as an Arabic tutor, counting Eli Smith among his pupils.

When the British took the decision in 1844 to employ al-Shidyaq to create a new translation, they knew of American plans to produce a new Bible version.[40] Considering that translations of the Bible were undertaken by several of their associates, American work was not initially framed as competition. The British did not proselytise with intensity in the Levant at the time and seem to have also misread the possibilities in the market. Lee reports to the Foreign Bible Committee that the Levantine region is ripe for a new, British translation of the Bible to Arabic:

> The Syriac Christians [the Maronites] would receive gladly a version of the Old Testament made first from the Hebrew, that the Greek Christians [meaning the Greek Orthodox] could well be disposed to read it, that the Mohammedans would refer to it with interest. But what would be most acceptable of all, especially to the Clergy, would be a new translation from the Hebrew accompanied with a concordance.[41]

This prosaic analysis of the market and of the wishes and needs of the Bible-reading public counted on demographic potential without any profound analysis of the undeclared expectations of potential buyers. Lee misread a region that he never visited, and assumed, without any substantive material nuance, that a translation would be well received. This misreading would permeate the entire process of translation, from the moment they chose to hire al-Shidyaq for the work, to the process of translation that they agreed upon, to the production process and the publication of the book. In contrast to the dilettante translations that were being made by theologians everywhere, the project into which al-Shidyaq was recruited was expected to produce a flagship translation, and for that, large institutional funds were allocated.

Al-Shidyaq had demonstrated his superior Arabic skills in Malta, where he authored and translated forgotten works on Arabic grammar and vocabularies, and translated a variety of Christian literature, including *The Book of Common Prayer* with George Badger (1815–88). His command of Arabic impressed his employers who considered his skills unsurpassed by any of the expatriate Arab employees they had at their service. The BSPCK had set up a Foreign Translation Committee at Cambridge, which included Lee, as well as four other members, whose job was to ensure that all translation work undertaken on behalf of the Society was audited for quality in all stages of production. Lee's colleagues in the committee included Thomas Hartwell Horne, the librarian at Cambridge and the university commissary Thomas Harrison. As non-experts in Oriental languages, they relied upon Lee's opinion on the progress and quality of the work. Al-Shidyaq's relationship to this setup was directly with Lee, whom he served in the capacity of assistant. This explains why Cambridge's archives only scarcely carry a trace of him.[42] His absence from the employment records suggests that any relations he had there besides Lee were informal.

The Foreign Translation Committee decided to hire al-Shidyaq despite a letter of caution about his morally unorthodox conduct having been sent by the British Bishop of Gibraltar stationed in Malta. Keen on securing his services, they repeatedly yielded to his persistent financial demands, from continuing to cash his Maltese salary as a supplement to his British income, to his frequent requests for a raise.[43] They saw in his excellent command of the language a scarce resource that was sure to imbue their Bible with an elevated value.

At the same time, the Americans were already making progress on the translation: work on the text had begun, experiments with font were well under way and Smith was contacting various European Orientalists soliciting feedback for the drafts being produced. The BSPCK and their

Foreign Committee were among the bodies and scholars Smith had con-
tacted and the American samples were once discussed in the minutes of
the Committee. Lee, who reviewed the font that was prepared by Smith,
reported to his colleagues that the font was 'a copy – a very good one
indeed – of the peculiar handwriting of the Maronites of Mount Lebanon,
and therefore not generally accepted by readers of Arabic'.[44] This opinion
on a font that was superior to any Arabic font in British possession, and
particularly better than the font that the British would eventually use in
their translation, reveals the beginnings of a competition over the Bible, in
an expanding market.

We know from al-Shidyaq's own writings about his quarrels with
Lee. Lee in turn did not share with the committee his problems with
al-Shidyaq, who had no respect for Lee's knowledge of Arabic. As
al-Shidyaq explains, Lee perceived that 'the language of the Arabs is not
scripted like other languages. Rather it is an artificial and florid language,
with much grammar and limitations unlike the languages of Europe'.[45] In
al-Saq as well as in his European travelogue, he shares these exaspera-
tions with the reader even though, as I maintained elsewhere, al-Shidyaq
won all his arguments with Lee, who concurred to his authority as the
best Arabic speaker in missionary employment.[46] Yet the translation itself
reveals that the process deployed in the al-Shidyaq-Lee version was unfit
to compete with the subsequent translations produced by the Americans
and the Jesuits in the decade to come.

Protestant Rivalries over Arabic Bible Publishing

Despite advertising their version as a direct translation from Hebrew
and Greek, the text reveals that al-Shidyaq worked from the King James
Bible.[47] The concepts that he selects for the text reveal a relationship to
English but not necessarily to Greek, and some of the problematics of
the KJV are reproduced in his translation. Take the concept *epieikis* in
Philippians 4:5 which is translated as 'moderation' in the KJV, to read
'Let your moderation be known unto all men. The Lord is at hand'. It was
rendered by al-Shidyaq as *iqtisadikum* or 'economy' instead of the more
accurate *hilmikum* or 'clemency'.[48] Also his translation of 1 Peter 5:13
reflected the King James's erroneous addition of 'church' in 'the church

الـكتب المقَدّسَة
وهي
كتب العَهد العَتِيق
قَد تُرجمَت حَديثاً من اللّغـة العبرانيّـة الاصـليّة
وكتبُ العَهد الجديد لرّبنا يسُـوع المسيح
قَد تُرجمَت حديثاً من اللّغـة اليونانيّـة الاصليّـة
إلى العَرَبيّـة
بنفقـة الجمعيّة الانكليزيّـة
المعروفة بجَمعيّة ترقية المعارف المسـيحيّـة

طبعَها العَبد المفتقر الى رَحمة ربّه وليم واطس
في لندن المحروسَة سنة ١٨٥٧ مسيحيّة

Figure 1.1 Al-Shidyaq Lee Hebrew Testament, title page.

that is at Babylon, elected together with you, saluteth you; and so doth Marcus my son' thereby replicating an earlier interpretative liberty taken in St Jerome's Vulgate, which nevertheless does not exist in the Textus Receptus, the original witness for the King James Bible.

Most telling of the use of the King James is al-Shidyaq's translation of the names of the Greek gods in Acts 14:12 and 19:35, Jupiter and Mercurius, into 'utarid (Greek: *dia*) and mushtari (Greek: *ermi*), rather than attending to other more appropriate synonyms, like, *zafs* or *zus*, for the former or *hirmiz*, for the latter, as was customary for Arabic Bibles, even in the Latin BSA. This rendition selected Arabic planet equivalents instead of making a connection to the names of Greek gods (of which Arabic equivalents exist, or in the case of the SBV, the BSA and many other Bible versions, they were borrowed from Greek). These examples reveal that al-Shidyaq most certainly consulted the KJV during his work. We can further infer that since al-Shidyaq was neither a Greek nor a

كِتَابُ العَهْدِ الجَدِيدِ

لِـــرَّبِّنَا يَسُوعِ المَسِيحِ

قَد تُرْجِم حَدِيثًا مِنَ اللّغَةِ اليُونَانِيَّةِ الأَصلِيَّةِ

إِلَى العَرَبِيَّـــةِ

بِنَفقَـةِ الجَمعِيَّةِ الانكليزِيَّةِ

المَعرُوفَةِ بِجَمعِيَّةِ تَرقِيَةِ المَعارِفِ المَسِيحِيَّةِ

―――――――

طَبَعَهُ العَبْدُ المُفتَقِرُ الَى رحمةِ ربِّهِ وليم واطِس
فِي لُندُنَ المَحرُوسَةِ مَثَّلُانَةَ مسيحِيَّةِ

Figure 1.2 SL, New Testament, title page.

Hebrew scholar, it was Lee's responsibility to make comparisons with the original languages. Perhaps Lee was cut short in his editorial work by his premature death in 1852. His successor in the Foreign Translation Committee as well as the chair of Hebrew and Arabic at Cambridge, was Prof. Thomas Jarrett.

Lee's death effectively dissolved al-Shidyaq's duties of 'physicking the foul of breath', or '*islah al-bukhr*' his parodic expression for his work as an Arabic tutor and Bible translator at Cambridge. When the translation was finally published in 1857, two years after al-Shidyaq had published *al-Saq* in Paris, and five years after he circulated his critique on the Bible, *Mumahakat al-Ta'wil fi Munaqadat al-Injil* (Disputations on the Interpretation of the Gospel), it was already doomed to fail. Not only were al-Shidyaq's publications too controversial for a Bible translator, but the translation's reliance on the KJV, as well as the deployment of the faulty font typical of Brian Watts printing press work, rendered this

Figure 1.3 SL, beginning of Matthew.

version impoverished as a philological endeavour and did not advance any improvements on printing Arabic texts at a time when serious research was being done on Arabic book design elsewhere.[49] With the publication of the SBV in 1860, this Bible was discontinued and British missionaries took the American Bible as their authoritative Arabic version. Since then, the al-Shidyaq-Lee version has become a curiosity, to be consulted by Bible scholars but of no liturgical value for believers. We find traces of it in the Jesuit Bible that was published a decade after the SBV. The Jesuit translators would eventually use it to improve their Arabic style in choice phrases and words.

The American Successors

In the early 1820s, and thanks to American efforts, the BSA emerged as the most sold Bible version in Arabic.[50] Other versions that they also sold, albeit less successfully, were from the London Polyglot Bible (ca 1657)

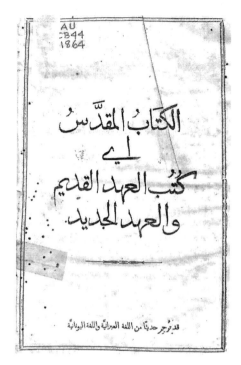

Figure 1.4 Smith Bustani Van Dyck, title page of the Continuous Text.
Source: Near East School of Theology.

and the so-called Newcastle translation of 1811.[51] Dealing in various versions of the Bible, the missionaries first tested the market and learned about the tastes of local readers who acquired their books.

Commoditisation bolstered a Protestant practice centred around Bible reading. Their faith in reading as the pathway to conversion thus required that Bible copies be available, and that the work of translation conform to the tastes of most readers, in the style and material production of the text. Distributing a Bible that was associated with the Roman Church ran counter to their ambitions and revived a history of confrontation and competition that went as far back as the Reformation. The BSA was indeed a popular Bible, and in their pragmatism, they made do with selling it without the deuterocanonical books for a time, but it is a Bible that was an unintended consequence of the Reformation. It had been conceived as a response to the translation of portions of the Bible that were made by Thomas Erpenius in

Figure 1.5 SBV, beginning of John. Source: NEST.

1616,[52] and that began to flood the Levant in the seventeenth century. Also then a *firman*, Bible burnings and the threat of excommunication were deployed to deter the local population from engaging with the Protestants.[53] This history was present for the American newcomers, and in their altercations with the Catholic Church, frequent reference was made by both groups to the Council of Trent and the history of the Reformation as the most relevant narrative that informed the relationship between the evangelists and the churches that were under protection from Rome. A new translation was thus becoming necessary for the authentication of the Protestant message and its competitive edge in Arabic.

Their plans to prepare their own translation of the Bible emerged out of their desire to cultivate circles of Bible readers outside the influence of the Eastern churches. The market, they believed, was ripe for such labours. Rufus Anderson, Smith's supervisor and the foreign secretary of the ABCFM exclaimed that the 'continued existence of large bodies

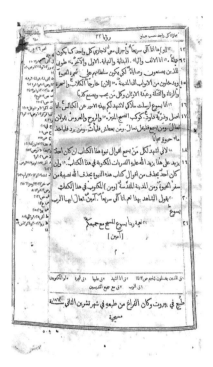

Figure 1.6 SBV, last page of Revelation, indicating Beirut, November 1864 as publication city and date. Source: NEST.

of nominal Christians among these Mohammedans, is a remarkable fact ... should spiritual life be revived among them a flood of light would illuminate the Turkish empire, and shine far up into Central Asia revived among them'.[54] Identifying the local Christians as the first priority in their operations, the missionaries hoped to teach a more righteous path than that which the Eastern Churches preached. Only through a transformation from a mere nominal identity to a rigorous practice of reading and engaging the Bible would Syria regain its former Christian glory as the land of Christ. But the local Christians were not the only audience, and plans to convert Muslims certainly existed, but they were channelled through a strategy of Bible commoditisation, where exchange and trade were the main feature of their communication with the locals.

Improvements in print technology were timely for their ambitions.[55] These improvements which enhanced the efficiency and lowered the costs

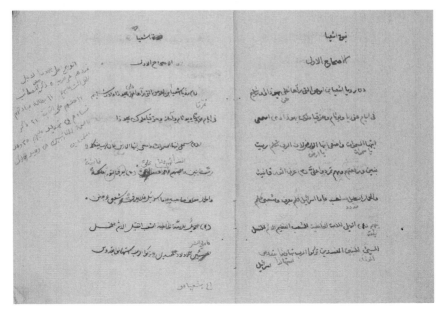

Figure 1.7 SBV, manuscript probably in Bustani's handwriting with edits from Smith. Source: NEST.

of Bible publishing helped the missionaries reformulate the relationship that binds Bible readers to the authority that maintains its foundational role as scripture. If in the past, the Bible had remained limited in its circulation and was disseminated mainly through oral liturgies during church service, the modern Bible distinguished itself through the democratisation of access to the continuous text, and the erasure of the line that separated Church elites from the laity. Their version differed from the competition in its superior font, layout and the simplicity of its visual execution. It also succeeded in producing a uniform translation that used a uniform vocabulary for concepts, in an Arabic that was standardised and that conformed with Muslim expectations of the stylistic quality of foundational texts.

It was perceived as a 'homegrown' Bible. When it entered the market, it was sold at plummeting rates for every reprint. In the American Bible Society catalogue, the price of the 1864 copy of the Smith al-Bustani Van Dyck (SBV) was set at $2.75.[56] Writing in 1872, Rufus Anderson, the Foreign Secretary of the ABCFM reports that 'the price of the reference edition was fixed at ten piasters and of the pocket edition at five, or about forty and twenty cents, which placed them within reach of nearly all who could read'.[57] By 1896, a similar, improved and vowelled, copy sold for 6 piasters.[58] Considering that in 1861, a cook's monthly salary at the mission was $5/month (or following Anderson's formula, 15 piasters), then indeed this Bible was available to most people, even those who were just learning to read.[59] But it was for the quality of its philological intervention and the logics of its strategies of translation that the SBV distinguished itself from similarly priced versions of the Bible.

Translating the Bible

Upon arriving in the Levant, the American missionaries abandoned their initial plan of translating the Bible from the King James Version (KJV). This version served as the main source text for Bible translations executed by Anglophone missionaries in many regions in the world. In places where Bibles were being introduced for communities that were not familiar with Christianity, there was no a priori expectation by local readers about what the source text of the Bible ought to be. In China, New Zealand and other locations, the biblical source text was even less a point to ponder. In some of those locations, such as parts of America, New Zealand and parts of Africa, Christianity had no strong presence. In India, and despite the continuous presence of Christianity there less than a century after the birth of Christ, their low numbers vis-à-vis the other religions and sects curtailed the impact of Christianity and relegated it to the status of minority religion. In those locations, the KJV accelerated the process of translation, for it did not require the profound philological training in ancient languages that a translation from original witnesses would compel. It sufficed to send a missionary whose acquaintance with the Bible was not steeped in Greek and Hebrew, but who had other skills, such as medicine, or printing, depending on the needs in the new field. When they first arrived in the Mediterranean, the missionaries thought that the KJV would be a good source text for vernacular Bibles in the region. Commenting on the Turko-Armenian translation, Jonas King wrote on August 31, 1830: 'Most of the translations must obviously be made from the English tongue, and there are very few persons, born in the Levant, who have a competent acquaintance with that language'.[60] The Eastern

Christians, as the missionaries were soon to discover, were versed in a variety of languages that had a long tradition of Bible translation. Also, the original witness text was never an issue that Arabic translations of the Bible cared much about, for witnesses could come from any of the ancient languages of the churches. The region's linguistic polyphony in both its ancient and modern mix of languages confounded the American labour of proselytisation. Relaying the linguistic hardships of missionary work, Rufus Anderson, wrote:

> The Maronites and Syrians spoke the Arabic language but employed Syriac alphabet in writing. The Armenians, to a large extent, spoke the Turkish language, but used Greek alphabet. The Greeks in Asia generally spoke the Turkish language but used the Greek alphabet. The Grecian Jews spoke the Grecian language, the Spanish Jews the Spanish, the Barbary Jews the Arabic, but all three used the Hebrew alphabet. Then too, the worship of the Syrians, Greeks, and Armenians was in the ancient languages of those nations, which were in the most part unintelligible for the common people.[61]

Such heteroglossic communities, whose Bibles were still read in ancient tongues and who had been translating into Arabic since at least the eighth century, would consider the KJV too young to have carried any authority as a source text. So, in 1832, the Armeno Turkish NT was published by William Goodell and Bishop Dionysius, who declared it translated from the 'original Greek'.[62] Similarly for Arabic, the translation required a sound scholarly approach steeped in the languages of the region. These new insights about the long history of the Bible in the region forced them to abandon their plans to translate from the KJV in the Eastern Mediterranean, and to send missionaries that were philologically capable of working from original biblical languages.

To resolve this discrepancy with other locations, the Americans stipulated that the alternative should remain connected to the KJV, through the resolution to use the family of Greek New Testament manuscripts known as the Textus Receptus, the received text, known in Arabic as *al-nass al-maqbul*, the accepted text. This textual source was collated by Desiderius Erasmus in 1516 and was the text that Martin Luther used for his own translation. The decision to use it in the nineteenth century emerged at a crucial time in the history of biblical scholarship in the West. As James Turner writes, since the beginning of the Renaissance, and crucially with the advent of the Enlightenment in the eighteenth century, the authority of the Erasmian text was unhinged, and 'philologists aimed to build a new, more reliable' source text for biblical scholarship. They also worked to develop 'a new understanding of the history of the New Testament text'.[63] These studies eventually revised the belief in the primacy of the Textus Receptus as a source text, and philologists began to collate and publish different versions of the Greek NT that they posited were more ancient, and therefore more legitimate. Their work also included a revision of ideas about how the gospels were authored, reconstructions of biblical geography and archaeological explorations, and finally, a revision of the taxonomies that organise the manuscript families with consequences on how 'to make sense of variant readings'.[64]

This revolution in biblical study, and the questioning of the authenticity of the Textus Receptus as the most ancient text, had been storming through Europe since the eighteenth century. As philologists were aware, including the scholars connected to the Syria mission, this Greek text was no longer convincing as the most ancient manuscript, and new versions were being collated all over Europe from other manuscript traditions of the New Testament that attested to being more ancient, and therefore more authoritative than Erasmus's most famous collation.[65] The choice to nevertheless use the Textus Receptus was legitimised for the central role this source text had played in the Protestant Reformation, as the source text that Martin Luther relied on when he prepared his own translation of the New Testament to German. Thus, the Bibles that came out in Modern Greek, Armenian, Arabic and Italian were all translated from this source text and not from the KJV. The Maltese Bible was the only exception. Unlike the other languages, Maltese had a lowly status as a vernacular and the missionaries sought to revamp that status. Before they began to translate the Bible, they published an English–Maltese lexicon and grammar, the Americans then translated the Maltese Bible from the KJV, closely following the example set by British missionaries stationed among oral tribes.[66] The choice to translate from original languages was the beginning of a philological journey that would extend beyond knowledge of Hebrew and Greek towards a profound learning of Arabic and its long literary history.

Market Potential is Muslim

The Americans sought to reform how the Bible had been traditionally received by the laity. They therefore had to contend with the minor position of this scripture for Arabs. They reasoned that in a language where the shadow of the Qur'an looms large, greater impact would be achieved through conformity to the trends of the elite majority, rather than through recourse to the linguistic practices characteristic of weak groups. As the sociologist Ahmad Beydoun observes, conforming to linguistic norms signifies 'the strength of the general bonds that structure the group and the forceful presence of its culture among other cultures as well as the intensity of its resilience in the face of hegemonizing cultures'.[67] The Americans sought in standard Arabic an assertion of strength, and argued the case for a standard register of Arabic as an ideological necessity for the work of proselytisation.

This new Bible was expected to circulate widely and transcend the dialectical variations typical of pre-*nahda* Bibles, an efficient decision that would result in only one translation for all Arabic readers. So rather than choosing to translate the Bible into the various dialects of the Arabic cluster, the Americans selected a standard form of Arabic as befitting the concept of the vernacular that Protestants adhered to and sought to propagate.[68] This ambition to propagate the Bible widely further encouraged the missionaries to conceptualise *fusha* as a style of writing that appeals to educated Muslims.[69]

In the study that Eli Smith undertook on the conditions of the market of Arabic Bible translation, which he attached to the proposal he sent to the ABCFM office in Boston in 1844, he reports that the vernacularisation of the Bible in Arabic dates back to the late seventh century.[70] As a consequence of the Arab conquests in the Levant that led to the defeat of Byzantium and the continuous rule of Muslims over Christians and other minorities in the long history of the Islamicate Empire,[71] those translations were blamed for faulty language, ideological corruption, and incompetent dissemination. As he claimed, all the available Bibles that they were circulating were written in inadequate Arabic, and had been translated by different hands, which produced a diverse phraseology and idiom. As he wrote:

> The structure of the sentences is awkward, the choice of words not select, and the rules of grammar are often transgressed. We have been ashamed to put the sacred books of our religion, in such a dress, into the hands of a respectable Muhammedan or Druze and felt it our duty to accompany them with an apology.[72]

By emphasising the linguistic register of earlier Bible translations, Smith was departing from deliberate linguistic choices of style that were institutionalised in earlier translations, and particularly in the BSA version. Instead, he adopted the long-held Muslim view that there is a *rakaka*, a lameness of speech, in the Arabic style of the Bible.[73] Christian Bibles were not traditionally measured for worth according to what Muslims thought of their Holy Book. And Muslims did not generally reject the Bible's claims to universal truth based on linguistic issues. At the height of Christian–Muslim polemic, in the ninth century, about the veracity of the Bible, Muslim scholars were mostly concerned with theological difference rather than with grammatical variation, even if such variation was sometimes thrown in for rhetorical gain.[74] Shifting the focus towards the style of writing, Smith was motivated by ambitions to proselytise amongst the Muslims.

In the directives he received from Rufus Anderson in 1826, just before he was to embark to Malta, Smith was instructed that his influence should be genial, and 'stream out, like an electric fluid, and dart from mind to mind, till thousands and millions feel the exciting power'.[75] Muslims as well as Christians were to be subject to such divine charm, and for that the Bible had to wear a suitable linguistic dress. Following the example of Luther, who was 'not only concerned about explaining what individual words mean but especially about recognizing what they cause to happen',[76] Smith was concerned with impressing Muslims, with the hope of converting them to Christianity.

Smith and his group were motivated by a wish to proselytise amongst the Muslims because of the sheer size of the market. In the *Missionary Herald*, the periodical published by ABCFM, the number of Arabic-speaking Muslims was often provided to justify the need for a new translation of the Bible. In 1847, five years after the decision to translate the Bible was taken, and work had begun, the *Missionary Herald* published an article that presented to its American readers and donors the exciting challenge to undertake a new translation to Arabic. As they wrote:

> Calculate if you can the magnitude and responsibility of such an enterprise. It is a blessed work to give the word of God to a hundred thousand dwellers in the little islands of the Pacific, or to the few thousand tribes that roam over our own wild forests, even though these islanders and these tribes seem hastening to utter extinction. But the Arab translator is interpreting the lively oracles for the forty million of an undying race, whose successive and ever augmenting generations shall fail only with the final termination of all earthly things. Can we exaggerate such a theme?[77]

The greatest number of the forty million being counted in this appeal for sympathy and donations at home were of course Muslims, and it is with them in mind that Smith made his proclamations about what constituted good Arabic. These Muslims, as the missionaries also reported in the *Herald*, were scornful of the Bible because of its lowly language and the fallen state of its Arabic-speaking Christians. In July 1835, the *Missionary Herald* wrote:

> The Mohammedan confidently asserts the Koran to be more excellent than the Bible, and his own religion than the gospel. In vain do we reply, that the native Christians have lost the knowledge and spirit of the gospel, and that their immoral lives are therefore in no sense the effect of the gospel. The Mohammedan has never seen any other effect, and he will not read the Bible to correct the evidences of his senses and perhaps too of his painful experience. He treats the holy book with the contempt he feels for its professed followers.[78]

With an eye on sheer sales and the potential to convert Muslims through acts of reading, Smith decided to adopt a style that could adequately compete with the Qur'an, the scripture that prides itself on having been revealed in the Arabic language.[79] He had to contend with this Arabic by conforming to some of its features, particularly in grammar, but departed from it lexically and in the prose style of its delivery. Smith began working on a new translation in 1848 and, as the American Orientalist Isaac Hall writes, without his persistent vision, this edition would not have materialised. Hall credits him with being 'the first to assert . . . that a new translation of the Bible was indispensable'.[80] He built his argument for a new translation by selecting standard Arabic for the writing style to appeal to the tastes of influential Muslims, but by departing from the rhymed prose typical of the Qur'an,[81] and by employing an updated vocabulary that rejected arcane words not easily available for the majority of Arabic readers. Style thus became a carrier of the desire to penetrate the market and reach out to Muslims as well as to Christians.[82]

What was new about this attitude towards Arabic was the desire to no longer mark the Bible as belonging to a variant register of written Arabic, as was typical of earlier Bible versions that were being sold by the missionaries, but rather to write their scripture in a style appealing to Muslims. The new simple design eased readability, which was also facilitated by introducing the more expensive vowelled editions which guaranteed that phonetic rendition was standardised according to the rules of Arabic grammar.[83] This last detail stabilised the text in ways that it never enjoyed previously. To create vowelled editions in Arabic, even today, is a time-consuming process, and has therefore always been reserved for special kinds of texts where standard aural readings are as important as the text itself, especially in texts like the Qur'an, lexicons, or poetry. Prose genres usually remain unvowelled, and Bibles were previously produced in unvowelled editions. This new design was also facilitated by the novel introduction of a Western style punctuation system. Full stops and paragraph breaks reinvented the text in modern ways, and together with vowelling, guaranteed that the phonetic rendition was regulated by the book makers, so that readers everywhere would translate the ink on the page in as much as of a standard aural experience as possible. Together with very wide dissemination, these new editorial decisions about the look and style of the text inspired common solitary reading practices which impacted and transformed the reader of the new Bible. No longer was the Bible to be learned through liturgy, nor was reading any more taught through two or three Bible books.[84] Rather, the new standard form of the Bible produced new readers that were hailed to become acquainted with a standardised Bible that had arrived at its present form through statistical data about what could entice the largest number of Arabic speakers to read the Good Book.

Upon the publication of the SBV's vowelled edition in 1871, Van Dyck proudly exclaimed that '[t]hose who are aware of the fact that, but a few years since, this people could with difficulty be induced to accept the Bible *gratis*, will be able to duly appreciate this fact, that so many copies have been *sold* within so short a period'.[85] In the same report, Henry Jessup also rejoiced that

> the whole Mohammedan world can read the New Testament of the Bible. They constantly objected to the old translation as not being the word of God, because it was not correct Arabic, and the Arabic is *a sacred language*. A Mohammedan in Sidon on seeing the vowelled edition of the New Testament, gave out word that the lost *Enjeel* . . . was found.[86]

These jubilations were intended for American donors, whose financial support guaranteed technological upgrades at the press. By 1864, six thousand copies of the SBV had been distributed, thereby turning it into a veritable best seller.

The SBV did not create a market for books, but it transformed the market that was already there; it standardised the text of the Bible and made the continuous text (a label that covers all the books of the Bible as arranged by Luther into one tome) available for the first time, at a cheap price. Through the stability of print, this Bible seemingly resolved the suspect instability of the manuscript Bible, and so ensured that all copies of the Bible were absolutely unified at the point of exchange with the reading public. It has become a sacrosanct text for the churches – such as the Greek Orthodox, Egyptian Coptic, and various Arab Protestant denominations – that have repeatedly refused suggested improvements on translation identified by many current biblical scholars.[87] Moreover, it claimed to have gone back to the Greek and Hebrew sources and to have jumped over the hundreds of Arabic translations that preceded it. This was a clear break from previous practices, where manuscript Bibles circulated in openly intertextual channels as opposed to claiming a rupture from other texts.

Conclusion

As a product that cut across the emerging sectarianism in Lebanese communities, in a form that was ameanable to the inherited tastes of literati who were accustomed to manuscripts, this Bible was promoted as *modern* precisely because the translators managed *to select how it continued a tradition*. As a result, when the translators claimed to have excluded the earlier translations of the Bible from their reference list and to have translated only from the original Bible languages, which the title page identified as Greek and Hebrew, they were implicitly claiming their superiority over the competition. What may have also helped bolster the superiority of this Bible in the eyes of the local readers was Van Dyck's status as a man of learning and a great medical authority with excellent, non-patronising relations to the native communities of Syria. When his support for the thought of Charles Darwin at the Syrian Protestant College cost him his job,[88] he went on to work closely with the Greek Orthodox community, where he helped them found their first hospital,[89] which remains a major medical institution in Lebanon to this day. Despite the diverse reasons that explain its popular reception, the SBV's success resounded for Arab Christians and had an impact, not only on democratising access to the Bible, but also on transforming the foundational position that turned the Bible into what it is today: a major bestseller in the world of books.

This new Bible was outfitted in a new dress, tailored to fit with a modern sensibility that was increasingly adaptive to the proliferation of modern commodities. The evangelical dress adapted the capitalist model of exchange and formulated the practice of reading within an alimentary view on the benefits of a consumption that leads to conversion. The Bible was straited into its commoditisation through the deployment of tactics of governance and state building that enabled it to enter an emergent political economy, that is, an overdetermination of economic frameworks in the political and social relations and negotiations between people. The sheer availability of the Bible that the American missionaries secured for the Arabic language produced a new problematic of religion as the site of the colonial encounter.

The publication of the SBV in 1860 coincided with the outbreak of civil war between Druze and Christians in Mount Lebanon. As Makdisi writes, the missionaries perceived the massacres as

> symptomatic of a 'native' Oriental world inherently segregated by religion and race, and unable to modernize on its own accord . . . [It was certainly] incomparable to anything that had occurred in America, which was itself in 1860, of course, on the brink of civil war, and which had by then a well-documented history of religious and race riots, to say nothing of slavery and the massacres of Indians.[90]

The missionaries maintained the fiction that Christian morality was a liberating force that must shape the modern period. While Southern slavery can in no way be compared to the minority question of Arab domains, this is exactly the analogy that shaped the imagination of American missionaries during this period, in the sense that Arab Christians were viewed as shackled to the yoke of heathen Mohammedans, enslaved against their will in a society that exploited their labour and silenced their rights and their voices.

The *savoir* of the American missionaries met its pragmatic realities then when the seismic shifts in the sectarian balance threatened the very sovereignty of the Ottomans over Mount Lebanon and Syria. The massacres against Christians in 1860 helped dissipate some of the tensions between the Protestants and the Catholics. The Maronites were no longer considered papal frauds by the American Protestants, who now represented them as the hapless Christian minority of the East, in need of Western protection against the Muslims. Their contribution came in the shape of a freshly translated and printed New Testament, that was donated to Christian refugees who took shelter in many places around Beirut, including the Protestant church and schools. For the Catholic elites who witnessed the Protestant response to the murder of Christians, the war might have stoked a jealous fear that would culminate in a new Jesuit translation of the Bible. As the Jesuits took the decision to produce a new Bible, their rivalry awoke the history of the Reformation and the fundamental differences in the approach to scripture as text, a development to which I will now turn.

Notes

1. Quoted in Johann Strauss, 'Langue(s) sacrées et recherche de langue sacrée(s) dans l'Empire ottoman au XiXe siècle' in Hiéroglossie: Moyen âge latin, monde arabo-persan, ed. Jean-Noel Robert (Tibet, Inde: Collège de France, 2019) 115–52, 116.

2. Appadurai, *The Social Life of Things*, 13.

3. For the situation in Istanbul and the multilingual communities the Protestants encountered there, Johann Strauss has an excellent article that testifies to the pragmatics of linguistic decisions in the effort to provide the widest possible dissemination of the Bible. See 'Langue(s) sacrées et reherche de langue(s) sacrée(s) dans l'Empire ottoman au XIXe siècle'. For local missionary efforts within Britain, see Leslie Howsam, *Cheap Bibles: Nineteenth-Century Publishing and the British and Foreign Bible Society* (Cambridge: Cambridge University Press, 1991). For American missionary local initiatives, see the five-volume collection of essays *A History of the Book in America*. (Chapel Hill: University of North Carolina Press, 2000–10). Especially see James N. Green, 'The Book Trade in the New Nation', vol. 2, 75–127; David Paul Nord, 'Benevolent Books: Printing, Religion and Reform', vol. 2, 221–46; Paul G. Gutjahr, 'Diversification in American Religious Publishing', vol. 3, 219–28. Scholarly interest in translation of the Bible around the world is witnessing a surge. On the Greek translation of the Bible in that period, see Miltiadis Konstantinou, 'Bible Translation and National Identity: the Greek Case', *International Journal for the Study of the Christian Church* 12, no. 2 (August 2012):176–86. On the nineteenth-century Chinese translation of the Bible to Mandarin see George Kam Wah Mak, *Protestant Bible Translation and Mandarin as the National Language of China* (Leiden: Brill, 2017).

4. On New Zealand, see Donald F. McKenzie, *Bibliography and the Sociology of Texts* (Cambridge: Cambridge University Press, 1999); On Swahili, see Johannes Fabian, *Language and Colonial Power: The Appropriation of Swahili in the Former Belgian Congo, 1880–1938* (Cambridge: Cambridge University Press, 1986). On the various Latin American indigenous

languages, see Lars Kirkhusmo Pharo, *Concepts of Conversion: The Politics of Missionary Scriptural Translations* (Berlin: De Gruyter, 2017).

5. The Bible today boasts more than a thousand translations.

6. On the pre-modern Bible languages, see Manuel Jinbachian, 'Introduction: The Septuagint to the Vernaculars', in *A History of Bible Translation*, ed. Philip A. Noss (Roma: Edizioni di storia e letteratura, 2007), 29–57.

7. Heather Sharkey, *A History of Muslims, Christians, and Jews in the Middle East* (Cambridge: Cambridge University Press, 2017), 205.

8. Albert Hourani, 'Ottoman Reform and the Politics of Notables', in *The Modern Middle East: A Reader*, ed. Albert Hourani, Philip Khoury, and Mary C. Wilson (London: I. B. Tauris, 2009), 83–110.

9. Michel Foucault, 'Governmentality', in *The Foucault Effect: Studies in Governmentality*, ed. Graham Burchell, Corin Gordon, and Peter Miller (Chicago: University of Chicago Press, 1991), 87–104.

10. Ibid., 100.

11. See the scraps and notes in Eli Smith's personal papers. 'Demographic Notes on the Population in the Levantine Region', and 'Demographic Notes on the Sectarian Demography and Geographical Distribution of the Population in the Levantine Region', Eli Smith's Personal Papers. ABC 50, Houghton Library, Harvard University, Cambridge, USA.

12. Sharkey, *A History of Muslims, Christians, and Jews in the Middle East*, 221.

13. Letter from Rufus Anderson to Smith before he left to Malta, pre 1830, ABC 60, Houghton Library, Harvard University, Cambridge, USA. 11 pages, 3.

14. Andreas Feldtkeller and Uta Zeuge-Buberl, *Networks of Knowledge: Epistemic Entanglement initiated by American Protestant Missionary Presence in 19th century Syria* (Stuttgart: Franz Steiner Verlag, 2019).

15. Letter from Rufus Anderson to Eli Smith and Dwight, 19 January 1830, ABC 60, Houghton Library, Harvard University, Cambridge, USA. 21 pages, 11.

16. Ibid., 10.

17. Ibid., 12.

18. Eli Smith, Josiah Conder, and H. G. O. Dwight, *Missionary Researches in Armenia: Including a Journey through Asia Minor, and into Georgia and Persia, with a Visit to the Nestorian and Chaldean Christians of Oormiah and Salmas* (London: G. Wightmann, 1834), lxiii.

19. Quoted in Mehmet Ali Dogan, 'American Board of Commissioners for Foreign Missions (ABCF) and "Nominal Christians": Elias Riggs

(1810–1901) and American Missionary Activities in the Ottoman Empire' (PhD Dissertation, Utah, University of Utah, 2013), 50–1.

20. Mehmet Ali Dogan, 'From New England into New Lands: The Beginnings of a Long Story', in *American Missionaries and the Middle East: Foundational Encounters*, ed. Mehmet Doğan and Heather Sharkey (University of Utah Press, 2011), 13.

21. Sharkey, *A History of Muslims, Christians, and Jews in the Middle East*, 208.

22. Pierre Bourdieu, *Outline of a Theory of Practice*, trans. Richard Nice (Cambridge: Cambridge University Press, 1977), 171.

23. Heather Sharkey, 'Introduction: American Missionaries and the Middle East, A History Enmeshed', in *American Missionaries and the Middle East: Foundational Encounters*, ed. M. A. Dogan and H. J. Sharkey (University of Utah Press, 2011), ix–xliii, xx.

24. William R. Hutchison, *Errand to the World: American Protestant Thought and Foreign Missions* (Chicago: University of Chicago Press, 1987), 52.

25. Geoffrey Roper, 'Arabic Printing in Malta 1825–1845: Its History and Its Place in the Development of Print Culture in the Arab Middle East' (Dissertation, Durham, Durham University, 1988), http://etheses.dur.ac.uk/1550/. 77.

26. Ibid., 123.

27. Makdisi writes a history of the relations that bound the Americans to the natives through the story of As'ad al-Shidyaq. See Makdisi, *Artillery of Heaven*.

28. Roper. 'Arabic Printing in Malta (1825–1845)'.

29. For details about the polemics that were written that accompanied Bible burning and anathema expulsions from the community, see Makdisi, *Artillery of Heaven*, 96–102.

30. John Owen, *The History and Origin and First Ten Years of the British and Foreign Bible Society*, vol. 1 (London: Tilling and Hughes, 1816), 788.

31. I checked these rare books in person in Calcutta in December 2018. See also Jurji Zaydan who mentions the Orientalists that were publishing Arabic texts in Calcutta in his history of Arabic literature. Zaydan, *Tarikh 'adab al-Lugha al-'arabiyyah*, 1359.

32. Claudius Buchanan, *Christian Researches in Asia, with Notice of the Translation of the Scriptures into the Oriental Languages* (New York: Largin and Thompson, 1812), 119.

33. Arvil Powell, 'The Legacy of Henry Martyn to the Study of India's Muslims and Islam in the Nineteenth Century', *Cambridge University*,

Henry Martyn Centre, n.d., https://www.cccw.cam.ac.uk/wp-content/up loads/2017/07/Powell-Dr-Avril.pdf. Accessed: 28 September 2019.

34. McKenzie, *Bibliography and the Sociology of Texts*, 82.

35. Roper, 'Arabic Printing in Malta;' William A Canton, *History of the British and Foreign Bible Society* (London: John Murray, 1910), vol. 2, 279.

36. Bernard Heyberger, *Les chrétiens du Proche-Orient au temps de la Réforme catholique Syrie, Liban, Palestine, XVIIe-XVIIIe siècles* (Rome: École française de Rome, 1994), 476.

37. Roper, 'Arabic Printing in Malta 1825–1845', 91.

38. Canton, *History of the British and Foreign Bible Society*, 287.

39. David W. Kling, 'The New Divinity and the Origins of the American Board of Commissioners for Foreign Missions', in *North American Foreign Missions, 1810–1914: Theology, Theory, and Policy*, ed. Wilbert R. Shenk (Grand Rapids: William B. Eerdmans, 2004), 11–38, 17.

40. Horne, Lee, Harrison, Guretono, 'Minutes of Meeting of the Foreign Translation Committee', 28 November 1844, Bible Society Archive, University of Cambridge, UK.

41. Horne, Lee, Harrison, Guretono, 'Minutes of Meeting of the Foreign Translation Committee', 9 November 1844, Bible Society Archive, University of Cambridge, UK.

42. Geoffrey Roper, 'Ahmad Faris al-Shidyaq and the Libraries of Europe and the Ottoman Empire', *Libraries and Culture* 33, no. 3 (Summer 1998): 233–48, 238.

43. Rana Issa, 'Al-Shidyaq-Lee Version (1857): An Example of a Non-Synchronous Nineteenth-Century Arabic Bible', in *Senses of Scripture, Treasures of Tradition: The Bible in Arabic among Jews, Christians and Muslims*, ed. Miriam L. Hjalm (Leiden: Brill, 2017), 305–26.

44. Horne, Lee, Harrison, Guretono, 'Minutes of Meeting of the Foreign Translation Committee', 13 November 1848, Bible Society Archive, University of Cambridge, UK.

45. Ahmad Faris al-Shidyaq, *Al-Wasitah ila ma'rifat 'ahwal Malta wa kashf al-mukhabba' 'an funun Urubba* (Beirut: Kutub, 1866), 131.

46. Issa, 'Al-Shidyaq-Lee Version (1857)'.

47. See the original title page of al-Shidyaq-Lee Bible, *Al-Kutub al-Muqaddasah*, 2 vols. (London: William Watts, 1857).

48. ἐπιεικής occurs in the Arabic translation of Aristotle's *Rhetoric* in a way that emphasises the meaning of 'clemency' as an extra-legal category of

jurisprudence. In Phil 4:5 the SL translates ἐπιεικής from KJV, where it is rendered as moderation. The SL use of *iqtiṣād* (*economy*), which fails to accurately capture the Greek, but remains faithful to the KJV. The SBV translation of this word into *ḥilm* (gentleness, clemency, mildness) approximates the lexical definition in Trench Synonyms where it is defined: 'going back from the letter of right for the better preserving of the spirit (a relation between theology and jurisprudence). The archetype and pattern of this grace is found in God" (Accordance Bible Corpus). This word is translated as *Güte* by Martin Luther and *Sanftmut* by Franz Eugen Schlachter. For the Greek corpus of texts, I checked 'GlossGA - Glossarium Græco-Arabicum', http://telota.bbaw.de/glossga/. Accessed 1 October 2019.

49. Dagmar Glass, *Malta, Beirut, Leipzig and Beirut Again: Eli Smith, the American Syria Mission and the Spread of Arabic Typography* (Beirut: Orient-Institut der Deutschen Morgenländischen Gesellschaft, 1998). Andreas Feldtkeller and Uta Zeuge-Buberl, *Networks of Knowledge.*

50. Roper, 'Arabic Printing in Malta', 76.

51. Ibid., 39.

52. On the BSA, see Paul Féghali, 'The Holy Books in Arabic: The Example of the Propaganda Fide Edition', in *Translating the Bible into Arabic: Historical, Text-Critical, and Literary Aspects*, ed. Sara Binay and Stefan Leder, Beiruter Texte Und Studien 131 (Beirut: Ergon Verlag, 2012), 37–52. On Erpenius and his Bible, see Mordechai Feingold, 'Learning Arabic in Early Modern England', in *The Teaching and Learning of Arabic in Early Modern Europe*, ed. Jan Loop, Alistair Hamilton, and Charles Burnett (Leiden: Brill, 2017), 33–55.

53. Roper, 'Arabic Printing in Malta, 68. See also a similar episode of Bible burning in Egypt, this time with the SBV Bible burned in 1867, Sharkey, 'American Missionaries, the Arabic Bible, and Coptic Reform in Late Nineteenth-Century Egypt', in *American Missionaries and the Middle East*, 242.

54. Rufus Anderson, *History of the Missions of the American Board of Commissioners for Foreign Missions, to the Oriental Churches*, vol. 1 (Boston: Congregational Publishing Society, 1872), 2–3.

55. Hala Auji, *Printing Arab Modernity: Book Culture and the American Press in Nineteenth Century Beirut* (Leiden: Brill, 2016).

56. American Bible Society, *Annual Report of the American Bible Society*, vol. 4 (American Bible Society, 1871).

57. Anderson, *History of the Missions*, 193.

58. Presbyterian Church in the U.S.A. Board of Foreign Missions and Beirut American Mission Press Syria, 'Illustrated Catalogue and Price List of Publications of the American Mission Press' (Beirut, Syria Mission Press: 1896).

59. A. L. Tibawi, *American Interests in Syria, 1800–1901: A Study of Educational, Literary and Religious Work* (Oxford: Clarendon, 1966), 158.

60. Kamal Salibi and Yusuf Quzma Khuri, *The Missionary Herald: Reports from Ottoman Syria, 1819–1870*, 5 vols. (Amman: Royal Institute for Inter-Faith Studies, 1995). 2: 42.

61. Rufus Anderson, *History of the Missions*, 75.

62. 'Mediterranean: Malta' *The Missionary Herald*, 23 January 1832, 2. For the historical conditions of the period of translation of the Turko-Armenian Bible, see Cemal Yetkiner, 'At the Center of the Debate: Bebek Seminary and the Educational Policy of the American Board of Commissioners for Foreign Missions (1840–1860)', in *American Missionaries and the Middle East: Foundational Encounters*, 69.

63. James Turner, *Philology: The Forgotten Origins of the Modern Humanities* (Princeton: Princeton University Press, 2014), 115.

64. Ibid., 116.

65. Tuska Benes, *In Babel's Shadow: Language, Philology, and the Nation in Nineteenth-Century Germany* (Detroit: Wayne State University Press, 2008); Bruce Metzger and Bart E. Ehrman, *The Text of the New Testament: Its Transmission, Corruption, and Restoration* (Oxford: Oxford University Press, 1964).

66. See McKenzie's discussion of Maori Bibles for a history of missionary practices working with oral languages, McKenzie, *Bibliography and the Sociology of Texts*. Also see Fabian's study of colonial linguistics in Africa, Fabian, *Language and Colonial Power*.

67. Ahmad Beydoun, *Ma'ani al-Mabani: Fi Ahwal al-Lughah wa A'mal al-Muthaqqafin* (Beirut: Dar Annahar, 2006), 32.

68. Stephen Sheehi, 'Towards a Critical Theory of Al-Nahḍah: Epistemology, Ideology and Capital', *Journal of Arabic Literature* 43, no. 2 (2012): 269–98.

69. There are important exceptions to the standardisation of the Bible in Arabic. One such case was supervised by British missionaries that Sharkey has covered. See Heather Sharkey, 'Sudanese Arabic Bibles and the Politics of Translation', *The Bible Translator* 62, no. 1 (January 2011): 30–6.

70. Hall, 'The Arabic Bible of Drs. Eli Smith and Cornelius V. A. Van Dyck'; Van Dyck and Smith, 'Brief Documentary History'.

71. I borrow the term 'Islamicate' from Marshall G. S. Hodgson, for the room it makes to account for the entangled histories of Muslims, Christians and Jews who continuously coexisted under Islamic rule that spread over the Levant and neighbouring regions. See *The Venture of Islam: Conscience and History in a World Civilization* (Chicago: University of Chicago Press, 1974).

72. Smith, 'Brief Documentary History', 1–2.

73. Sidney Griffith, 'The Gospel in Arabic: An Inquiry into Its Appearance in the First Abbasid Century', *Oriens Christianus* 69, (1985): 125–67. This view would continue well into the twentieth century, most notably in Taha Hussein's proclamation that Arabic Bibles are not written in good Arabic. Taha Hussain, *Mustaqbal al-thaqafa fi Misr* (Cairo: al-Hindawi, 1938, 2014), 283.

74. Sidney Griffith, 'The Gospel in Arabic'.

75. Letter from Rufus Anderson to Eli Smith, 22 May 1826, ABC 60, Houghton Library, Harvard University, Cambridge, USA. 11 pages, 6.

76. Johannes Von Lüpke, 'Luther's Use of Language', in *The Oxford Handbook of Martin Luther's Theology*, eds. Robert Kolb, Irene Dingel and L'Ubomir Batka (Oxford: Oxford University Press, 2014), 152.

77. *The Missionary Herald*, 1847, vol. 43, 192.

78. *The Missionary Herald*, 1839, vol. 35, 40.

79. The Qur'an, 16:103.

80. Hall, 'The Arabic Bible of Drs. Eli Smith and Cornelius V. A. Van Dyck', 283.

81. Contrast with the Bible in rhymed prose that was published in the fourteenth century. 'Abd Yashu' al-Subawi, *Anajil 'Abd Yashu' al-Subawi* (Jounieh: Al-Maktabah al-Būlusiyyah, 1318).

82. Sheehi was first to observe the vehicular function of standard Arabic for the circulation of capital. See Sheehi, 'Towards a Critical Theory of Al-Nahḍah'.

83. Semitic languages are written with consonants and long vowels. Short vowels are often not given in a text. A vowelled text is thus a text where the short vowels are visible.

84. Accounts that most Christian readers acquired literacy through reading Psalms and the Book of Matthew are sprinkled across the literature. One

such account is Shafiq Jeha, *Tarikh al-Ta'lim w al-Madaris fi Bishmizzin: 1850–1951* (Beirut: Beirut International Book Capital, 2009). Also see Ahmad Faris al-Shidyaq, *Leg over Leg.*

85. American Bible Society, *Annual Report of the American Bible Society*, 130.

86. Ibid., 129.

87. The late Baptist scholar Rev. Ghassan Khalaf has provided recommendations for a new translation that, as he explained to me privately, have met with resistance from churches that use this Bible version because they are habituated to its idiom. See Khalaf, *Adwa' 'ala tarjamat al-Bustani Van Dyck (Al'ahd al-jadid)* (Beirut: Jam'iyat al-kitab al-muqaddas, 2009).

88. The Darwin crisis in the Medical School of the Syrian Protest College, today known as the American University of Beirut, is a story of monumental impact on the course of Arabic literature and modernity. See Marwa Elshakry, *Reading Darwin in Arabic, 1860–1950*. Makdisi refers tangentially to this crisis in *Makdisi, Artillery of Heaven*; also see Jeha, *Darwin and the Crisis of 1882 in the Medical Department.*

89. Van Dyck's work as a medical doctor with the Greek Orthodox community was formalised in 1878, where he helped found what continues to be known as St George's Hospital.

90. Makdisi, *Artillery of Heaven*, 170–1.

2

Bible Competition

The arrival of American missionaries in Beirut was a world apart from the pre-nineteenth century history of Bible translation. The American commoditisation of the Bible contested the authority of other religious communities and dragged them into the fray of competition. The Catholics were especially vexed with the Americans and identified them as the most dangerous contenders for Christian leadership. American zeal awakened the history of the Reformation and old seventeenth-century Catholic tricks like Bible burning, excommunication, and official complaints to the Ottoman and Western authorities were tried in this new context to little effect. To complicate matters for the Catholics, the Americans distributed a version based on the bilingual Arabic-Latin Catholic Bible from 1671, Biblia Sacra Arabica. American salesmanship and ardour, as well as their serious interest in educating the locals and converting them to their reading practices, qualified their competitive advantage.

Competition between the Catholics and the Protestants was not the product of the nineteenth century. But at this time, competition became a market force, wedded to a commodity, when in the past it had been embodied in religio-political rivalry over turf and over who has access to the production as well as to the reading of the Bible.

Competition between the Jesuits and Protestants in the nineteenth century took advantage of the emergent colonial political economy that favoured imported commodities over local labour. The spirit of free trade was spreading, and in the Ottoman Empire, it was inaugurated by the Balta Liman Agreement of 1838, with the emerging British colonialists.

This agreement, like the *Tanzimat* edicts signed in the same year, facilitated the movement of American missionaries in the Levant, as members of the British millet, and thus protected by an agreement that allowed them to trade in the Empire. Describing the impact of this agreement on British and Ottoman political relations, Necla Geyikdağı writes that the agreement 'conferred upon British merchants not only the status of "most favoured nation" but also that of 'most favoured domestic merchants'.[1] Through this agreement, the British were referred to as a *millet*, a term that legally recognised the group by the state, and was thus discreetly included alongside other *millets* (sects or nations), that resided within the Ottoman domains. The American missionaries, who counted as part of the British *millet* gained tremendously from the Balta Liman agreement.

In its details, the agreement guaranteed the interests of Britain to become the main trading partner of the Ottoman government. The agreement expected the Ottoman state to levy a 12% tariff for local exports, while they taxed commodities entering Ottoman regions on British ships at 5%. British products, as well as products from the British colonies, flooded into Ottoman stores. The agreement opened the Ottoman market up to the global economy, meanwhile in Britain, Ottoman goods had to sometimes confront 60% tariffs on imports into the kingdom, through policies of protectionism that the British imposed to shield local industries from international competition. While the Ottoman state increased its revenues from taxes due to this agreement, the Ottoman craftsmen could no longer compete or survive in a market dominated by British consumer goods.[2] The difference between Ottoman and British cities and their relation to the economy could not be more pronounced. Describing London's financial district, the City, a few years after the signing of the agreement, al-Shidyaq writes

> No one steps in except to work and to earn, and no tongue wags except for profit and utility. No sun rises and no lamp is lit except in pursuit of a living. Hearts are moved only to earn and to acquire. So you see each and every person with their eyes and mouth gaping, wide open, to devour the world and everything in it. You stumble through its corridors across brokers talking to themselves as they go about their business.

Here you meet youth already veterans in management, even supervisors; likewise you find seasoned veterans who possess the energy and eagerness of the young. Whichever way you turn, you encounter voracious countenances – their internal and external senses steered completely by their ambition toward accumulation and hoarding. There is not a single corner of the globe that this district does not supply with merchandise and work.[3]

The bustle that al-Shidyaq describes was so powerful that 'no producer [was] left who could compete with British goods protected by the Ottoman state'.[4] The agreement was disastrous for the capacity of the Ottomans to develop their own industry, but the state was oblivious to the difficulties it was instating, for the tax revenues that were agreed upon increased, while the income of the craftsmen came plummeting down. In 1881, the Ottoman economy crashed; Istanbul accrued major debts, or to put it differently, Britain achieved its aims to undermine the Ottoman state through the domination of capital.

The Ottomans' slide into the political economy of globalisation had unlucky consequences for the empire. The transformation in how commodities were exchanged, and the increasing dependence in the Ottoman Empire upon goods coming from the *ingliz*, the Anglophones of Britain and America shaped in key terms how the Bible became commoditised and the consequences of this commoditisation on its textual reception. Like other goods produced by the *ingliz*, the Bible was cheaper than what local craftsmanship could offer by way of book making. With the free movement of English merchants and goods in Ottoman domains, the presence of the missionaries and their wares could no longer be curtailed with the weakening favour of Roman and French diplomats with the Ottoman courts (and the impact these weakening ties would have on the Catholic Arabs in the Levant). The Anglophone activity, whether of the commercial or missionary kind, was now legally protected by law even when religious conversion became an 'imperial headache', as Selim Deringel translates.[5]

For the Bible, this legal transformation between the *ingliz* and the Ottomans enabled the possibility of its commoditisation. It redirected the age-old competition between Protestants and Catholics towards an increase in its production, and an attention to the quality of its translation and printing, to prepare it for capitalist outperformance in an emerging market for Bible books. The law of capitalist competition governed both parties unequally. The American publishing ventures set the standard; Catholics had to follow and emulate if they were to have any competitive advantage in the market.

The accumulationist perspective underscoring American economic interests transformed competition into what Karl Marx defined as 'the immanent laws of capitalist production' which were felt 'by each individual capitalist, as external coercive laws'. Competition, as Marx observes, compels the capitalist to constantly extend 'his capital, in order to preserve it, but extend it he cannot, except by means of progressive accumulation'.[6] This accumulation was embodied in the obsession with the downward pricing of the Bible especially after the Jesuits published the New Testament in 1878. From 1872 to 1898 the SBV version depreciated in cost from 10 to 6 piastres, at a time that saw great currency devaluations. This drop in prices was aided by the increase in production.

The size of production was a source of pride for the missionaries. Documenting a bygone period, Henry Jessup writes in 1910 that at the opening of 1859, Dr Van Dyck had 'the whole of the new translation of the four gospels in type. Five thousand nine hundred and sixty-two volumes and tracts were issued from the press in 1858, and 3,638,000 pages were printed'.[7] A few years earlier, Isaac Hall quoted Van Dyck's testimonial account:

> We made here electrotype plates of four sizes of the entire Bible, one vowelled entire; three sizes of the New Testament, one vowelled; and one set of vowelled Psalms, 12mo: in all, between 10,000 and 11,000 plates. Some of these were made after I left the Press, and by oversight of proof-reader were not compared with the standard copy which I had left there for that purpose.[8]

The fixation on the numerical and the choice of items that impress a perception of efficiency, like the plates or the number of pages, or the size of the printed book, suggests for the reader that the market is being flooded, and that prices are going lower and lower. The promise is that the Bible is within reach of most people. The Americans were what Weber would characterise as 'favourably situated for production to underbid their rivals on the selling side'.[9]

The Jesuit Bible

When religio-politics no longer worked as a means of competition, the Catholics had no other recourse but to beat the Americans at their own game and prepare a new translation of the Bible. Jesuit missionaries returned to the Levant in 1831 after a long period of absence.[10] They had not been there since they went dormant in 1777. Back then, Rome had become aloof to their activities and refused to extend them any support or protection and they were unwanted by the Ottomans. The Protestants had met the same fate at the time, and circulation of printed Bibles was halted even before it began. The contrast with the nineteenth century is instructive, for it allows us to reflect on how competition begins to regulate the flow of commodities. With the open peddling of the Bible in village squares and cities, the Jesuits came with the intent to compete, and to regain ownership of the means of production not just of the Bible, but of all other commodities and services that the Americans sought to market. They rivalled the Americans in all their endeavours and started providing education and healthcare services to Maronites and Oriental Catholics. By 1848 they had founded the famous Jesuit Press, in 1875 they founded St Joseph University and then in 1878 they published a new version of the New Testament that departed from the 1671 version.

In their new version, the Jesuits reasserted the concept of tradition through recollecting Rome's response to the Reformation in their set of meetings that took place between 1545 and 1563, known as the Council of Trent. Their reinvigoration of the concept of tradition confirmed the symbolic capital of Rome as a church that has endured for centuries in the East. The Jesuits would then go on to demonstrate that, like the Protestants, they could translate the Bible through recourse to modern philology, but that their competitive edge is not in flaunting modernity, but in echoing tradition. The Jesuits resignified the concept of tradition in modernity to bestow authentic distinctions and pedigree, against a sect that they faulted for lacking the patina of age.

If the Bible was the centre of Protestant activity, it was not the same for the Jesuits. When they came in, they focused on a variety of cultural activities that could adequately compete with the Protestants. Like them, they started schools, opened a printing house, health services and eventually also a university. Like them, they also translated the Bible. Competition was what centred their activities. In the words of Van Dyck,

> The Jesuits have issued a translation, made by them with the assistance of Ibrahim al-Yazigi, son of Dr Smith's former assistant, and printed in three large octavo volumes. It is a fair translation generally, and only differs in very slight particulars from mine (so far as I have traced it) – and that only for the sake of differing from the Protestant Version.[11]

The Jesuit continuous text was published in 1881 and according to American accounts, they sold it at an even cheaper price than the SBV.[12] It was a collective effort that included seven theologians and literary scholars, and is often associated with the names of Ibrahim al-Yaziji, the Jesuits Josef Van Ham, Auguste Rodet and Ambrosios Monnot.[13] Through their close reading of the SBV and the strategic choices they made to distinguish their work from the Protestant translation, the Jesuits succeeded in bracketing the influence of the Protestants on their constituencies.

In the introduction to the Jesuit Bible printed in Lebanon, the SBV is proclaimed to have prompted a new Catholic translation, where the Jesuits 'corrected' the 'falsifications' of the Protestants in the text of the Holy Books. In the introduction to their Bible, the Jesuits write, the Protestants:

> permitted their hands to manipulate the Divine Books through deviations and omissions. They translated and published the Bible in this condition and distributed it to the far ends of Syria (*al-bilad al-shamiyyah*) and other nations. They adorned it in the eyes of people through good printing and beautiful font. They made it cheap to persuade the good people to desire it and buy it, blinding them to what disastrous traps lay in it.[14]

Claiming that the Protestants seduced the people through packaging their translation with superior font and printing, the Jesuits laboured to excel especially in designing the package and produced a text that is stupendous in the time taken for its design and layout. As the introduction of the 1897 edition of this Bible points out, the font was designed especially for the translation, in a step that learns from the Americans but clearly exceeds their exquisite attention to detail. 'We took for it the best Arabic font in the eyes of scribes, the so-called Constantinople font, that has since become well known in most places'.[15] In addition to the font, this Bible exhibited intricate work in the design of embellishments used in the text, including section markers and the insistent use of rosettes rather than Western-style punctuation. Each book of the Bible had its own unique section marker, and each chapter had its own unique rosette design. The folio size of the master copy used expensive and thick paper and opens with several pages that display the seals of Rome in both Arabic and Latin, in gold, red and blue. For smaller editions, thin and durable paper was deployed, and the arrangement of the text in two columns made it possible to publish the entire Bible as a continuous text. Visually, the

Figure 2.1 Jesuit Bible, Rome's Endorsement in Preface.
Source: Bibliothèque Orientale.

إِنْجِيلُ
رَبِّنَا يَسُوعَ ٱلْمَسِيحِ

Figure 2.2 Jesuit Bible, title page. Source: Bibliothèque Orientale.

profuse Catholic taste asserted its difference from the spartan savours of the Protestant textual aesthetic.

The choice embellishments signal the efforts of the Jesuits to present themselves as upholders of tradition. In her work on printing practices in the nineteenth century, Hala Auji argues that the Jesuit publications initially 'resembled scribal works, at least in the manner in which they were organized and their emphasis on calligraphic techniques'.[16] These continuities were deliberately orchestrated by the Jesuits, who emphasised tradition as a strategy of translation and book production. As they mentioned in the introduction of the first edition, their Bible was translated from the original Hebrew and Greek. 'We had it collated meticulously and compared it to the old versions in the Church', namely the Syriac translation and the Greek version known as the Septuagint as well as the Latin version that 'has been depended upon since an ancient time and that is fixed by the Council of Trent'.[17] In the 1897 edition, the introduction further states that

Figure 2.3 Jesuit Bible, icon prefacing the New Testament.
Source: Bibliothèque Orientale.

the footnotes and appendices that were attached at the end of the translation interpreted the difficult passages in 'accordance with the teachings of the Church Fathers'.[18] The mention of Trent in the last decades of the nineteenth century frames the new translation within the problematics of the Counter-Reformation and its stipulations about the position of scripture in church life. Yet the meaning of Trent was markedly different from its mention in the introduction of the Biblia Sacra Arabica version of 1671.

The Polemics of Bible Translation between Protestants and Jesuits

Rome approved the proposal submitted by the Jesuits for a new translation of the Bible to Arabic in 1871. Al-Yaziji's magisterial Arabic produced an elevated literary style, classical and simple, without a trace of the BSA's Christian Arabic. Jesuits were well attuned to how the SBV was marketing itself, by claiming that it went back to original Bible sources. The deployment

Figure 2.4 Jesuit Bible, Matthew, title page and beginning.
Source: Bibliothèque Orientale.

of 'original' texts was intended to advance a claim to authenticity that was extremely innovative at the time. Having picked up on how authenticity was being constructed by the SBV, the Jesuits attest to have translated from the original languages 'Hebrew and Greek'[19] when only a century earlier, the historian and literary figure, Jirmanos Farhat (1670–1732),[20] Maronite patriarch of Aleppo, includes an entry on *injil* (Gospel) in his famous lexicon *Ahkam al-I'rab*, 'Mathew wrote it in Hebrew . . . Marcus recounted it from Peter in Latin . . . Lucas in Greek . . . and John in Greek'.[21] What this tells us is that the original languages of the Bible were not common knowledge even amongst wide sections of the Eastern Arab Church elites. Even though the BSA version states its source languages,[22] the concept of the original text was not even that important, in accordance with the decrees of Trent. The translators of the BSA write in the introduction that 'all Bible texts have been corrupted somehow . . . and that not even the Hebrew or

Figure 2.5 Jesuit Bible, Matthew, first and last page of Chapter 3.
Source: Bibliothèque Orientale.

Greek text is absolutely perfect'. They even contended that Arabic was one
of the famous languages of the Bible prior to the sectarian strife amongst
the churches. Since then, copies of the Arabic Bible have become full of
mistakes or even lost.[23] With the publication of the SBV, such a permissive
view of the parent text was no longer possible. On the Jesuit Bible title
page, we read that this text was translated from the Hebrew and the Greek.

Before they began work on their versions, the Jesuits published
a polemic claiming that the SBV contained outright falsifications of
the biblical message. In a series of articles in their journal *al-Mashriq*,
detailing what they found offensive in the SBV, the Jesuit Van Ham,
accused the Protestants of deliberately attacking the Catholic creed in
their translation. The Protestant response initially came from the convert
to Protestantism, Mikha'il Mashaqqah, a man who closely worked with
Eli Smith and who readily participated in polemic with the Catholics,

Figure 2.6 Jesuit Bible, Luke, title page and beginning.
Source: Bibliothèque Orientale.

whenever opportunity arose. Entitled *Kashf al-Awham 'amman Mazzaqathu al-Siham* (Exposing the Delusions of Those Who Were Torn by Arrows), Mishaqqa's polemic was appendixed in Van Ham's 1871 book, كشف المغالطات السفسطية ردا على ما أشهره حديثا أحد خدمة الأبروتستانية ضد بعض الأسفار الإلهية (*Exposing the Sophist falsifications in response to the recent publication of one of the Protestant servants against some of the Divine Books*). In this polemic, Van Ham summarises the position of the Catholic Church toward the Bible as follows:

> St Augustine said, 'I only believe in the Book because the Sacred Church commanded me to believe in it.' The Protestants take the opposite view. They do not accept that God bestowed authority on the leaders of His Divine Church. They also do not believe that every believer must subject his mind to the teachings of the Church. They refuse to accept that

Figure 2.7 Jesuit Bible, Luke, beginning of Chapter 2.
Source: Bibliothèque Orientale.

outside the Holy Book there is a Tradition that includes the word of God
... they have no path to reaching Truth based on God's word; this word
disciplines the mind and the will through its infallibility. Therefore, the
condition of the Protestants in defining the canonical books is dread-
ful. We are on a stable continent, whereas they are under the sway of
earthly, historical and critical knowledge – always shaky.[24]

With tradition as the backbone of their method of translation, the Jesuits
then went on to attack the scientific objectivity of the Protestants and contended that it was no more than a cover for ideological assertion. In another
polemic published by the same author in 1872, entitled *Kashf al-Tala'ub w
al-Tahrif fi Mass Ba'd Ayat al-Kitab al-Sharif* (Exposing the Falsifications
that Touched Some Verses in the Noble Book), Van Ham writes that if one

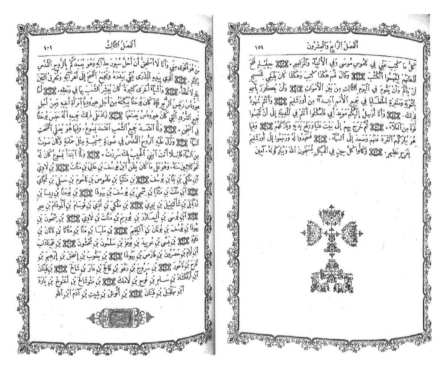

Figure 2.8 Jesuit Bible, Luke, last page of Chapter 2.
Source: Bibliothèque Orientale.

reads the SBV version, one finds that they have indeed manipulated the
Word to their ends by 'cancelling the Catholic Truth from Divine verses.
But we thank God for the Divine Church that had prohibited the reading
of the book of heretics and the copies of the inventors'.[25] He then proceeds
to list the instances where the SBV has obliterated Catholic faith. As the
title of the book implies, Van Ham's polemic pertained to some verses
rather than to the entire translation. The complaints he inventories remain
at the level of the lexeme, whereas Van Ham and the Jesuits believed
the Protestants inserted their ideological biases into the text of the Bible.
Of the lexemes mentioned, the Greek term *presbýteros*, in James 5:14
is emphasised as an example of Protestant manipulation. Translated as
shuyukh in the SBV, and *qusus* in BSA rather than *kahana* as the Jesuits
eventually rendered it, this word testifies for Van Ham to the Protestant
rejection of the hierarchy of the Catholic Church. After explaining that the

Protestants do not revere this important Catholic office, he then offers the Catholic interpretation whereby, he argues, 'the language of the Holy Book means by this word, men who God bestowed with priestly authority'. It signifies 'a chief, teacher, and caretaker of souls on behalf of God'.[26] He responded to Mashaqqah as follows: 'you claimed in your fifth reply that the word *shuyukh* does not signify the *kahanut* and that this is a matter of belief and not a matter of translation ... By God, who is not both a theologian and a translator at once? Are you not aware, friend, that one of the most singular characteristics of a translator is his use of words that signify the intended meaning in belief? Otherwise, what is the benefit of the translation?'[27]

What the Protestants did not possess in tradition, they compensated for in claims to modernity, about philology and finesse in Arabic printing. The SBV translator Cornelius Van Dyck's response, which was published in the weekly of the Syrian Mission, *al-Nashra al-Usbu'iyya*, mounted a cool-headed critique that remained completely steeped in philological evidence. In six articles, entitled 'Irtida' al-Siham 'ala al- Yasu'i Fan Ham' ('The Arrows Hit Back the Jesuit Van Ham'), published in five issues between 17 December 1872 and 7 January 1873, Van Dyck makes a compelling philological argument, based on the Greek text of the Textus Receptus, that elucidates the differences between *presbýteros* and *hieroí* or *hiereîs*, where he contends, the former means elderly, while the latter means priest and that in James 5:14, the former – not the latter – is found in the original Greek text.[28]

Similar arguments were made for other lexemes, such as *cheirotonéō* in Acts 14:23, 'and when they had ordained them elders in every church, and had prayed with fasting, they commended them to the Lord, on whom they believed', which the Jesuits eventually translated as فعينا شيوخاً في كل كنيسة وصليا وصاما ثم استودعهم الرب الذي آمنوا به. Another instant is the concept of *gynē* in 1Cor 9:5: 'have we not power to lead about a sister, a wife, as well as other apostles, and as the brethren of the Lord, and Cephas?' translated as أما لنا حق أن نستصحب امرأة مؤمنة كسائر الرسل وإخوة الرب وصخر؟. In the first instance the SBV translates the word as *intakhaba*[29] and in the second as *zawjah*, as in the KJV quoted here. This is an important doctrinal difference between the two churches, and its interpretation was a point of contention even in Luther's time. The difference has consequences for how the church is organised, particularly how priests come to office: whether by election from the parish, or by appointment from the church leaders. The second point, also a salient conflict in Luther's time, affects the celibacy stipulation enforced by the Catholics. By objecting that *cheirotonéō* is treated as if it is an election, in the Greek sense, instead of the Catholic meaning of 'bestow the authority of priesthood',[30] and his dissatisfaction with the SBV's suggestion that the apostles had wives,[31] Van Ham is not simply arguing about mere words, but is defending an entire historical doctrine that had to be reiterated in the Counter-Reformation. There were other differences that Van Ham could have selected, but his strategic repetition of Counter-Reformation arguments bolstered his position as a keeper of tradition.

Van Dyck responded with the authority of philology that the SBV is an accurate version, if not the best of translations. He defends his translation of *cheirotonéō* as *election* by providing lexical evidence.[32] Knowing how it irritates the Catholics to question the creed of celibacy, Van Dyck proceeds to mount an intricate criticism on the suggestion that Peter was unmarried. Through textual and philological means, Van Dyck argued that Peter was in fact married. He appealed to the morality of the nineteenth century reader to judge whose interpretation is the more plausible one, he writes:

Our opponent rejects our translation of *adelfĕn gynaîka* as sister-wife where he finds cause to reject that Peter was married and that his wife accompanied him on his travels. He also opposes our suggestion that the apostles and brothers in God were married and that their wives accompanied them on their travels. We beseech the reader: which of the two conditions is purer and farther from suspicion: that the apostles were accompanied by wives, or that they were accompanied by women who were not their wives? They cannot deny that Peter was married because the Bible mentions that his mother-in-law was sick and that Jesus cured her in Matt 8:14. That his wife accompanied him is clear from his first letter 5:13 where he says 'She that is in Babylon, elect together with you, saluteth you; and so doth Mark my son' [In this verse] the word 'church' is added by the Roman church and has no existence in any of the Greek originals. This confirms that this verse refers to his wife.[33]

However, the philological accuracy of Van Dyck and his partners only bolstered what Van Ham argued two years ago: namely that the Protestants accord more authority to human knowledge than they do to tradition. As Van Ham itemised the lexical issues he had against the SBV, he also made use of philology to support his arguments. Unlike his adversary though, he ultimately subordinated philology to tradition to demonstrate for his readers the Catholic creed that while science is amiable and useful, its truths do not form the cornerstone of faith. Faith, for Van Ham and the Maronites, must always root itself in the authority of tradition. The tradition that Van Ham restored, touched at the heart of the Catholic institutional structure. In a phrase, Van Ham's philological arguments intended to protect the sanctity of the priesthood, its institutional appointments, and the celibacy of its priests and in another example not mentioned here, the supremacy of the Virgin Mary.

Even though the American team handled this campaign with great ease, Van Ham managed to reiterate important pillars of the Catholic creed. He succeeded in his campaign precisely because he was able to frame the Protestant argument as deriving from mere human rationality while he promoted his own dissatisfaction with the SBV based on the authority of tradition. The debate that Van Ham had started worked to bolster the tenants of the church in the eyes of lay Catholic readers. By focusing on a choice of lexemes and treating them through the lenses of philology, and then through asserting their meaning in tradition, Van Ham's reception of the SBV reminded his readers about the creeds of the church. He did not flag other faults that he might have encountered upon reading, but rather he selected them well and cleared the way for a new Catholic translation that could supersede the BSA as well as the SBV. When it finally came out, the translation was subsidised to the extent that it was cheaper than the SBV despite the more laborious and expensive decisions that were made in the text. Through the concept of tradition, the Jesuits connected modern Bible translation to a long history of Catholic Arabic Bibles and countered the problem of a Bible reform through demonstrating how Reform looks like from the point of view of tradition. The Jesuit's success guaranteed that the local Catholic churches had its own Bible version and did not have to rely on a Protestant version that was produced primarily to convert them.

The Biblia Sacra Arabica: A Contrasting Catholic Case

In 1516, Selim I occupied the domains of *Bilad al-Sham*, initiating four hundred years of Ottoman rule over the Levant. His reign witnessed the expansion of Ottoman contact with Europe. In 1535, the king of France, François I, signed the first Capitulations agreement with Sultan Sulayman that, among other commercial and military exchanges, allowed French citizens to move freely in Ottoman domains.[34]

For the Maronites and other local Christian churches, Ottoman rule came as a mixed blessing. Under Ottoman rule, the Christians developed cultural and civil autonomy as a religious minority, in exchange for higher taxes and exemption from military service.[35] The Ottoman government visibly favoured the Orthodox community and provided their patriarchs with more powers than they had enjoyed under the Byzantine Empire. As Gregory Jusdanis notes, 'in addition to being the head of the church, [patriarchs] assumed the secular leadership of Orthodox people, responsible for both their pastoral needs and a host of civil practices such as education, marriage, and inheritance'.[36] The Maronites did not enjoy the same indulgences from the state, but with the opening up to Europe, they were able to bolster their networks with France and Rome, twining trade to the durable relations that their communion with Rome had afforded them since the era of the Crusades.[37] As Marshall Hodgson notes, the Maronites Catholic connection invigorated their contact with France and Rome under the Ottoman interest in Europe, and emerged as main agents for Ottoman political and diplomatic contact with Europe.[38]

The bolstered position of the churches was impenetrable to the young Protestant Church. As Henry Jessup recollects

> About thirty years after the death of Luther, the German Protestant divines opened correspondence with the patriarch of Constantinople, but he rejected their overture with contempt. The Greek Church 'knew not the day of its visitation.' For three hundred years after that time, with the exception of the sending of papal legates, hardly a movement was made in Europe towards modifying the state of the Eastern Churches.[39]

The English, who also tried to proselytise, advanced just as little. Through the newly established English Levant Company in Aleppo (1581), they entertained ideas about proselytisation among the Company's local employees.[40] Through its channels, Protestant Bibles began to appear in Aleppo and other places in the Ottoman Levant. These copies were based on the earliest Protestant Arabic versions: the New Testament (1616) and the Pentateuch in Arabic (1622), prepared by Dutch Orientalist Thomas Erpenius after he returned to Leiden.[41] The *London Polyglot*, issued between 1654 and 1657, was another Protestant version that also headed East,[42] as was Solomon Negri's *Psalter* that he published along with Athanasius Dabbas's cooperation with Negri on a New Testament version that was published by BSPCK in 1717.[43]

In that period, church elites often discovered Arabic Bibles printed in London or Amsterdam, which they rounded up and burned in town squares.[44] But they also sought other means to balance their burnings of the Bible. Local churches began to study the viability of venturing into printing new translations of the Bible. Of the local projects, Meletius Karmah's proposed translation of the Pentateuch (which however did not materialise) was an early local attempt at a new translation. Of those Bibles that were published, Macarius Ibn al-Za'im's translation of the Psalms is noteworthy as an example that combines a new translation with printing.[45] Before he aided the Protestants in gospel translation, he travelled to Romania in search of a rich patron to sponsor a new Bible translation project. Dabbas's travels resulted in the publication of two liturgical books, financed by the Wallachian ruler Constantin Brâncoveanu, as well as in the acquisition of a printing press that he promptly transported to Aleppo. In 1705 and 1706, Dabbas published Psalms and the Gospels, the latter portioned for 'all the Sundays and Saturdays as well as for the feasts of the church and must thus be classified as an Aprakos Gospel'.[46]

Catholic authorities in Rome reacted differently and employed several means to counter the Protestant incursions on Bible publishing. They instructed their local printer Abdallah al-Zakhir to publish attacks against the Protestants. They further mobilised their networks in England and, in 1736, they secured an order from the King of England that forbade the Chairman (in Arabic transcriptions: Tsharmin, Skirmin) of the Levant

Company to proselytise and ordered him to abandon his ambitions to mercantile gain.[47] Meanwhile, they worked hard on producing a new and improved translation of the Bible.

Biblia Sacra Arabica Sacræ Congregationis de Propaganda Fide jessu edita ad usum ecclesiarum orientalium (1671) is an Arabic–Latin Bible printed in Rome to reverse the infiltration of Protestant Bibles in the Levant. The work of translation had started fifty years earlier. But the decree that made it possible dates to the Council of Trent and the history of the Counter-Reformation. This version was famous for its style, which syncretised earlier local translations with innovative translation work done by Levantine scholars in Rome for the benefit of the Maronites and other Eastern Catholic Churches.

When Rome finally decided to assert its authority over the Oriental dominions, it applied its force under the rubric of the Council of Trent. This council, which took place in the northern Italian city of Trento between 1545 and 1563, was the major event in structuring the Catholic response to Luther's Protestant revolution. In Trent, Rome articulated a pragmatic position on its approach to scripture and its vernacularisation, as well as taking strategic decisions relating to its satellite churches. Following the dictates of Trent, a 'seminary scheme' was initiated to 'repair the slender theological formation of most parish priests by introducing instruction in the Holy Scripture'.[48] For the Maronites, this resulted in the founding of the Maronite College in Rome around 1584–5.[49] A press belonging to the college was established and run by Ya'qub Qamar. Trent stipulated a scholastic approach to a canon of texts that make up the Catholic repertoire and insisted that scripture is not the sole textual source of its authority. Placing scripture 'alongside other forms of authority for Christians' the conveners at Trent disrupted and clarified that its observation of scripture did not emulate the Protestant proclamation of Martin Luther in 1521 when he declared himself to be 'captive to the Word of God', a proclamation that consolidates in the phrase *Sola Scriptura* (by the Book alone). The Catholics 'gave the "traditions" of the Catholic Church, its accumulated corpus of teaching, parity of authority alongside the Bible, which Protestants regarded as the uniquely authoritative word of God'.[50] Replicating Calvin's conception of the Holy Spirit as the author of scripture, the Catholic leaders attending Trent extended the work of the Holy Spirit to all aspects of church doctrine. Amidst Lutheran charges that the notion of tradition conferred arbitrary authority on the Pope, the Council's equalisation of tradition with the Bible drove a deep wedge between Trent on the one hand and, on the other, the whole Reformation movement based on scripture, its all-sufficiency and inerrancy.[51]

This side-lining of scripture remarkably energised the production of new Catholic Bible versions in various languages, including Arabic, and changed how vernacular Bibles were produced and circulated in earlier times. The scholastic approach determined the translation decision taken in distinctive ways. As decreed by Trent, the canonical books of the Bible were reaffirmed according to the decrees of the Council of Florence. This recuperation of the Florentine arrangement of the Bible's books was a direct rejection of Erasmus's critiques of St Jerome's Vulgate Bible.[52] As the Council decreed, Jerome's was the most perfect of versions because of its 'long use'.[53]

The BSA was the most thorough elaboration of the dictates of the Council of Trent in the vernacularisation strategies adopted in Arabic translation. Its translation was undertaken by more than one translator and is sometimes referred to by the name of its chief translator and supervisor, the Maronite Archbishop of Damascus Sarkis al Ruzzi (Latin: Sergius Risius). Two other translators of the BSA also worked on the *Paris Polyglot* (1628) (Yuhanna al-Ma'madan al-Hasruni, who later became Royal Interpreter and professor of Syriac and Arabic at the Royal College, and Nasrallah Shalaq al-'aquri), and the third, Ibrahim al-Haqlani, was Emir Fakhreddin's ambassador to the Grand Duke of Florence.[54] To commence the work of the translation, al-Ruzzi collected and copied various texts from existing Arabic manuscripts in monasteries in Mount Lebanon and the Syrian Anti-Lebanon, before he travelled to Rome. Once the manuscripts were incorporated into the BSA reference apparatus, they were burned, for they 'were corrupt and full of error'.[55] When the team started, they 'read the older Arabic texts (*nusus*), compared them to Hebrew and Greek and chose the best and most accurate. Then they corrected what was corrupt and incongruous, taking the Latin Vulgate as their guiding principle'.[56] The version was a bilingual, Latin–Arabic edition, in three volumes, and in folio. As such, its presentation suggests that its readership was comprised of the educated elite and speakers/learners of Arabic and Latin, while its folio size indicates that it was to be read in church libraries and not in the privacy of one's home.[57] The BSA did not ever enter the market, and remained a gift to be bestowed on newly appointed Maronite patriarchs, who would receive crates that included, in addition to BSA and other Bible versions, 'ornaments, liturgical instruments as well as money'.[58]

The BSA was the first printed Bible to be officially adopted by the Maronites, and while it was not the last, local printing remained limited and the Bible manuscript market continued to thrive without discernible competition from the new technology. Protestants were keen to read this Bible, as is attested to by the existence of this Bible version in the original print in most historically Protestant libraries and universities. This version remained in continuous use for Protestant Bible projects all the way until the nineteenth century, when the plans to translate their own version became more concrete.

Writing about this version, and as part of the preparation for a new translation of the Bible by the BSPCK, the Damascus-born London resident Salomon Negri (Sulayman Ibn Ya'qub al-Shami al-Salihani)[59] sent a letter to a member of the BSPCK in London in May 1725, in which he described what came to be the official British and American opinion on the BSA. Salomon Negri detracted from the perfection of the BSA version because,

> as it is made from the Vulgar Translation by the Maronites (a People little versed in the true knowledge of the Arabick language), all understanding Men among the Eastern Nations have rejected it; besides, this Edition is distributed only among those of the Romish communion, and is therefore sent by the Congregation from Rome, to their Missionaries in the Levant.[60]

In the rivalries of the Reformation, the new printed Bible was produced with the seal of Rome on its front page, clearly indicating that it was authorised by the church and not by a Protestant clandestine incursion. Rome's seal signalled the authenticity of the Bible available to readers, but it also separated the place of Bible production from the market of circulation. This guaranteed that the Protestant Bibles remained of marginal circulation and ultimately failed in producing a community of readers.

The Bible as Gift Exchange

Marcel Mauss writes that through gifts exchanged, the giver 'has a hold over the recipient in the same way that he, as its owner, has a hold over a thief. Because the [gift] is animated by the *hau* of its forest, of its territory'.[61] Attached viscerally to its 'place of origin', the gift is animated with the soul of the giver and rooted in his territory. There is a clear difference between this exchange and commodity exchange. The origin of commodities is only secondarily crucial in the inscription of an object into commodity economy. Commodities become such not through ceremonial acts of giving, but because they are produced in larger numbers, for the purpose of dissemination and accumulation. In the seventeenth century, the Catholic Church reinscribed the Bible in a gift economy of awards for the benefit of their clerical class. Through the economy of the gift, Rome streamlined the satellite churches under its control and was not forced to succumb to the law of the market. Their Bible was not a site of competition, rather competition was about access to the people.

Whereas the Protestants entered the region at a loss as to whether to sell or gift the Bible, Rome succeeded in bracketing their rivalry with flair and largesse, crating the BSA and sending it to the new Maronite or Melkite Catholic patriarchs to congratulate them on their appointment. In this exchange, a little bit of Rome became embodied in those Bibles. The Bible was not simply scripture, but a gift of holiness that was to remind the receiver of his allegiances and to the power of Rome as a *catholic* church, that is, a church that has universal ambition and appeal.

Conclusion

The American Protestants departed from a model of exchange that acquires adherents through the obligations forged by the gift. They instead sought to instate a conversion model that challenges the hierarchical authority of the family and its demands for obedience. By capitalising on the dynamics of commodity exchange, they elected a model based on a transfer of ownership, one that does not expect allegiance based on the cultivation of an economy of obligations. They staked their mission on the radiance of scripture and of an assumption about the individuated agency of readers, those new owners of the Bible that were reading it, that like the Germans Ranke writes about, 'in their own vernacular tongue', and at their own pace, subordinating the text's temporality to 'the immediate interests of the day'.[62] The transfer of ownership that premises the Protestant model enables an incorporation of the Bible, into an embodied ownership, an ownership that makes the object native to the buyer and therefore subordinated to the quirks of individual context, and its quotidian rhythms. In such an individuated vision of readership, the cultivation of allegiance collapses into the confidence of *sola scriptura*, where the power of the text will impress the reader to transcend the textuality of the Bible so that it emerges as scripture, the central totem that congregates those readers into new practices of faith.

Whereas the American missionaries indoctrinated native readers of their Bible through its commoditisation and cheap price, the Jesuits diversified their Biblical products, publishing gift editions luxurious in design and fabrication, and reproducing the bond with Rome for a new epoch. They also sold smaller, subsidised editions that were cheaper than the competition. Theirs was the most handsome book to be found on the market, embodying such intricate labour, that its totemic power was *in excess* of its price, conspicuously untranslatable into monetary value and irreducible to the laws of accumulation.

Capitalising on tradition in their Bible, the Jesuits brandished a precious design that was incalculable in the price of the item. This way, even when a copy was bought from the market, the Bible partly functioned as a gift, carrying the souls of those unnamed designers of its textual topography and exquisite presentation. The Jesuits accepted the law of individuated readings that the Americans had introduced to Bible reading. However, they laboured to curtail the impact of autobiographical temporalities, which organise the textual experience of each reader differently on practices of interpretation. This curtailment was aided by the standardisation of key material details in the text: in language, layout and general design, while the continued production of gift processes of exchange became auxiliary to commoditisation and emerged as a distinguishing characteristic of the success of Jesuit Bibles on the market.

Notes

1. V. Necla Geyikdagi, *Foreign Investment in the Ottoman Empire: International Trade and Relations 1854–1914*, Library of Ottoman Studies (London: I. B. Tauris, 2011), 23. See also Peter Hill, *Utopia and Civilisation in the Arab Nahda*, 11–14.

2. Geyikdagi, *Foreign Investment in the Ottoman Empire*.

3. Ahmad Faris al-Shidyaq, 'The Travelogues of Ahmad Faris al-Shidyaq', trans. Rana Issa and Suneela Mubayi, *A Public Space* 27 (2019): 36–57.

4. Geyikdagi, *Foreign Investment in the Ottoman Empire*, 22.

5. Selim Deringil, *Conversion and Apostasy in the Late Ottoman Empire* (Cambridge: Cambridge University Press, 2012), 39–40.

6. Karl Marx, *Capital*, trans. Samuel Moore and Edward Aveling (London: Wordsworth Classics, 2013), 413.

7. H. H. Jessup, *Fifty-Three Years in Syria*, vol.1 (New York: Fleming H. Revell Co., 1910), 155.

8. Hall, 'The Arabic Bible of Drs. Eli Smith and Cornelius V. A. Van Dyck', 280.

9. Max Weber, *Economy and Society: An Outline of Interpretive Sociology*, vol. 1 (Berkeley: University of California Press, 1978), 93.

10. Heyberger, *Les chrétiens du Proche-Orient*, 264–75.

11. Quoted in Hall, 'The Arabic Bible of Drs. Eli Smith and Cornelius V. A. Van Dyck', *Journal of the American Oriental Society* 11 (1885): 280.

12. John Orne, 'The Arabic Press of Beirut, Syria', *Bibliotheca Sacra* 51, no. 202 (1894), 281–97.

13. For the full list of the translators see Paul Féghali, *Al-Muhit al-jami' fi al-kitab al-muqaddas wal-Sharq al-qadim* (Beirut: Pauline Bookstore, 2009), 341. See also Johann Strauss that provides more details about how the process came into being and conceived collaboratively in three different Catholic cities, Rome, Lyon and Beirut. Strauss, 'Langue(s) sacrées et recherche de langue(s) sacrée(s) dans l'Empire ottoman au XIXe siècle', 133. The NT was published in 1877 and the full Scriptures in 1881. Georg Graf, *Die Christiche Arabische Literature bis Frankischen Zeit* (Freiburg: Herder Forlag, 1905).

14. Jesuit Translators, 'Al-Muqaddimah', 5.

15. Ibid., 1.

16. Auji, *Printing Arab Modernity*, 81.

17. Jesuit Translators, 'Al-Muqaddimah'.

18. Ibid.

19. Ibid., 6.
20. For more on Farhat, see Abdulrazzak Patel, *The Arab Nahdah: The Making of the Intellectual and Humanist Movement* (Edinburgh: Edinburgh University Press, 2013), 43–58.
21. Jirmanus Farhat, *Ahkam Al-I'rab fi lughat al-a'rab*, ed. Rochaid de Dahdah (Marseille: Imprimerie Carnaud, 1849). In the introduction to BSA, no such errors were made, perhaps because it was translated and printed in Rome. Farhat by contrast was writing in Aleppo.
22. Jesuit Translators, 'Al-Muqaddimah'.
23. Introduction to BSA. This view is indeed one that is held by biblical scholars of various denominations. In his historiography of the Bible, Jinbachian asserts that Arabic is so ancient and widespread in Bible versions that it can be counted as a secondary language, at par with Armenian, Georgian and Syriac. See Manuel Jinbachian, 'Introduction: The Septuagint to the Vernaculars'. Also see the published letters of Archdeacon Travis. There, we find that he used the Arabic Bibles to defend the inclusion of 1John 5:7 and 8 in subsequent editions, after Erasmus dropped these verses from his famous Textus Receptus. Richard Porson, *Letters to Archedeacon Travis: In Answer to His Defence of the Three Heavenly Witnesses, I John v 7* (London: T & G. Egerton, 1790).
24. Yusuf Van Ham, *Kashf al-mughalatat al-sufastiyyah raddan 'ala ma 'ansharuh hadithan 'ahad khadamat al-'brotstantiyah did ba'd al-'asfar al-'ilahiyyah* (Beirut: Jesuit Press, 1870), 8–9.
25. Yusuf Van Ham, *Kashf al-tala'ub wal-tahrif (Fi mass ba'd 'ayat al-kitab al-sharif)*, 6.
26. Ibid., 23.
27. Mikha'il Mashaqqah, 'Kashf al-'awham 'amman mazzaqathu al-siham', in *Kashf al-mughalatat Al-sufastiyyah raddan 'ala ma 'ashharuh hadithan 'ahad khadamat al-brotstantiyah did ba'd al-'asfar al-'ilahiyyah*, ed. Yusuf Van Ham (Beirut: Jesuit Press, 1870).
28. Cornelius Van Dyck, 'Irtida' Al-Siham 'Ala al-Yasu'i Van Ham, 4th Response', *Al-Nashra Al-Usbu'iyyah*, 7 January 1873.
29. Ibid.
30. Van Ham, *Kashf Al-Tala'ub Wa Al-Tahrif*, 33.
31. Ibid., 37–8.
32. Cornelius Van Dyck, 'Irtida' Al-Siham 'Ala al-Yasu'i Van Ham, 2nd Response', 24 December 1872.

33. 'Irtida' Al-Siham 'Ala al-Yasu'i Van Ham, 6th Response', 7 January 1873, 14.

34. Thomas Philipp, 'Bilad Al-Sham in the Modern Period: Integration into the Ottoman Empire and New Relations with Europe', *Arabica* 51, no. 4 (October 2004): 401–18, 403.

35. Mehmet Sinan Birdal, *The Holy Roman Empire and the Ottomans: From Global Imperial Power to Absolutist States* (London: I. B. Tauris, 2014).

36. Gregory Jusdanis, *The Necessary Nation* (Princeton: Princeton University Press, 2001), 113.

37. Kamal Salibi, *Al-Mawarinah: surah tarikhiyyah* (Beirut: Dar Nelson, 2011).

38. Hodgson, *The Venture of Islam*, vol. 3, 126.

39. Jessup, *Fifty-Three Years in Syria*, vol. 1, 81–2.

40. Bruce Masters, *Christians and Jews in the Ottoman Arab World: The Roots of Sectarianism* (Cambridge: Cambridge University Press, 2001), 75.

41. Ronny Vollandt, *Arabic Versions of the Pentateuch: A Comparative Study of Jewish, Christian, and Muslim Sources* (Leiden: Brill, 2015), 117–18.

42. Ibid., 109–32.

43. John-Paul Ghobrial, 'The Life and Hard Times of Solomon Negri: An Arabic Teacher in Early Modern Europe', in *The Teaching and Learning of Arabic in Early Modern Europe*, ed. Jan Loop, Alistair Hamilton, and Charles Burnett (Leiden: Brill, 2017), 310–31, 314.

44. Roper, 'Arabic Printing in Malta', 67.

45. Hilary Kilpatrick, 'Meletius Karmah's Specimen Translation of Genesis 1–5', in *Translating the Bible into Arabic: Historical, Text-Critical, and Literary Aspects*, ed. Sara Binay and Stefan Leder, Beiruter Texte Und Studien 131 (Beirut: Ergon Verlag, 2012), 63–74; Hilary Kilpatrick, 'The Arabic Culture of Christians in Syria in the 16th and 17th Centuries', in *Contacts and Interaction: Proceedings of the 27th Congress of the Union Européenne Des Arabisants et Islamisants Helsinki 2014* (Leuven: Peeters, 2017), 221–31; Carsten-Michael Walbiner, 'Macarius Ibn Al-Za'īm and the Beginnings of an Orthodox Church Historiography in Bilād al-Shām', in *Le role des historiens orthodoxes dans l'historiographie* (Balamand: Universite de Balamand, 2010), 11–29.

46. Carsten Walbiner, 'Melkite (Greek Orthodox) Approaches to the Bible at the Time of Community's Cultural Awakening in the Early Modern Period (17th–18th Centuries)', in *Translating the Bible into Arabic: Historical, Text-Critical, and Literary Aspects*, ed. Sara Binay and Stefan Leder, Beiruter Texte Und Studien 131 (Wüsburg: Ergon Verlag, 2012), 53–62, 59.

47. Heyberger, *Les chrétiens du Proche-Orient*, 476.

48. Michael A. Mullett, *The Catholic Reformation* (London: Routledge, 1999), 39.

49. Salibi, *Al-Mawarinah*, 216.

50. Mullett, *The Catholic Reformation*, 39.

51. Ibid., 44.

52. The Council of Florence had decreed that the Holy Spirit proceeds from the Father and the Son and not through the Son as the Greek original read. For more on the Council of Florence, see Oskar Skarsaune, 'From the Reform Councils to the Counter-Reformation – the Council as Interpreter of Scripture', in *Hebrew Bible/Old Testament: The History of Its Interpretation*, ed. Magne Sæbø (Göttingen: Vandenhoeck & Ruprecht, 1996), 319–28.

53. Mullett, *The Catholic Reformation*, 40.

54. Kamal Salibi, *A House of Many Mansions: The History of Lebanon Reconsidered*, (Berkeley: University of California Press, 1988), 184. Paul Féghali, 'The Holy Books in Arabic: The Example of the Propaganda Fide Edition', in *Translating the Bible into Arabic: Historical, Text-Critical, and Literary Aspects*, ed. Sara Binay and Stefan Leder, Beiruter Texte Und Studien 131 (Beirut: Ergon Verlag, 2012), 37–52; Paul Féghali, *Al-Muhit al-jami' fi al-kitab al-muqaddas*, 341.

55. Wahid Qaddura, *Bidayat al-tiba'ah al-'arabiyyah fi Istambul wa Bilad al-Sham*, (Riyadh: Matba'at al-Malik Fahd), 69–73.

56. Féghali, *Al-Muhit al-Jami' fi al-Kitab al-Muqaddas,* 341.

57. Qaddura notes that bilingual books were mainly for a Western audience whereas Arabic-only books were for the Arab Christians. Based on what we know of the language skills of elite Christians, namely that they were well versed in both Latin and Italian, I maintain my suggestion that the bilingual books were luxury items that had a limited Arabic readership. Qaddura, *Bidayat al-tiba'ah al-'arabiyyah,* 59.

58. Heyberger, *Les chrétiens du Proche-Orient*, 406–7.

59. Ghobrial, 'The Life and Hard Times of Solomon Negri'.

60. Salomon Negri, 'An Extract of Several Letters Relating to the Great Charity', May 1725, SPCK Collection Archive, Oxford Bodleian Library, UK. 6.

61. Marcel Mauss, *The Gift: Expanded Edition,* trans Jane I. Guyer and Bill Maurer (Chicago: Hau Books, 2016), 71.

62. Leopold von Ranke, *History of the Reformation in Germany*, trans. Sarah Austin, vol. 2 (London: Longman, Green, Brown, and Longmans, 1845), 93.

3

Standardising Arabic

My teacher, Sheik Asaad, was a Maronite, and formerly a student in Ain Waraka. He has been much with the Patriarch, at Canobin, and is one of the most intelligent men I have met with on Mount Lebanon. He was with me from morning til night, and hours were spent by us every day in discussing religious subjects.

One day, after a long discussion with him about the Roman Catholic and the Protestant churches, he took up a New Testament, written in Carshun and Syriac, and opening it said, 'The first passage I cast my eye upon shall be for the English.' The chapter to which he happened to open, was Luke 1 and he read, beginning at the top of the page, as follows; 'the word; it seemed good to me also, having had perfect understanding of all things from the very first, to write unto thee, most excellent Theophilus; that thou mightest know the certainty of those things wherein thou hast been instructed.'

He seemed to be struck with the passage, as the first word was 'the word,' and remarked, that it was very appropriate, as we distributed the word.

Then closing the book, he said, 'Now I will open it, and the first passage shall be for the Pope.'

On opening, the first word that met his eye was '*Unclean*,' and he read as follows; 'the unclean is gone out of a man, he walketh through dry places, seeking rest; and finding none, he saith, I will return unto my house, whence I came out. And when he cometh, he findeth it swept and garnished. Then goeth he, and taketh to him seven other spirits, more wicked than himself, and they enter in, and dwell there, and the last state of that man is worse than the first.' (Luke 6. 24–6).[1]

This is an account by Jonas King to the periodical *The Missionary Herald* about the conversion of As'ad al-Shidyaq. As'ad, brother of Ahmad Faris al-Shidyaq, was the first Arab convert and martyr to Protestantism. In this scene we encounter him performing an *istikhara*: a practice of scriptural reading that seeks to intuit the future. Akin to prayer, as it solicits *khayr* and grace, but with a clear intention to plead assistance in decision making or hope for a small miracle that decides the course of the future, an *istikhara* is a ritual that is not exclusive to Christians. It consists of a random scriptural reading that rests on assumptions about the agency of God and requests His intervention in the world.

While the tale communicates As'ad's state of grace, it also distinguishes him from the missionaries who rejected superstitious handlings of the Bible. For them, As'ad belonged to a world they sought to convert by transforming its relation to scripture. He was an ideal convert who readily accepted 'the Bible as a transformative text'.[2] The randomness in the *istikhara* reading approach relinquishes control and transposes it onto God so that not only will He affect action in the world, but He directs the reader's fingers to the select page for the prediction. The prediction itself is unpacked allegorically in the service of a self-interest that the missionaries worked to replace with otherworldly commitment. The reform that the missionaries preached required a reconfigured relationship between readers and scripture. This reconfiguration was on two planes: at the level of reading and interpretation and at the temporal relation to scripture. Temporally the *istikhara* assumes the Bible's transitive influence on the natural world. An *istikhara* for them was anachronistic because it sought 'from the Bible not statements about the truth of the world but directives for efficacious action in this world'.[3] This is a handling of the Good Book that was granted no quarter in the evangelical methods of reading.

The missionaries rejected beliefs that subjected the power of the Bible to a symbolic realm requiring hermeneutical intervention (by clerics) for its unveiling. Following Calvin, they considered God's message as being manifest on the surface of the biblical text, but not itself conducting action in the world. Olivier Millet argues that in its co-emergence with the Renaissance, Calvinist theology learned from humanist and scientific discourse the value of transparency. [4] For them the Bible is no longer a web of allegorical signs requiring interpretation, but a message that is always relevant and indissociable from its literal and spiritual senses. Unlike the *istikhara*, the new way of reading the Bible fixed the temporal trajectory of interpretation in philology, in the study of biblical language historically, to translate the Bible to manifest its relevance for the present time. As'ad's conversion narrative underscores a transformation in the reader's agency in the *istikhara*, having come to Jonas King ready to convert.

The ceremonial *istikhara* exhibits As'ad's agency in manipulating the act of interpretation towards a form of prediction. His agency carries forward transitively, rupturing him from his community and ushering him into his conversion towards a new modality of scriptural reading that bases itself on solitary reading acts in the encounter with the divine. Through this commitment to a new form of reading, As'ad became the first convert and martyr to Arabic Protestantism. His conversion narrative served a model for the other converts who were being invited to adopt *sola scriptura* (by book alone) as their new creed. I argued in the previous chapter that the rivalry between the older church and the newcomers changed in kind when the Bible became an exchange commodity. In this chapter, I will explore how the Protestants advanced a new language of ideology that was designed to impress future converts and persuade them to engage in solitary readings of the Bible as the cornerstone of their faith.

Turning the Bible into an exchange commodity shifted the framing of the Bible as a book of scripture. How the reader was expected to accept its divine status changed. Scripture, as Wilfred Cantwell Smith makes clear, is not a genre of text. Its location at the heart of its community differs in kind from how other texts are treated. Cautioning scholars not to neglect this distinction, Cantwell Smith calls for 'a new understanding of scripture [as] the recognition that no text is a scripture in itself and as such. People – a given community – make a text into scripture, or keep it scripture: by treating it in a certain way'. [5] This treatment is what interests me in this chapter, particularly in how the commoditisation of the Bible affected a change in this relationship both for the producers and the readers. This change in textual design has had historical precedents that are more ancient than the Protestants, and each time such a transformation occurred a new scriptural relation was forged with the Bible. According to Cantwell Smith, Luther's translation and canon reform rehashed aspects of scripture that were salient in the past. As formal elements of scripture, the translation of the Bible into continuous text was first undertaken by St Jerome, while the finality of the canonisation of a book that belongs to the genre of scripture was proposed by the first generation of descendants after Muhammad, who collated the Qur'an. Luther's addition came through his instrumental dependence on print technology. Although print technology is clearly more effective than scribal methods, it was the Qur'an that first depended on decontextualisation and dissemination for its doctrinal constitution of the Muslim community.[6] Through coupling decontextualisation with dissemination, the Muslims, and later Luther, enacted processes of fetishisation of scripture that centred reading as an act of faith. For reading to emerge as a pious gesture, the manner of the book's production came to matter. The textual content had to become standard, and variations were tantamount to heresy. This is particularly true of the Bible, a scripture where variation was the standard and not the rule. With Luther's dependence on print technology, the Bible was produced in its most stable form, and variations became highly significant and policed – whether these were in the books considered to be canonical, what phrasing to use, or where to place the punctuation.

Labouring to commoditise the Bible, the Protestants had to ensure that reading practices were synchronised to control and limit as much as possible the room for interpretation. Through exploring the language of the translations and the material presentation of the book, I extract aspects of these synchronous reading practices as they were produced linguistically, as evidence of the transformation in the semiotic ideology that governs the Bible when it is still a text, as it is being prepared for exchange and before it is placed in the hands of its community and is received as scripture.

Calvinist Translation and Semiotic Ideology

In his study of the semiotic ideology of Calvinist missionaries and converts in Indonesia, Webb Keane explores how material objects of religious practice, which include an understanding of language as a material object, transformed the notion of agency amongst the Sumbanese and reduced it to a notion that only admits the living human subject as agent. By thus intervening, the Protestants excluded any fetishisation of objects that rendered them idolatrous. Instead, they emphasised the *sola scriptura* doctrine and foregrounded the logocentric semiosis of a notion of agency as anthropocentric. This notion of agency, as Keane shows, has repercussions for how the sacred is framed and reproduced. The capacity of the Calvinist Protestants to decontextualise their faith turned the Bible into a fetish – a supreme object that exceeds its temporal and spatial coordinates. As he writes, the Calvinist textual practices, from liturgies to prayer and Bible reading,

> underwrite a certain entextualization of the world ... This mode of objectification brings out aspects of language that are not anchored or dependent on a particular context. It allows language to be extracted from one context and inserted into another.[7]

Keane rejects the concept of fetish that typifies how Protestants perceived the people they worked to convert. As with their judgement of the 'nominal' Christians of the Levant, the Protestants among the Sumbanese that Keane studies were much concerned with rejecting local practices of faith for their fetishistic 'misattribution of agency'.[8] What irritated the Protestants about the Christians of the Levant is that their approach to the scriptural word was idolatrous rather than interpretive, in other words, the agency for transforming a situation was with the incantation (like with Asad's *istikhara*) while they would insist on the human locus of agency. To convert the Levantine Christians, the Protestants had to change their relation to the Word. Scripture had to be wrested from the mouths of the clergy and relocated to the solitary readings of the individual believer. How this transformation was brought about had to nevertheless bestow some agency to the text, in other words, produce a text capable of directing how it must be read, and control that reading as much as possible. In this chapter, I question the control over the individual reading performance the text enables through its peculiar method of production.

To contextualise how the Protestant translation departed from its predecessors in the Arabic tradition, I first explore the notion of simple speech and vernacularisation in the historical context of biblical revelation that culminates in Luther's revolutionary translation of the Bible to German. This conceptual understanding of how the Christian creeds relate to vernacular Bibles is important in relation to a tradition of vernacular Arabic Bibles whereby Luther's vernacularisation practice comes to seem neither so novel nor revolutionary. This brings me to the need to nuance how we study the linguistic history of Arabic in relation to religious groups. I parse this part of the argument into two historical narratives, one providing a brief history of the language styles deployed in the Biblia Arabica tradition and the other going through a quick historical account of the emergence of normative Arabic writing in the ninth century. Describing the history of Christian writing against the normative tastes of the dominant Arabic writers, I explore the ideological discrepancies between the two groups that made Christians choose variant forms of Arabic for their religious texts and why the decision to translate the Bible into standard Arabic in the nineteenth century is a significant one that greatly impacted how readers were produced by the Protestant enterprise.

When the Protestants arrived in Syria, they saw local Christians misattribute agency by expecting supernatural powers from certain objects such as icons, relics, as well as Bible veneration. Their belief in the exclusivity of the Bible for faith contrasted with the fetishist practices they identified in so-called 'nominal Christians' who as fellow missionary, William Thomson reported, were at fault for 'their perverted bias of some human minds to idolatry'.[9] A translation of the Bible, they reasoned, could acquire life in the hearts and souls of new converts who would be drawn to reading it. Disciples of Calvin, the American missionaries regarded the Bible as a translation of the word of God in historical time.[10] This understanding of the labour of translation enabled the missionary translators to lay claim to an abstracted form of agency that transcended the spatial and temporal limits of the individual, mortal body by connecting it to primordial time, so ancient that it nears the atemporal. Through philological acts of historical rootedness, some of this atemporality is looped back into the historical. Through their philological interest in the historicity of language, the Protestants gave fresh relevance to the origins of the Bible, and they sought to access the power of the divine as a historically concrete event that could nevertheless transcend its historicity through the conduit of translation. This conception of the origin's power shapes the target text and forges it into the most effective means of acting in a world of competing mediators.

The missionaries who came to Syria were preoccupied with Muslims as potential converts, but also as contenders to a logocentric discourse that dominates the greatest proportion of their mission geography. The tone of their encounter with Islam was inaugurated with Luther's own attempts at becoming the first translator of the Qur'an to German. In his 1542 preface to of a Latin Qur'an translation by Theodor Bibliander, Luther equates Muslims and their prophet with the errors of the Jews and the pagans as he encourages readers to use their encounter with the book as an opportunity, 'to separate ourselves in prayer from the Turks, from the Jews, and from the other nations, and to invoke the eternal and true God, the creator of all things, the Father of our Lord Jesus Christ, who was crucified for our sake and raised from the dead'.[11]

When the Americans arrived to the Levant, they shared Luther's belief in the exceptional creed of his faith. But to separate themselves from Muslims and the Muslim approach as well, they had to exercise extreme nuance and specification in the encounter with Arabic as a language that is so often tinged with the sacredness of the Qur'an. Protestants had to find solutions that would allow them to rival, through their own publication of a Bible in Arabic, Muslim language ideology and its veneration of Arabic as a sacred language based entirely on its being the language of the Qur'an. For some dominant Muslim creeds, Arabic's sacredness became an argument to refute the translatability of the Qur'an and facilitated a language ideology that strictly polices grammar rules and semantic expression. The dominant Muslim view is that the author of the Qur'an is '*ar-rabb*, the Lord, or *Allāh*, one of the ancient gods of Arabia, not Muhammad or some other human being'.[12] This belief lent the text its sacred power and transformed it into scripture. For Luther, scripture rested on translation, or the conception of language as a mediating vessel where the divine can communicate in a language that humans understand. The cleavage around the un/translatability of scripture, between the Christian Bible and the Qur'an is based on inverse approaches to language. Whereas the Qur'an is the inimitable word of God, the Bible announces itself as a translation of divine word. For Protestant Christians, neither Arabic nor any other language, including the original languages of the text were inherently divine. Yet to compete for souls, the Bible had to be defined against the Qur'an, and its edification of Arabic, and had to find solutions for the demands of high register that the Qur'an's sacred language associates with the scripture. Their solution was to reinvent Arabic as a vehicular language, as standard and correct as it is simple and clear. Luther's conception of language style and the premium he placed on vehicular registers became the method through which to think of what language register would be suitable for a new Arabic Bible.

Competing with the Qur'an

In 1530, Martin Luther made an argument about the importance of Bible vernacularisation, in his famous 'Open Letter on Translating'. In the letter he accused the Catholic Church in Rome of gross incompetence in handling the Bible, in preaching it and in allowing people to comprehend its message. He wanted a translation that could reach the people, in their own language. For the Germans who were the readers of Luther's translation, the German version of the Bible that he prepared spoke to the plebeians rather than to the church masters. This move to vernacularise the Bible was at the intersection of a crucial milestone in the history of knowledge, and the fate of religiosity and secularity since the Renaissance. The proliferation of printing and new modes of book dissemination coincided with the Protestant foregrounding of individual readings of the Book as a cornerstone of faith. *Sola scriptura* was a doctrine that turned its back on Rome and attended instead to the people. Squarely standing with his face to the people, Luther said:

> We do not have to ask about the literal Latin or how we are to speak German – as these asses do. Rather we must ask the mother in the home, the children on the street, the common person in the market about this. We must be guided by their tongue, the manner of their speech, and do our translating accordingly. Then they will understand it and recognize that we are speaking German to them.[13]

He listened closely to them, and composed in their registers and speech, guided by a verse from St Paul in the first epistle to the Corinthians: 'So it is with you. Unless you speak intelligible words with your tongue, how will anyone know what you are saying? You will just be speaking into the air'.[14] Easy to understand! That's how Luther wanted the New Testament to distinguish itself from the other texts around it. As Johannes von Lüpke argues,

> Luther believed that the task of theology is that of linguistic theory, which claims to take over all traditional forms of linguistics and renew them. By referring to the Bible's linguistic world, in the school of the Holy Spirit and with his rhetoric, theology learns and teaches simultaneously a '"new dialectic" and a "new grammar" . . . and is intent on distinguishing God and human beings from each other in the medium of language and on bringing them together in an eternal, continuous new conversation'.[15] For Luther an adequate translation of the Bible was vernacular, and the simplification of scripture's language was the touchstone of his concept of calling.[16]

Like Luther, Calvin also sought the divine through a profound commitment to translation. Addressing kings and princes in his preface to Olivétan's French Bible about how to facilitate the spread of the new church, Calvin advises them to see to it that the Bible 'is not prohibited and forbidden to any Christian freely and in his own languages to read, handle, and hear this holy gospel, seeing that such is the will of God'.[17] Those tongues by which the Bible shall come to be are not to be confused with God's word. Calvin writes, 'When the scripture speaks of the Word of God, it certainly were very absurd to imagine it to be only a transient and momentary sound, emitted into the air'.[18] Yet because it is a transient sound and not only a state of grace, the biblical text shall be retranslated back into relevance for each era. Calvin was writing against the edicts of the Council of Trent that offset the Catholic Counter-Reformation and which in its second decree states that no translation of the Bible shall take place and,

> no man trusting in his own wisdom . . . dare to interpret the Holy Scripture contrary to that sense which holy mother church, to whom it belongs to judge of the true sense and interpretation of the Holy Scripture, has held and holds.[19]

Thus any work of translation shall happen within the direct control of the mother church, Rome. I showed in the previous chapter how in the seventeenth century, this control succeeded in driving out the early wave of Protestant missionaries from Syria. In the nineteenth century, the rivalry with the Catholics came one more time to the fore, when Calvin's American descendants travelled beyond the small towns and cities of New England to settle and evangelise in the world.

Arabic posed a unique encounter for the American missionaries with the complex diversity of the Arab and other ethnic inhabitants who spoke the language. Stabilised as it is in the Qur'an, the language also attested to a millennium-long history of Biblia Arabica, of Arabic Bibles in translation since at least the seventh century. Unlike the Qur'an's sacralisation of Arabic and edification of its elevated register, the Arabic Bible tradition translated its scripture into a speech that followed a stylistic doctrine of simplicity. For centuries, Arab translators of the Bible let themselves be governed by a theological commitment to simplicity as it was writ in the Bible. They understood the Revelation of the New Testament in *koine* Greek as the first elaboration of the divine edict of speaking to believers in simple and clear speech.

Revealed in *koine* Greek, the vehicular dialect of the uneducated masses of the early Roman empire, the gospels' simplicity of speech was the conduit for Bible dissemination and spread of the Christian religion. Simplicity served the Bible's oral circulation in Mass and in spiritual guidance. Its subsequent translations to Latin, with St Jerome's *Vulgate* written in a common variety of Latin that had much currency, vulgar as in ordinary and most common, a vehicular tongue of Latinate masses, to the Syriac *Peshitta*, translated *simple*, a simple and most widespread form of the Syriac varieties of tongue. In all those cognates, the Bible's language has been identified for being so common as to be vulgar, and so simple as to be known as *al-basita* (literally: the simple one). Christians in the Levant often turned to their own indigenous dialects to translate the Bible, and sought a clarity that was rooted in Syrian Arabic and called it a naiveté, a *sadhaja*, continuous with a linguistic lineage inspired by the New Testament and particularly by St Paul's pronouncements, including the verse in his second letter to the Corinthians 11:6: 'But though I be rude in speech, yet not in knowledge; but we have been thoroughly made manifest among you in all things'.

In the nineteenth century, biblical simplicity in Arabic had to grapple with the dominance of linguistic practices deriving from the Qur'an, which also evolved a preference for simplicity, albeit through the concept of *fasaha*, a feature associated with the classical and normative variant of Arabic, which literally means the 'cream of milk' and metaphorically means clear and simple speech. In the Qur'an, in the Sura of the Bees, it is written that this Holy Book was sent in 'clear Arabic speech'.[20] A proclamation that shares with St Paul the demand for clarity of speech that lets the ideas become visibly manifest, the edict that the Holy Book shall be understood by the believers without the mediation of translators and commentators on the Holy Word. Deriving their linguistic ideologies from the Qur'an, the linguists evolved the concept of *fasaha* through claiming the highest eloquence to their scripture, the finest model of Arabic, in a similar way to the sacrosanct fate that beset St Jerome's translation into Latin. According to Ibn Jinni, *fasaha* is a deliberate inclination toward impressive clarity, selected, through grammatical and lexical *qiyas* (derivation and deliberation), from amongst the foundational Arabic dialects of the Desert, for its rhetorical strength: its effect on the ears of the listener.[21] At the intersection of modern history and a long tradition of Arabic Biblical translation, Arabic language ideology was about to change in the negotiations that the missionaries undertook when they decided to present the Bible in *fusha* Arabic disregarding an entire tradition of Biblia Arabica. To understand this innovation in the biblical style, I will now go over some of the scholarship on Arabic historical linguistics and particularly on the styles deployed in Christian literature, to elucidate the new translations of the Bible in the rupture they enact with Christian biblical tradition.

Variations of Arabic in a Historical Context

Coming into being in South Palestine, two centuries after its translation to Latin, the Arabic Bible has proliferated in hundreds of translations and thousands of manuscripts.[22] These Bible versions have borrowed from each other and utilised a variety of source texts, including Greek and Hebrew, but also Coptic, Syriac, Latin and Armenian. In Arabic, the definition of a *simple* biblical diction has varied across time. These translations deployed varieties of Arabic: the dialectical variants of certain regions; calques of Greek, Syriac and other syntactical norms in literal translations; eclectic diction translations in Middle Arabic variants; as well as totally domesticated forms that were produced in the classical *fusha*, reaching an epitome in the rhymed version emulating the Qur'an that was completed by 'Abd Yashu' al-Subawi in 1318.[23]

Nevertheless, most of the Bible versions were written in a variant Arabic and did not follow the normative tastes of Arabic grammar and writing style. This nonconformity with stylistic and grammatical conventions was so prevalent that sociolinguists have spent decades studying the phenomenon in order to divine its underlying syntax, to little theoretical effect.[24] The contention of sociolinguists like Joshua Blau, Benjamin Hary and others is that a language variant, termed Christian Arabic, can be discerned and its grammar deduced. For the sake of this grammar, Blau studied hundreds of New Testament manuscripts from monasteries in South Palestine and discovered that Christian Arabic 'contains features separating it from Middle Arabic varieties'. Middle Arabic is a variety of Arabic that combines colloquial with *fusha* and is used for less official and more popular genres of text,[25] and Blau's contention upon reading hundreds of Bible versions is that those Bibles display a variety special to them, a variety that is so different from Middle Arabic that it can be termed Christian Arabic. More recently, the term Christian Arabic gained theoretical relevance in the work of Benjamin Hary and Martin Wein. Reasserting the analytical strength of underscoring religious identity in the study of language, and partly motivated by Hary's expertise in Arabic historical linguistics, they argue that 'since religions (or secularisms) are intrinsic parts of human society and communication, language varieties could be analysed for their religious associations and described as religiolects'.[26]

Kees Versteegh proposes otherwise: that rather than deploying religious identity to catalogue dialects, one ought to consider that people tend to use writing styles selectively. For him, Middle Arabic is variant enough of a scribal style to render such theological identifications of writing style superfluous. As he notes, Christian writers 'were less constrained by the norms of the written language than Muslims and were relatively free in expressing themselves by writing in a form of Arabic that contained more vernacular forms',[27] but this does not amount to them having developed a unique writing style. For our purposes, this scholarship elucidates the great variety of writing styles that exist in the Biblia Arabica tradition. The variety is a norm so proliferant that it has prompted scholars like Hary and Wein to suggest a subfield in the study of language, a field that earmarks *religiolects* as the main object of its analysis. The contrast between the Arabic found in canonical Christian texts differs widely from how Muslim religious literature is written. The normative style of the dominant group exerted such power that the concept of *religiolect* helps us to reflect on why such contrast in linguistic behaviour exists between religious groups. To understand what motivated the Christians to write and translate in the way they did over the centuries, I will now turn to a brief account of the history of the emergence of the normative style of Arabic's canonical literature.

Following the expansion of the Islamic Empire in the seventh century, and the adoption of Arabic as the language of administration in Damascus and Baghdad, the Islamisation of the Empire came to rest upon the ideological claims of the Qu'an's inimitability, which was effectively normalised through a process of codification and standardisation of the Desert dialects in linguistic scholarship. Grammatical scholarship supervened upon these ideological claims and laboured by accepting their assumptions. A normative variant of Arabic was first codified in the ninth century, and while its connection to the Qur'an was not yet so clear, it singled out the dialects of the Arabian Desert for grammatical mapping and codification as the best examples of Arabic speech. The codification was not meant to be prescriptive in the beginning. Foundational grammarian Abu Bishr 'Amr ibn 'Uthman ibn Qanbar Al-Basri Sibawayhi (c. 760–96), who wrote the first Arabic grammar, was simply describing those dialects that harked from the desert and that had such a prestigious status. His decision to codify the desert dialects was related to the exalted status of the desert in the Islamic imagination as the birthplace of Muhammad and the Qur'an. The Qur'an after all was revealed in one of the most vehicular

variants of these dialects. Sibawayhi's dependence on the Bedouin dialects as object of study would eventually pave the way for grammar to be
embroiled in interpretations of the Qur'an.[28] It did not take long for the
grammarians that came after him to draw a link between those dialects
and the qur'anic text. This link brought grammar to questions of law and
sharia. Eventually, the soundness of Arabic in relation to Bedouin dialects
translated into a disproportionate reliance on the Qur'an for grammatical
and lexicographic reasoning. Codifying Arabic speech was in effect a
standardisation of a vernacular variety of Arabic at the expense of all other
modes of speaking and writing in the language. For the medieval linguists,
this vernacularisation process participated in safeguarding the centrality
of the Qur'an as a supreme text, around which Arabic was made to orbit.
With the intention of bolstering the claims of the Qur'an's linguistic inimitability, most grammarians and lexicographers limited their examples and
witnesses in their books to 'only two sources of literary Arabic',[29] the
Qur'an and pre-Islamic poetry. This latter source was ideal for the insistence on the temporal as well as geographical supremacy of the qur'anic
context. At the height of its Imperial domination, Arabic thus acquired
an enduring normativity for its high registers. On the opposite end of the
spectrum, those groups that remained on the fringes of the courtly *majalis*
of letters did not reproduce or conform to normative expectations in their
use of the language. Instead, they were more prone to deploying local
varieties of speech.

The desire for distinction from the dominant grammatical convention
was not only motivated by religious difference. As Nelly Hanna, Humphrey
Davies, Madiha Doss, Jerome Lentin and others have shown, there are
many examples of the existence of a variant style that mixes classical and
dialect, indeed even a proliferation of this mixture in the pre-modern literary landscape that defines texts that were not traditionally assimilated into
the canon – and these include folk tales, letters, contracts and other such
examples of less formalised literary genres.[30] These lax styles of writing
disregarded the prescribed rules of Arabic grammar that were deduced
from studying the Qur'an. Anyone could deploy this variety for writing,
including canonical literary and religious figures, and its deployment was
not a sufficient indicator of the learnedness of the writer. In the case of

biblical literature, which largely deployed such variant styles – prompting many sociolinguists to promote arguments about religiolects and Christian forms of Arabic – the readiness to adopt *lahn* (variant dialect) worked towards solidifying group relations and distinguishing Christian identity from the typical expectations of writing in the dominant (and Qur'an-inflected) idiom. As Hilary Kilpatrick rightfully argues, summarising the complex linguistic practices of the local Christian churches under one broad Christian Arabic religiolect occludes giving nuanced attention to how different Christian communities approached literary Arabic in their writings, based on their location vis-à-vis Muslims and other competing Christian neighbouring communities. While we can point out the pre-dominance of Middle Arabic as a literary style for religious texts and some epistolary practices (also among Muslims), some of those writers also performed well in the high *fusha* registers.[31] What the Bible allows us to index is thus not a generalisable observation about Christian Arabic. As Ronny Vollandt cautions, the persistent linguistic exploration of the Arabic Bible eludes its abstraction to a generalisable theory because,

> The focus on linguistic features is often done at the expense of an analy-
> sis of their translation technique and a study of their embeddedness into
> the context of related theological, exegetical and grammatical traditions,
> of which biblical versions have always been an inextricable part. The
> same holds true for their *Sitz im Leben*, i.e., investigation as to how
> these translations were used in the liturgy, education, or apologetics, as
> this factor strongly conditioned the strategy followed by the translator
> in transferring particular structures, proper names, or concepts from the
> source language into the target language.[32]

In short, focusing on the linguistic features alone does not address the questions of how these translations came into being or what context they mediate. They are studied outside a historical framework and are examined according to a grammatical logic that is nevertheless impossible to codify, given its profuse variance. Rather, through the nuances of historical context, we can examine how, under Protestant supervision, the Bible was produced in the normative variant of the language, and how this variant stabilised the reading practices of the text. These decisions about which writing style to use enabled the Bible to acquire attention and sacrality, not through *illuminati* Bible productions and ritual handlings, but through the insistence on solitary readings of the text.

The history of the Bible's writing style mediates the ideological dynamics that shaped variant modes of writing in Arabic, particularly in how a legacy of *koine* simplicity was apprehended to respond to the changing needs and political visibility of its community of readers. When the Bible was translated to Arabic in the seventh century, its translators displayed a veneration for the original text in Greek which resulted in what Uwe Vagelpohl called 'a highly text-centred approach' that interfered with legibility in the target language.[33] This literal approach emphasised the sacredness of the source text. With the spread of Arabic as a lingua franca amongst the peoples of the Levant, translations of the Bible began to proliferate amongst the biblical communities. Sidney Griffith justifies the impetus for translating the Bible into Arabic according to their use within those communities. As he writes, 'the earliest Christian translations obviously had a liturgical function as well as a role in theology and controversy; the earliest Jewish translations seem to have been made more for study, for discussion and controversy rather than for liturgical proclamation'.[34] In the ninth century, a more reader-centred approach in biblical translation emerged, most notably with Sa'adya Gaon al-Fayyumi's (882–942) *Tafsir*, a Judeo–Arabic translation of the Pentateuch that, despite its use of the Hebrew alphabet 'succeeded . . . in overcoming the excessive literalism in the earlier versions and their perceived stylistic clumsiness and infelicity'.[35] While such able translators stand out for their mastery of Arabic, most translations of the Bible were produced for consumption within biblical communities and did not conform to the standard register. Instead, translators chose what can be termed a *koine* Arabic to mirror the common speech of the biblical communities who were the primary readers of these translations. Even when print technology was introduced for Bible dissemination in the seventeenth century, the Arabic translations of the Bible continued to favour a Middle Arabic variant;[36] unlike the European case, where standardisation processes consequent upon print singled out the urban variants of emerging European capital cities. Appropriating Luther's linguistic strategies, the Counter-Reformation

Arabic Bible produced in Rome upheld this dictum of *naiveté*, and twined vernacularisation with divine calling, to satisfy the demands of a different political economy than Protestant commoditisation of the Bible with the Western Church.

The idiom of the Roman version, the BSA, is particularly noteworthy because the translators of this version justified their deployment of Middle Arabic through arguments about *koine* simplicity being a theological imperative of Bible translation. In the introduction to this Bible, the writing style was identified as 'Christian Arabic', a variant of the language that did not conform with Arabic writing conventions as a symbolic assertion of the identity of Christians as distinct from the dominant use of Arabic. They wrote:

> In this Arabic copy you will find some utterances that are not in concord, and even contradictory to the rules of the Arabic language (*al-lughah al-'arabiyyah*): male gender instead of female, single numeral instead of plural, plural instead of dual . . . the reason for this was the naiveté (*sadhaja*) of the speech of Christians (*kalam al-masihiyyin*), which became a kind of language (*lughah*) special to them. This is not only in the Arabic tongue (*lisan*) but also in Latin, Greek and Hebrew where the early prophets and apostles neglected the standard of expression (*qiyas al-kalam*). The Holy Spirit did not want to yoke the expansiveness of the divine word (*al-kalimah al-ilahiyyah*) within the norms of grammar (*al-farayid al-nahawiyyah*). The Holy Spirit bequeathed to us the heavenly secrets without eloquence or adornment, but with easy words so that humans shall dedicate their force and talent to their miraculous salvation.[37]

For these Christians, naiveté of speech was one of God's graces, and His way of directing the faithful to a ritual of salvation. Serving Christians that live amongst a majority of Muslims, the elite local scholars that worked in Rome on this translation asserted a linguistic identity for themselves – negatively – by departing from the normative rules of grammar and style imposed by Muslims on what constituted handsome writing.[38] In their translation, departures from eloquence are typical, and even the most eloquent of the gospels, that of John, speaks in a Middle

Arabic characteristic of the Levant. In John 1:17: 'For the law was given by Moses, but grace and truth came by Jesus Christ', they translate: من أجل أن الناموس بموسى أعطى والنعمة والحق وجبا بيسوع المسيح. Sometimes the lameness is obvious, as in John 10:30: 'I and my Father are one', that states: أنا والأب واحد نحن, or John 14:10: 'Believest thou not that I am in the Father, and the Father in me? The words that I speak unto you I speak not of myself: but the Father that dwelleth in me, he doeth the works', الكلام الذي أكلم لكم أنا به لست أتكلم به من عندي بل أبي الذي هو حال في هو يفعل الأعمال. (compare this last verse to the succinct translation of the SBV: الكلام الذي أكلمكم به لست أتكلم به من نفسي لكن الآب الحال في هو يعمل الأعمال).

In this translation we can still find the unstable orthography of the word 'Allah' that would not become fixed before the nineteenth century. See for example, John 10:33: 'makest thyself God', تجعل نفسك ألاها. As a Levantine text, this Bible also displays unmistakable Damascene inflections of certain verses such as John 11:11: 'Our friend Lazarus sleepeth', حبيبنا نايم, or in this colloquial archaism in John 15:8: 'Herein is my Father glorified', أركون هذا العالم to mean the Lord glorified. This departure paralleled their own geographical distance, outside the Arab world and away from *milieus* of educated Muslims.[39] Differentiating themselves from the linguistic identities of strong groups, Christian Maronites wrote in *lahn* as an assertion of difference and non-assimilation to the dominant grammar that is gleaned from the Qur'an's 'centripetal force' on written Arabic.[40] I will explore *lahn* at length in the following chapter. For now, it suffices to note that seventeenth century Maronites preferred linguistic variance, and this variance enacted a form of negative strength, a refusal of norms for the sake of subversive group cohesion. The interest in writing in variant styles endured until the nineteenth century. With the arrival of the evangelical missionaries, language politics began to change.

How *Koine* was Reinvented in *Fusha*

Quoting Eli Smith, the American Orientalist Isaac Hall notes that prior to the American missionary interest in Arabic Bible translation, 'little [was] known of Arabic versions of the New Testament. The Gospels seem to have been in Arabic since the seventh century, and other books since the ninth and tenth'.[41] Smith laboured to fill this gap in American Biblical scholarship on the tradition of *Biblia Arabica* when he collected his reference library, which included Bibles in Syriac, Judeo–Arabic and various ancient Arabic versions. This translator and his cohort knew that the vernacularisation of the Bible was so ancient that it preceded the Reformation's linguistic radicalism by centuries. In the case of Arabic, the missionaries re-inscribed the vernacular to match 1) the expectations of the local literary elites and 2) the necessity to transform the Bible into an exchange commodity that could rival the fetishist veneration of church tradition that separates the Bible from lay readers. This re-inscription diverged from one of the persistent theological approaches to biblical language in Arabic, particularly the dominant presence of dialectical variation in the written rendition of the text. Like Luther, the Americans sought impact, and they reasoned that in a language where the shadow of the Qur'an looms large, impact would best be achieved through conformity with the trends of the elite majority, and not through recourse to linguistic practices characteristic of weak groups. The industrial press enabled the missionaries to achieve their objectives and produce a Bible version within reach of the general population. This new Bible was expected to circulate widely and transcend the dialectical variations typical of pre-*nahda* Bibles, an efficient decision that would result in only one translation for the dialectically diverse Arabic speaking world. Through syntactical adherence that nevertheless deployed a language both simple and clear, the Americans reinvented a standard form of Arabic as a writing style befitting the concept of the vernacular that Protestants adhered to and sought to propagate. This ambition to propagate the Bible widely further encouraged the missionaries to conceptualise *fusha* as a style of writing that appeals to educated Muslims.

Smith searched for a suitable style amongst the Muslims and spoke to many local interlocutors about what this style might be. The textual apparatus he compiled for the work of translation displays a heightened awareness of the region, with works that not only contain signature Arabic Bible manuscripts of continuous texts, lectionaries and portions of the Bible from a variety of sources, but also choice works of Arabic topography, medicine and history that were to provide the Arabic vocabulary for the flora and fauna, words about the body and disease, and other such glossaries as were needed to fully illuminate the Arabic Bible.[42] As David Grafton observes upon examining this collection, Smith and his successor Van Dyck 'availed themselves of the latest biblical scholarship, including what were to become controversial resources'.[43] Smith even laboured to produce a new Arabic font that would appeal to the tastes of Muslims. For that, he gathered calligraphic samples from various scribes in the region which he then sent to Leipzig, to the workshop of Christian Bernhard Tauchnitz for development, and later to Homan Hallock, the missionary printer, to be punch cut.[44] This font, which became known as the American Font, was superior to any other printing font on the market. Its readable and simple typography, known as *nashki*, which emulates an early Arabic font used for copying administrative documents and books, was also sold to other presses which were setting up business in the region.[45]

Smith is also clear that he favoured a qur'anic turn of phrase. He argued that, by adhering to the rules of classical Arabic:

> we are able to avoid, in a great degree, giving the work the savor of a local dialect, which would be impossible were we to descend to the vulgar language of conversation. We also bear in mind that the work is designed for a race, only a small portion of which are Christians; and consequently, are on our guard in reference to the many words which are current among Christians, in a meaning not sanctioned by Mohammedan usage, lest by using them we convey a wrong idea to a Mohammedan mind.[46]

With an eye on the Muslims, Smith laboured to appeal to their tastes and succeed in attracting them to his Bible version. Smith died before he was able to see the translation through to completion, and his successor, Cornelius van Dyck, went further in ensuring that the translation was palatable to Muslims. Van Dyck employed the Azhari sheikh Yusuf Al-Asir as copy-editor in 1858,[47] who vowelled the entire manuscript while combing through to eliminate chance 'foreign idioms'.[48] As Van Dyck clearly pointed out, 'all native Christian scholars decidedly objected' to the adoption of 'idioms and expressions peculiar to Muhammedans'.[49] Van Dyck accepted this argument and revised all the proofs to ensure that 'a simple but pure Arabic, free from foreign idioms' was adopted.

Different historians of the period have often credited the Bible translations of the *nahda* with modernising the language. But what is this modernity, which had as its main contribution the deliberate choice of a style that departed from Middle Arabic and revival of interest in the classical syntax? Was there a more immediate impact of the Bible translation on Arab literary life? And in what way did it 'modernise' the language as is often claimed? One can find partial answers to these questions by examining how the SBV systematised its translation choices in the text. In its methodical application of particular lexemes to denote specific Christian ideas, the SBV managed to construct a uniform Christian glossary that was chosen in contradistinction to the concepts that can be found in the Qur'an.

The glossary shows how the construction of Christian identity in the nineteenth century was mainly a process of semantic inclusion and exclusion, which had not been fully present in earlier versions of the Arabic Bible. It is important to note that much of what I refer to here as 'qur'anic lexemes' had in fact been incorporated into the Arabic language through centuries of inter-confessional exchange among Arabic speakers. The dramatic transformations in Christian epistemological concepts mediated the heightened context of sectarian separations that were shaping the socio-political world of the nineteenth century Levant. The most significant shifts were in the adoption of the Gregorian calendar and concepts referring to time as well as the moral world of the Bible, in the shift in geographical names from *sham* to *suriyya* as well as the topographical labels of Bibleland.

Re-inventing Christian Arabic

Buoyed by the ABCFM directive that all translations of the Bible must depend on the *Textus Receptus* of the New Testament,[50] or *al-nass al-maqbul*, as its original witness for the New Testament, Smith backpedalled the *Biblia Arabica* canon, favouring an overwhelming focus on etymological relations between *koine* Greek, Syriac and Arabic. The records mention that he submitted a full translation of the New Testament to the mission board on 5 April 1855 and that he was almost done with the Book of Isaiah by the following year.[51] His successor Van Dyck alleged that Smith did not limit himself to the Textus Receptus and had made use of the advances in biblical scholarship that were radically transforming the Enlightenment landscape in Europe and were questioning the authority of the Textus Receptus as the most ancient Greek text.[52] The truth-claims of this allegation derive from the rise of etymology as a philological practice concerned with the historical origins of language and Smith's acquaintance with the most famous Orientalists working in Germany. Benjamin Smith, Eli Smith's grandson, accused Van Dyck of distorting the facts when he claimed that Smith's original witness was 'Hahn's recension of the Greek, but he adopted various readings from Alford and from Tregelles, as far as the work of the latter was published'.[53] Even if it is correct that Van Dyck's allegation was self-serving, it shows the extent to which etymological arguments were destabilising the field of biblical studies.

Etymology supplied the new translation of the Bible with new concepts, revived from ancient biblical languages other than Arabic. It facilitated the strategic shift in the biblical glossary from sharing concepts and lexemes with the Qur'an. It also ensured that the New Testament kept in step with the Greek text earmarked by ABCFM, advances in biblical philology were reduced to lexical history, which bracketed off the complex histories made possible by textual critical questions about the oldest biblical manuscripts. This paradox divulges a process of indoctrination of Lutheran creeds and the Reformation context as the only historical framework that was institutionally acceptable in the nineteenth century. In the Arabic context, this insistence functioned as a synchronising device that created kinship relations between diverse languages by ensuring that all evangelical translations of the Bible stemmed from the same Greek witness, at the expense of honouring, or even knowing, the heteroglossic readings and translations that have contributed to the tradition of *Biblia Arabica*.

Temporal and Moral Worldviews

Perhaps the most influential of these changes was the shift in the calendar from the Islamic Hijri era to the Gregorian calendar that valorised a decidedly Western dating of biblical events. This shift in the calendar influenced Muslims and Christians alike, for the temporality of the state was fixed to the Hijri calendar.[54]

Other signs of introducing a Christian temporality came with such concepts as *al-khamsin*, an exact translation from Greek (Pentecost) and *'imad*: (baptism; a Syriac term) were also systematically adopted in the SBV, whilst in earlier Bible versions, including the BSA, those concepts had not been systematically rendered. The Shidyaq Lee (SL) uses those lexemes in addition to lexical synonyms that are in the Qur'an, and are also common amongst Christians, such as *sabagha*, a term for baptism that also means 'tint'. If we compare the original biblical languages, such as Greek or Syriac, we find that in the Peshitta, the word used is *a'med*, a translation of the Greek word *baptizo*. Both terms, *'amad*, and *sabagh*, would have been understood by a lay Arabic reader, as both are found in all the established lexicons I consulted. The SBV adopted *'amad* systemically, even though its synonym, *sabagh*, was also considered a Christian term by the Muslims in a religious context. As Lane's dictionary translates 'the term is used by the Christians as meaning: The dipping, or immersing, of their children (i.e., baptising them), in water'.[55] Likewise for the eighteenth century Christian lexicographer Jirmanus Farhat, *ṣibghah* was undoubtedly a Christian term. He writes that it is a synonym of *'imad* and then continues:

> *al-ṣābigh* is the title of John son of Zachariah because he baptised (*yaṣbugh*) with the *ṣibghah* of salvation, or because he *ṣabagh* the Lord Christ and the righteous. The Jews used to be baptised (*yanṣabighūn*) every day believing that man cannot live virtuously if he was not dipped in water every day.[56]

In his lexicon, al-Bustani also defines this term as Christian. On the other hand, in the SBV (unlike other Bibles), we find no trace of it whatsoever. Al-Bustani writes,

> *Sabagha* in water, *iṣṭabagh* that is *'amada*, baptised. Christian term. *Al-ṣābegh* الصابغ. The title of John the son of Zachary . . . and *al-ṣibghah* الصبغة is the type, *ṣibāgh* religion, sect. To Christians it is a metaphor (*'isti'ārah*) for baptism . . . In Surat Al-Baqarah (The Cow) الصباغ صبغة الله, His Grace. God's command to Muhammad, i.e., circumcision. Al-Jawharī said that صبغة الله is God's Religion. He said and it is said

that it originates from *ṣabgh* Christian children in their water . . . The
Christians used to dip *their children in a yellow* water (*yughmisun awla-
dahum fi ma' asfar*) that they called *ma'mūdiyyah* and they say that it is
for purification and with it they realise their Christianity.

Similarly, *al-khamsin* was adopted systematically, even though an earlier
more widely accepted term was also available (although both are borrowings). In the SBV, *al-khamsin* replaced the Christian Arabic *al-'ansarah*
which is a borrowing from Hebrew. In contrast, the SL used *al-'ansarah*,
a word that derives from the Hebrew feast of *hashu'it*, where it is a loan
word that comes from the Hebrew *'atsarah*.[57] The SBV preferred to translate the Greek into Arabic, a practice that I came to expect as I read
through this version. In established Arabic lexicons prior to the SBV,
khamsin and *'ansarah* were not recognised as Christian concepts. In fact,
al-Bustani's lexicon is the first text that defines these lexemes in terms of
their biblical meaning.

   The SBV also bestowed a distinctive uniformity on other concepts,
specifically ones that denote the moral and legal world of the Christian
faith, also selected against the Qur'an. Terms include *barr*: (just), *lahut*:
(Godhead), *anathema*, and *karaz*: (preach). These terms were used with
such systematic consistency in the SBV that they were emphasised for
their Christian conceptual significance. Compared to other Bibles, where
a host of synonyms were used to translate the Greek equivalents of these
words, the SBV Bible displays a remarkable consistency regarding
lexemes denoting the moral worldview of Christianity, which suggests
that the translators were consciously selecting what they believed would
befit Christian moral theology. Again, those concepts cannot be traced in
the text of the Qur'an, even though their synonyms are available, and in
earlier Bible translations some of those synonyms were used. A lexeme
like *anathema* for example in 1 Cor 12:3: 'Wherefore I give you to understand, that no man speaking by the Spirit of God calleth Jesus accursed',
was a pioneering entry into the Arabic Bible versions and a clear borrowing from Greek. لذلك أعرفكم أن ليس أحد وهو يتكلم بروح الله يقول "يسوع أناثيما"
Both the Jesuit Bible and the SL prefer to use terms of Arabic origin,
mubsal and *mal'un* in the respective versions.

SBV's translation strategy becomes even clearer in its systematic use of phrases like *ghayr mu'min*: (unbeliever), a concept which in Arabic had been represented by a single word: *kafir*. Unsurprisingly, the SL uses the more succinct phrase *kafir* while the SBV uses only *ghayr mu'min*. While both are common and synonymous terms, the word *kafir* is used persistently in the Qur'an to refer to unbelievers. In English translations of the Qur'an, *unbeliever* is often used, which has an identical meaning to *ghayr mu'min*, which calques the Greek prefix in *a-pistos*, meaning runaway slave or deserter and which the KJV calques as *apostate*, but shifts the semantic significance to mean *non-believer*. The Jesuit Bible oscillates between both terms. Ironically, as Arthur Jeffery tells us, *kafir* comes from the Hebrew *kofer* or the Syriac *kfara*.[58]

The word *karaz* (preach) was also introduced for the first time. This word did not exist with this meaning in Arabic lexicons prior to al-Bustani's work; it is only found as a term in falconry.[59] Even though it is officially used in the title of the Coptic Church *al-kiraza al-qubtiyya*, a reader un acquainted with the Christian tradition would find it too confusing a choice. The SL never used this word, opting instead for its Arabic equivalent *bashshar*.[60] The SBV uses *karaz* exclusively for preach. To mean the gospel, or good tidings, the SBV uses a derivation of *bashshar* (see for example: Acts 21:6; 2Tim 4:5; Rev 14:6). In Syriac, this word is *akrez*, which, Farhat notes, is the original etymology of the Arabic loan word. In Greek, which often functioned as a lexical source for Syriac, the term is *keruzai*. Baptist minister and Bible translator Ghassan Khalaf, who prefers simple and ecumenical theological concepts, writes against this lexeme, because it is routinely ignored by Muslim lexicographers even today, which might obscure an understanding of the text.[61]

The choices made in the SBV of the word *namus* from the Greek *nomos* (law) reveal the translators' ideological motivations. This word is systematically translated as *shari'a* by the SL in the Gospels, but in Paul's epistles, the SL switches to *namus*, for Mosaic Law. The SBV only uses *namus* throughout the NT yet systematically uses *shari'a* in the OT (see for example, Lev, Num, Deut). This distinction is not found in the KJV, and a quick OT check on the SL shows that it lacks uniformity in the treatment of the word. While *shari'a* has a decidedly Islamic connotation because of the historical tendency to associate *law* with the Islamic faith, *namus* on the other hand has long been associated with the other monotheistic faiths.[62] In the latest Catholic translation of the Bible, the word *namus* was dropped in favour of the more ordinary term, *shari'a*. The word exists in both the Greek and Syriac. We find Ibn Sina speaking of *namus al-tibb* in his reference to the Hippocratic Oath, and al-Jurjani defines the word as a synonym for *shar'*.[63] *Shari'a* is defined by Farhat as: 'What God sanctioned for his people as *halal* and *haram*. *shari'a* (law) of nature from Adam until Moses. The law of justice from Moses until the Lord Christ. The law of virtue from Christ to the arrival of the Antichrist, when the Time arrives and the laws are annulled'.[64]

This definition does not differentiate between *namus* and *shari'a*, and it is the one that al-Bustani summarises in his lexicon when he writes: '*Ishtara' al-shari'a* اشترع الشريعة, instituted, established the law. And from it is *tathniyat al-ishtira'* تثنية الاشتراع (Deuteronomy), which is the fifth chapter of the Torah'. Despite this, the title of Deuteronomy in the SBV is the short version *tathniyah* تثنية. Like the Jesuit Bible, the SL used the full phrase: *tathniyat al-ishtira'*. Again, what distinguishes the SBV's lexemes from the other translations is that they are not to be found in the Qur'an. Whereas most of these words are recognisable to Arabs as words with a history of long use, the translators deliberately chose these words in their biblical translation because they did not have corresponding meanings in the Qur'an. The lexemes become even more interesting when we examine biblical topology, especially because the Levant has traditionally been associated in the Western imagination with the Bible's place of origin. The biblical topology shows how the strategic borrowing from Greek de-familiarised the Bible's topography as Levantine Arabs would have known it, in such terms as *btulmayis* for Acre in Acts 21:7 ولما أكملنا السفر في البحر إلى صور أقبلنا إلى بتولمايس فسلمنا على الأخوة ومكثنا عندهم يوماً واحداً. Whereas in this instance the BSA preceded the SBV in using Greek place names, the SBV attempted to revert back to the Greek in all the names of places even if a few places escaped such treatment. Such is the case with *Sur* in the same quote, where it was left in its most common designation instead of deploying the Greek *Tyros*. Nonetheless the scope of the change was great enough for a defamiliarisation to occur and for the land to be re-presented through its earlier biblical history, emphasising the landscape they came to settle in as *bibleland*,[65] excising how the land was named following the advent of Muslim rule.

Geographical and Spatial Concepts

While some of the place names in Bible translations continue to correspond to a large degree with their Greek names, those that had changed over time and no longer did so were subsequently changed in various Bible translations. The SBV resorted back to the Greek names and reproduced a missionary epistemology of the Levant as the living land of the Bible. The SBV Bible was the first translation I encountered in which *Syria* was rendered as *Suriyyah* and not as *Sham*, as this area was known in all earlier Bibles I consulted. In the Bible, *Suriyyah* was first introduced as the name of a biblical place in the SBV translation to designate the Greek term *suria*.[66] The new name was systematic and can be located whenever the region is referred to. Take for example Acts 18:18: 'And Paul after this tarried there yet a good while, and then took his leave of the brethren, and sailed thence into Syria', وأما بولس فلبث أياماً كثيرة ثم ودع الإخوة وسافر البحر إلى سورية. The SBV's use of the term was later followed by the Jesuit Bible of 1877. Medieval Arabic lexicographers often claimed that 'Sham' is derived from the word for *shamal* (left-wards), specifying that the area was termed as such because it was to the left of Mecca.[67] In earlier sources, like Yaqut al-Hamawi's geographical lexicon, the name 'Syria' is considered a Byzantine term for the region.[68] In present scholarship in the field, 'Syria' and 'Sham' are often conflated, and translations into English often do not recognise any conceptual differences between the two, although they are, historically, two distinct geopolitical concepts that indicate two varying conceptions of the nation. As Fruma Zachs argues, the invention of the political concept of 'Syria' in the nineteenth century was entangled with the *bibleland* trope advanced by the missionaries.[69] In 1848, when Smith embarked on translating the Bible, the missionaries were working on different fronts. In local use, the term was first taken up in Arabic by al-Bustani in the Beirut salons he helped to establish.[70] Yet the term comes into common parlance in the post 1860 era of civil war as Kamal Salibi has noted, but does not come into official Arabic political discourse before 1864, when the Ottoman name for the region was changed from *Wilayat of Damascus* to *Wilayat of Syria*.[71] The displacement of '*Sham*' by '*suriyyah*' reveals the impact that missionaries had in rearranging the map of the Levant.[72]

From the perspective of this region's natives, *Sham* was amenable to political investments especially in proto-nationalist articulations that posited the Arab identity of this region in opposition to the Turkish identity of its rulers. By the end of the seventeenth century, the term was being used by trans-sectarian *shami* elites who were eager to gain political autonomy from the Ottoman domains. In his work on the Arab national awakening in the eighteenth century, Steve Tamari analyses the emerging territorial conception among the Damascene literati. As he shows, '*Sham*' and '*shami*' were fashioned as ethnicities superior to the Turks of the Ottoman Empire at least two centuries earlier than the standard periodisation of nationalism in Syria as a modern ideology of the *nahda*. As he claims, the dissatisfaction with Ottoman rule among Muslim and Christian Arabs in the Levant began to give way to an ethno-political consciousness of *Bilad al-Sham* that set the Levantine Arabs as different, and superior, to their Turkish rulers.[73] The Muslim writers that he studies erase the sectarian distance that separated them from their Christian neighbours in the interest of fostering a proto-nationalist ideology.[74] In line with their usage, in the seventeenth and eighteenth century *Suriyyah* is distinguished from *Sham* because the former was a term that had Christian designations, while the latter, as Tamari shows, was a multi-confessional, ethnocentric, proto-national political identity. For the Eastern Churches, the former term was reserved for religious designations. It distinguished two of the fifteen church provinces, or metropolitanates (Provincia Syriae primae and Provincia Syriae secundae).[75] In the nineteenth century, we find that for Christians like al-Bustani, *Suriyyah* was preferred over *Sham* as an instrumental carrier of religious identity and political galvanisation.

Tamari's focus on the Muslim writers must thus be linked to the study on the Greek Orthodox community in the work of Carsten Walbiner. In Walbiner's work, we encounter a decidedly *shami* emergence among a major Christian writer, Macarius al-Za'im (d. 1675), the historian and

Orthodox Patriarch of Antioch. Residing in Aleppo, the Patriarch was also busy recollecting for his people a golden age that could be politically harvested. Walbiner cogently shows how the use of contemporary rather than older placenames allowed al-Za'im to construct a myth of origins that showed the 'bygone greatness and importance of the Patriarchate'.[76] In al-Za'im's worldview, earlier Christian historiographers recollected the past not because they were nostalgic. Rather, for him the recollections of the past provided society with a history of the community's presence and helped it to construct viable identities in the present. He framed his historiography as a continuation of the work of his predecessors, and imagined that his work was important because it instated new social relations and the political leadership (headed by the church, and him in it) at the top. For him, history was above all else a great teacher of moral relations between people. As he told his audience, the Greek *Suriyya* is their Arab *Sham*, and they are the inheritors of a great nation. While he did recall the historical names of the lands of *Sham*, it was only for the sake of historical illustration. However, for political clarity, al-Za'im used *Sham* to transmit his political vision for his society. Walbiner's direct quotations from al-Za'im show that this patriarch referred to his region as *bilad al-sham* even when he was quoting from the Bible, in an effort to question the legitimacy of Turkish rule by flying 'in the face of the fact that the message of Islam is universal and places submission to God above the multitude of linguistic and ethnic groups that make up the worldwide community of Muslims'.[77] Therefore, the instrumental use of 'Syria' as a modern national construction signals a rupture with proto-national practices that began to take shape in the seventeenth century. That this rupture took place at the lexical level in the SBV Bible is significant, for it identifies the emerging nationalisms of the nineteenth century in Lebanon as a sectarian construction and a political articulation of Christian identity.[78]

The SBV's terminology enacts a foreignisation strategy when it refers to the geographical region of the Bible through Greek nomenclature, for it makes visible the historical gap that separates the present natives from the historical events of Christianity. The historical biblical label for the landscape would have satisfied Issa Diab's proposition that 'proper names, names of places and concepts should not be translated so that the reader can follow the evolution of a religious manifestation across the history of the Holy Book'.[79] Writing from the position of a historian of religion, Diab expects that a translated Bible must conform to the demands of academic precision. In my view, such a suggestion disregards that the Bible has a scriptural role that informs its community's sense of identity. This is not a proposition for future translation work on my part but rather a suggestion that, in the nineteenth century, Arabic readers became more aware of the geographic importance of the Levant as the original location of the Bible. By looking at the evolution of place names, we can uncover some of the biases that translators inevitably follow. For example, the Peshitta renders biblical geography differently and in accordance with Syriac conventions. For a translation into Arabic, excluding the Peshitta from topographical selection marks a clear strategic choice, especially since Syriac continues to be a liturgical language in some of the Eastern Churches. In the SBV, meanwhile, we find a heightened sense of fidelity towards the original Greek text as the original manifestation of the word of God. It is with this assumption in mind that I frame the SBV's borrowing of lexemes of biblical geography from Greek. To shift the names of the geographical and regional markers in the Bible from conventional Arabic to Greek is a deliberate move towards re-inventing the Bible landscape to agree with perceptions of Anglophone newcomers. Put differently, the Bible was removed from the contemporary lives of the Arab Christian commu-nity and relegated to ancient history. Through their translation practices, the Protestants alerted their Arab readers that the Bible speaks of an age that was different in every way from the nineteenth century reality of Christian Arabs, who according to the missionary historian Henry Jessup were inhabiting this 'fallen, fallen Syria . . . Crushed down to the earth by ten thousand leaden weights of form and superstition, until thy once pure heart ceased to beat'.[80] By recollecting the Greek names of bibleland, the missionaries and their collaborators laboured to make Levantine Arabic speakers aware of the historical depth of their political and moral loss.

Proselytisation among Eastern Christians required the re-invention of two realities, in which the Church of St Paul was dialectically opposed to the plethora of Eastern Churches in the Levant and Egypt. The clear articulation of biblical origins coincided with a rising national sentiment among Lebanese Syrian Christians. This nascent political ideology complemented the missionary intervention by fully endorsing a new national myth that singled out the Bible for its mythical construction of national roots. In this re-invented geographical landscape, *sham* and *shami* Middle Arabic Bibles became relics belonging to a distant past.

As a rule, based in part on what the letters and pamphlets published by the missionaries inform us and partly on a tangible systematic trend, we can argue that the separation of Christian terminology from its Muslim counterpart was deliberate. Even though in the SBV Bible, we still find qur'anic words not replaced by Greek or Syriac terms, such as the word for fasting *sawm*, this appears to be an exception to the general aspect of the SBV. In linguistic terms, we can summarise the difference between the BSA and the SBV through the concept of a religiolect: whereas the religiolect constructed in the BSA Bible was a syntactical deviation from the normative rules of grammar, the SBV Bible did not deviate from normative standard Arabic. What it did instead was to offer a new set of lexemes that, taken as a totality, reveal that a conceptual enclave became possible in the Arabic language, in which sectarian politics took on semantic significance. In structuralist parlance, signifiers were shored up with new signifieds, and when a possible signifier was flagged as too domesticated in Arabic to be of any use, new ones were found by borrowing – mainly from Greek and, less often from Syriac.

Compared with the translation that al-Shidyaq worked on in Cambridge, which had been published three years before the SBV New Testament came into being, the effects of a systematic translation along sectarian lines stands out, particularly in the absence of such a selective systemic process in the SL. Al-Shidyaq's Bible version shows clear signs of his singular translation style. Al-Shidyaq inverted the decision to separate the biblical glossary from qur'anic phrases, and instead systematically chose lexemes that denote a shared theological glossary between Christians and Muslims. According to al-Shidyaq's reports about the translation process, his supervisor, Samuel Lee, loathed the qur'anic turn of phrase and thus its systemic presence in the text signals al-Shidyaq own politics of translation: namely, what he believed to be the function of a new Bible translation. Lee shared the opinion of the team in Beirut that concepts found in the Qur'an should not be used in the Bible.[81] As al-Shidyaq claimed in his travelogue, Lee suffered from a *hawas* (obsession) with avoiding constructions that resembled the qur'anic style and terminology to the point that 'each time he found a word that ends with *waw* and *nun*, or with *ya'* and *nun*, he would say it resembles the qur'anic style; so he would change it'.[82] Yet Lee was more pliant than al-Shidyaq admitted. Not only does this version show evidence of precisely such words in the text, but Lee also defended al-Shidyaq's opinions about how the register of Arabic which ought to be used for the translation must be the eloquent standard of *fusha*. As he informed the translation committee in one of the meetings,

> Mr. Fares fully concurred that it was important to avoid such vernacular Arabic as exhibiting colloquial peculiar to any particular countries or Districts, and to adopt a language, which, while it is gracefully accurate and grammatical, may yet be simple, and intelligible to all readers of Arabic.[83]

Indeed, the translation shows the extent to which this opinion set the style standard for the translation. Al-Shidyaq was interested in selecting lexemes that bring the conceptual level of the biblical world closer to the worldview of a Muslim public, resolving at the level of the lexicon the political sectarianism that was storming through his homeland.[84] With al-Shidyaq, words like *bi'ah* (church), for example in Matt 16:18: 'That thou art Peter, and upon this rock I will build my church' وعلى هذه الصخرة أبني بيعتي could be interchanged with *kanisa* in other locations, such as Acts 14:23: 'And when they have ordained them elders in every church', ولما عينا لهما قسوساً في كل كنيسة. Likewise other words such as *sunnah* (tradition), *siddiq* (just), *sabagh* (baptise), *kafir* (non-believer) and *shari'a* (law) were interchangeable with lexemes that become exclusive in the SBV, but were also used with enough consistency throughout the translation that they reveal how the issue of a Christian theological worldview was not one that al-Shidyaq was willing to exercise, contrary to the explicit wishes of his supervisor. Both those Bible versions worked towards simplification of the religious idiom, to satisfy the ideological position of the translator. The SBV excluded religious concepts that are mentioned in the Qur'an, while the SL worked towards a shared religious idiom.

With the decision to use *fusha* style in translation, the Americans promoted their new version by capitalising on its links to biblical antiquity, which effectively positioned Arabic as a modern vernacular that orbits around an ancient, and foundational, biblical standard, the Textus Receptus. The SBV was dressed in an Arabic that could circulate among Arabs beyond the Levantine region in which they worked. The major difference was the sacredness with which the language was treated. For the Protestants this encounter with a language ideology of veneration posed both a challenge as well as an opportunity. The challenge lay in the degree of education a scribe must attain before they could master the classical register. The opportunity was in the sheer number of Arabic speakers in the world.

The success of the SBV eclipsed both the SL and BSA versions. What both lacked were the translation practices that transformed how the Bible was presented as scripture. I have proposed that there was a shift in the fetishization processes from an object that was severed from the human labour that produced it, and which was fashioned as writ by the divine to its fetishisation as a commodity: contending for attention in a market not only reserved for the Bible but that also included the Qur'an, and all the other books whose value as literary texts were very much shaped by the centripetal force of the Qur'an as a scripture revealed in a holy tongue. The commodity fetish venerated the scientific acumen that brought this translation into the market, and thus emphasised the intellectual capital of the missionaries as the harbingers of scientific modernity. Science was here the fetish and the market was its realm.[85] This new fetish produced new readers through standardisation practices that deployed a normative and highly coded writing style as well as constructing a new conceptual worldview that highlighted for the reader how the values of the Protestants differed from their competitors, whether they be Muslim or Christian. The opportunity was a *translatio studii*,[86] a transfer of the symbols of authority from a waning Islamic culture to the ambitious Christian newcomers. I turn in the next chapter to one who carried out this task most successfully. Trained in the Protestant ways, Butrus al-Bustani would soon graduate from his reading assignments and into an authorial position, and in his legacy we shall see the features of the new reader begin to coalesce.

Notes

1. Jonas King, 'Remarks on Asaad Shidiak', *Missionary Herald*, March 1827, 68–9.
2. Makdisi, *Artillery of Heaven*, 105.
3. Webb Keane, *Christian Moderns: Freedom and Fetish in the Mission Encounter* (Berkeley: University of California Press, 2007), Kindle edition.
4. Olivier Millet, *Calvin et la dynamique de la parole: Étude de rhétorique Réformée*, (Paris: Slatkine, 1992), 61.
5. Wilfred Cantwell Smith, *What Is Scripture? A Comparative Approach* (Minneapolis: Fortress Press, 1993). Kindle edition, Chapter 1.
6. Cantwell Smith claims that the Qur'an is the last development we have in the notion of scripture as form and genre. Its quick process of canonisation and standardisation, its dissemination through oral as well as written literacy has not been surpassed even by Luther's Reformation. See Wilfred Cantwell Smith, 'The Study of Religion and the Study of the Bible', in *Rethinking Scripture: Essays from a Comparative Perspective*, ed. Miriam Levering (New York: State University of New York Press, 1989), 18–28.
7. Keane, *Christian Moderns*.
8. Ibid., Chapter 6.
9. This is a widespread pronouncement amongst missionaries. Thomson writes at length about it in his travelogue from Jerusalem. Thomson was on the board of the SBV and worked with some regularity with Smith and others. His trip to Jerusalem was initially instigated by his responsibilities as the main education administrator of the Syria Mission. See William Thomson, *The Land and the Book; or, Biblical Illustrations Drawn from the Manners and Customs, the Scenes and Scenery of the Holy Land* (New York: Harper, 1880), 487.
10. Keane draws attention to the difference between two German cognates for translation: *overzetting* and *vertaalt*, that frame 'the general Calvinist distinction between divine and human agency' where *overzetting* refers to translation as a textual method, and *vertaalt* makes 'meaning available in the world'. Keane, *Christian Moderns*, Chapter 6, ft. 8.
11. Sarah Henrich and James Boyce, 'Martin Luther—Translations of Two Prefaces on Islam: Preface to the Libellus de Ritu et Moribus Turcorum (1530), and Preface to Bibliander's Edition of the Qur'an (1543)', *Word and World* 16, no. 2 (Spring 1996): 250–66, 264–5.

12. Jan Retsö, 'Arabs and Arabic In the Age of the Prophet', in *The Qur'ān in Context: Historical and Literary Investigations into the Qur'ānic Milieu*, ed. Angelika Neuwirth, Nicolai Sinai and Michael Marx (Leiden: Brill, 2011), 281–92, 289.

13. Martin Luther, 'An Open Letter on Translating', (15 September 1530), 4. http://www.blackmask.com. Accessed 5 May 2021.

14. 1Cor 14:9, The New International Version, https://biblehub.com/.

15. von Lüpke, in *Luther's Use of Language*, 154.

16. Max Weber, *The Protestant Ethic and the Spirit of Capitalism*, trans. Talcott Parsons (London: Routledge, 1992), 85. One must also keep in mind that the dominance of the Lutheran linguistic beliefs in the master narrative of vernacularisation does not account for Bible versions that were produced in vernacular tongues long before the Reformation, in Europe or elsewhere.

17. John Calvin, 'Preface to Olivétan's New Testament (1534)', https://www.monergism.com/preface-oliv%C3%A9tans-new-testament.

18. John Calvin, *Institutes of the Christian Religion: Translated from the Original Latin, and Collated with the Author's Last Edition in French*, trans. John Allen (Philadelphia: Presbyterian Board of Publication, 1813), https://www.gutenberg.org/files/45001/45001-pdf.pdf, 450.

19. Quoted in ibid.

20. 16:103. Tarif Khalidi, *The Qur'an: A New Translation* (London: Penguin Classics, 2008).

21. Abi Fath al-Uthman Ibn Jinni, *Al-Khasa'is*, ed. Mohammad Ali Al-Najjar, 4th ed. (Cairo: al-Hay'ah al-Masriyyah al'Amah li al-Kitab, 1039, 2018).

22. Griffith, *The Bible in Arabic*.

23. Al-Subawi, *Anajil 'Abd Yashu' al-Subawi 1318*.

24. Blau, *A Grammar of Christian Arabic*; Kees Versteegh, 'Religion as a Linguistic Variable in Christian Greek, Latin and Arabic', in *Philologists in the World: A Festschrift in Honour of Gunvor Mejdell*, ed. Rana Issa and Nora Eggen (Oslo: Novus Forlag, 2017), 57–88.

25. Joshua Blau, 'Are "Judaeo-Arabic" and "Christian Arabic" Misnomers Indeed?', *Jerusalem Studies in Arabic and Islam* 24 (2000): 49–57, 55.

26. Benjamin Hary and Martin Wein, 'Religiolinguistics: On Jewish-, Christian-, and Muslim-Defined Languages', *International Journal of the Sociology of Language* 220 (March 2013): 85–108, https://doi.org/10.1515/ijsl-2013-0015, 88.

27. Versteegh, 'Religion as a Linguistic Variable in Christian Greek, Latin and Arabic', 88, 79.

28. Carter paraphrasing Johann Wilhelm Fück, see p.15. In many ways, Sibawayhi was a lot more reflective about Arabic dialects than the purists that proliferated in the nineteenth century. As Carter argues about him, 'The dominant characteristic of the Kitāb is its tenacious search for reasons for linguistic behavior, and the element of purism and preservation for its own sake is conspicuously lacking'. See Michael G. Carter, *Sībawayhi's Principles: Arabic Grammar and Law in Early Islamic Thought* (Atlanta: Lockwood Press, 2016), 222.

29. Kees Versteegh, *The Arabic Language* (Edinburgh: Edinburgh University Press, 1997), 53.

30. Joshua Blau, 'The Status and Linguistic Structure of Middle Arabic', *Jerusalem Studies in Arabic and Islam* 23 (1999): 221–27, 222; Joshua Blau, *Studies in Middle Arabic and Its Judaeo-Arabic Variety* (Jerusalem: Magnes Press, 1988), 209. For a similar definition see Jacques Grand Henry, 'Christian Middle Arabic', in *Encyclopaedia of Arabic Language and Linguistics*, ed. Rudolf de Jong Lutz Edzard (Leiden: Brill Online, 2014); and Jerome Lentin, 'Middle Arabic', in *Encyclopaedia of Arabic Language and Linguistics*, ed. Rudolf de Jong Lutz Edzard (Leiden: Brill Online, 2012); Nelly Hanna, 'Language Registers: What Did They Signify', in *Ottoman Egypt and the Emergence of the Modern World: 1500–1800* (Cairo: American University of Cairo, 2014); Sajdi, *The Barber of Damascus*; Madiha Doss and Humphrey Davies, *Al-ʿamiyyah al-misriyyah al-maktubah: 1401–2019* (Cairo: Al-Hay'ah al-misriyyah al-ʿammah lil-kitab, 2013).

31. Hilary Kilpatrick, 'The Arabic Culture of Christians in Syria in the 16th and 17th Centuries'.

32. Ronny Vollandt, 'Some Historiographical Remarks on Medieval and Early-Modern Scholarship of Biblical Versions in Arabic: A Status Quo', *Intellectual History of the Islamicate World* 1 (2013): 25–42, 36.

33. Uwe Vagelpohl, 'The ʿabbasid Translation Movement in Context: Contemporary Voices on Translation', in *ʿAbbasid Studies II*, ed. John Nawas (Leuven: Uitgeverij Peeters, 2010), 247. Also see Griffith, 'The Gospel in Arabic: An Inquiry into Its Appearance in the First Abbasid Century', 155. See also Franz Rosenthal, who described those texts as slavishly 'imitating Greek syntax', *The Classical Heritage in Islam* (Berkeley: University of California Press, 1975), 8. On this style also see Griffith, 'The Gospel in Arabic: An Inquiry into Its Appearance in the First Abbasid Century', 155.

34. Sidney Griffith, *The Bible in Arabic*, 203.

35. Ibid., 273.

36. Hikmat Kashouh, *The Arabic Versions of the Gospels: The Manuscripts and their Families* (Berlin: De Gruyter, 2012).

37. Introduction to the BSA.

38. Blau, *A Grammar of Christian Arabic.*

39. Contrast this Bible to Meletius al-Karmah's proposal to translate the Bible in a language that could stand up to the critical eyes of Muslims, to be produced amongst them and immediately serve to shift the critique that Christians write in *laḥn.* Kilpatrick, 'The Arabic Culture of Christians in Syria in the 16th and 17th Centuries'; Kilpatrick, 'Meletius Karmah's Specimen Translation of Genesis 1–5', 63–74.

40. Yasir Suleiman, *The Arabic Language and National Identity: A Study in Ideology* (Washington: Georgetown University Press, 2003), 35.

41. Hall, 'The Arabic Bible of Drs. Eli Smith and Cornelius V. A. Van Dyck', 278.

42. David D. Grafton, *The Contested Origins of the 1865 Arabic Bible: Contributions to the Nineteenth Century Nahda* (Leiden: Brill, 2016).

43. Ibid., 140.

44. J. F. Coakley, 'Homan Hallock, Punchcutter', *Journal of the American Printing History Association* 45.23, no. 1 (January 2003): 18–40. Andreas Feldtkeller and Uta Zeuge-Buberl. *Networks of Knowledge. Epistemic Entanglement initiated by American Protestant Missionary Presence in 19th century Syria* (Stuttgart: Franz Steiner Verlag, 2019), 139–70.

45. Auji, *Printing Arab Modernity.*

46. Van Dyck and Smith, 'Brief Documentary History', 10.

47. Al-Asir also wrote hymns for the Protestant church, three of which are still included in their hymn book. See *Kitab Al-Taranim al-ruhiyyah lil-kana's al-injiliyyah* (Beirut: The American Press, 1949), 388, 421, 423.

48. Van Dyck and Smith, 'Brief Documentary History', 23.

49. Ibid., 28. The late Rev. Ghassan Khalaf brought to my attention that the new Catholic translation that came out in the 1990s dropped *namus* and adopted *shari'ah* as the more natural Arabic word. Also see Samir Khalil Samir, 'Nahu mustalahat masihiyyah 'arabiyyah mu'asirah muwahhadah (Towards a Unified Christian Arabic Terminology)', in *Nahu mustalahat lahutiyyah masihiyyah 'arabiyyah muwahhadah* (Ghazir: Manshurat ikriliyyat al-batriyarkiyah al-maruniyyah, 2005), 11–18.

50. Metzger and Ehrman, *The Text of the New Testament.*

51. Van Dyck and Smith, 'Brief Documentary History', 23–5.

52. Ibid., 14–15.

53. Ibid. For B. Smith's letter, see "Letter to James Dennis" January 1885 in *The Henrietta Smith Archive.* Special Collections and Archives, American Univeristy of Beirut Library.

54. Before they adopted the Hijri calendar and then the Gregorian calendar, the Eastern Christians used the Julian calendar, which is shorter by eleven, twelve or thirteen days depending on the century.

55. Lane was translating from *al-Sahah, Taj al-arus,* and Abu Zayd al-Ansari. Edward William Lane, *Arabic-English Lexicon* (Cambridge: The Islamic Texts Society, 1984).

56. Jirmanus Farhat, *Ahkam Al-i'rab fi lughat al-'a'rab.*

57. The Talmudic name for the Hebrew feast of *Shavuot, or the Feast of Weeks.* In this holiday work is forbidden, hence the name *'atsarah,* or refraining.

58. Arthur Jeffery, *The Foreign Vocabulary of the Qur'ān* (Baroda: Oriental Institute, 1938), 138–9.

59. 'كَرَّزَ الصَّقْرَ: خاطَ عينيه وأطعمه حتَّى يَذِلَّ'. Al-Ma'any al-jami' (Al-maany.com, 2010), https://www.almaany.com/.

60. Cohen considers that /bshr/ to be a Protosemitic common root. David Cohen and J. Cantineau, *Dictionnaire des racines Sémitiques ou attestées dans les langues Sémitiques* (Paris: Mouton, 1976).

61. Ghassan Khalaf, 'Tarjamat al-kitab al-muqaddas ila al-'arabiyyah wal-mu'athirat', in *Translating the Bible into Arabic: Historical, Text-Critical, and Literary Aspects*, ed. Sara Binay and Stefan Leder, Beiruter Texte Und Studien 131 (Beirut: Ergon Verlag, 2012), 7–24, 20.

62. See Azmeh's discussion of the historicity of *shari'a* that dispels our modern tendency to assume the inertia of *shari'a.* Aziz Azmeh, *Al-'ilmaniyyah min manzur mukhtalif* (Beirut: Markaz dirasat al-wihdah al-'arabiyyah, 1998), 56.

63. Ibn Sina, 'Al-Qanun Fi al-Tibb', ed. Mohammad Ahmad Khalifa Al-Suwaydi (Al-waraq.net, 2003), http://www.alwaraq.net/Core/waraq/coverp age?bookid=94&option=1.

64. Farhat. *Ahkam al-i'rab fi lughat al-'a'rab.*

65. Rana Issa, 'Missionary Philology and the Invention of Bibleland', in *The Jerusalem Code*, vol. 3, ed. Ragnhild Zorgati and Anna Bohlin (De Gruyter, 2021). 309–27.

66. Khalaf mentions that Syria was a Roman province that included, among others, the region of Phoenicia. Ghassan Khalaf, *Lubnan fi al-kitab al-muqaddas* (Mansuriyeh: Dar al-manhal lil hayat, 1985), 210.

67. Jamal al-Din Muhammad ibn Mukarram Ibn Manzur, *Lisan al-'arab* (Beirut: Sader, 1290/2010).

68. Yaqut ibn-Abdullah al-Rumi al-Hamawi, *Kitab mu'jam al-buldan*, ed. Mohammad Ahmad Khalifa Al-Suwaydi (Al-waraq.net, 2003 1226), http://www.alwaraq.net/Core/waraq/coverpage?bookid=94&option=1.

69. Fruma Zachs, 'Toward a Proto-Nationalist Concept of Syria? Revisiting the American Presbyterian Missionaries in the Nineteenth-Century Levant', *Die Welt Des Islams* 41, no. 2 (2001): 145–73. Zachs conflates the two terms sometimes, see ibid., 159. Frenkel claims that *Sham* became an Islamic Holy land *only after the Crusades*, see Yehoshu'a Frenkel, 'Baybars and the Sacred Geography of Bilād Al-Sham: A Chapter in the Islamization of Syria's Landscape', *Jerusalem Studies in Arabic and Islam* 25 (2001): 153–70.

70. Zachs, 'Toward a Proto-Nationalist Concept of Syria', 158.

71. Salibi, *A House of Many Mansions*.

72. Issa, 'Missionary Philology and the Invention of Bibleland'.

73. Steve Tamari, 'Arab National Consciousness in Seventeenth and Eighteenth Century Syria', in *Syria and Bilad Al-Sham under Ottoman Rule*, ed. Peter Sluglett and Stefan Weber (Leiden: Brill, 2010), 309–21.

74. Reading similar texts, Heyberger reaches similar conclusions, albeit he makes clear the nuance of religious belonging that placed Muslims above Christians. Especially important is his reading of the Damascene Sheikh, Abd al-Ghani Al-Nabulsi (1641–1712). Heyberger, *Les chrétiens du Proche-Orient*.

75. Carsten-Michael Walbiner, 'Macarius Ibn Al-Za'īm and the Beginnings of an Orthodox Church Historiography in Bilād al-Shām', in *Le Role des historiens orthodoxes dans l'historiographie* (Balamand: Universite de Balamand, 2010), 11–29. See also Farhat's lexical entry for *Suriyya*, where he writes: '*suriyyah* is the name of two provinces one in Iraq, and it is the first *suriyyah*, and the second in *bilad al-sham*, and it is the second *suriyyah*'. Jirmanus Farhat, *Aḥkam Al-I'rab fi Lughat al-A'rab*.

76. Walbiner, 'Macarius Ibn Al-Za'īm', 17.

77. Tamari, 'Arab National Consciousness in Seventeenth and Eighteenth Century Syria', 315.

78. The first official use of *Suriyyah* as a term that refers to a modern national imagination comes from the joint collaboration between al-Bustani and Smith (as well as others) in their cultural salon known by the name of *Al-Jam'iyyah al-Suriyyah li al-'Ulum wa al-Funun* (1848–85), or 'The Syrian Arts and

Sciences Society'. For the collected papers given at this society Butrus al-Bustani et al., *Al-Jam'iyyah al-Suriyyah lil 'ulum wal funun* (Beirut: Dar al-Hamra', 1848). On the work of this society see Peter Hill, *Utopia and Civilisation in the Arab Nahda* (Cambridge: Cambridge University Press, 2020), 30–6, 42–7.

79. Issa Diab, 'Afkar lahutiyyah wara' ikhtiyar ba'd al-kalimat fi ba'd tarjamat al-kitab al-muqaddas al-'arabiyyah', in *Translating the Bible into Arabic: Historical, Text-Critical, and Literary Aspects*, ed. Sara Binay and Stefan Leder, Beiruter Texte Und Studien 131 (Beirut: Ergon Verlag, 2012), 25–44, 42.

80. Jessup, *Fifty-Three Years in Syria*, vol. 1, 81.

81. Jurji Zaydan flags the closeness that the missionaries kept to the Hebrew in the Old Testament. After the death of Smith, and following the resignation of al-Bustani from the translation team, Van Dyck continued the project alone, and seems to have remained quite close to Hebrew. Zaydan compares this Bible to the Jesuit version and thinks that the latter translators preferred a more eloquent and domesticated version even if a phrase here and a paragraph there were added or deleted. For studies on the literalness of the SBV, see Jurji Zaydan, 'Tarjamat Al-Tawrat', *Al-Hilal*, 1893, American University of Beirut; George Khawwam, 'Ilm al-naqd 'awthaq min al-naql: nazra naqdiyyah ila tarjamat Van Dyck min khilal al-zabbur 90:1–5', in *Yubil 150 Sana 'ala Al-tarjama al-bayrutiyya al-injiliyya lil kitab al-muqaddas: Ahamiyyatuh al-tarikhiyya w al-ijtima'iyya wal-lahutiyya*, ed. Rana Issa (Beirut: Near East School of Theology, 2018).

82. al-Shidyaq, *Al-Wasitah ila ma'rifat 'ahwal Malta wa kashf al-mukhabba' 'an funun 'Urubba*, 131.

83. Horne, Lee, Harrison, Guretono, 'Minutes of Meeting of the Foreign Translation Committee', 10 May 1847, Bible Society Archive, University of Cambridge, UK.

84. Issa, 'Al-Shidyaq-Lee Version (1857)'.

85. Marwa Elshakry, 'The Gospel of Science and American Evangelism in Late Ottoman Beirut', *Past and Present*. 196, no. 1 (August 2007), 173–214. Accessed: 15 October 2021. https://doi.org/10.1093/pastj/gtm006.

86. Stierle, 'Translatio Studii and Renaissance: From Vertical to Horizontal Translation'.

4

Butrus al-Bustani as Translator

The death of Eli Smith in 1857 disentangled Butrus al-Bustani from his engagements with the Syria mission, and his career as a Bible translator came to an end. Two years before Smith's death, this friend and mentor had left him a long letter explaining why his candidacy for the position of minister of the evangelical church in Beirut had been rejected. As Smith writes, al-Bustani had acquired a 'secular rather than spiritual' reputation, as a 'man of great intelligence', whose skills and contribution to the secular betterment of the people can be seen in his dedication to 'secular business whichever be of the literary kind that would leave for the pastorate a divided mind and heart which would certainly stand in the way of success'.[1] Fearing that al-Bustani may become too distracted by his literary pursuits from the work of the ministry, Smith might have triggered al-Bustani's release from the burden of spiritual responsibilities that he was carrying throughout his employment with the missionaries. Under no legal obligation to honour his contract upon the death of one of the signatory parties, al-Bustani left the Bible unfinished, in the care of Cornelius Van Dyck, his friend and colleague, who would carry out the task of the full translation of the continuous text mostly alone, aided only by the Muslim sheikh Yusuf al-Asir, as copy-editor. Al-Bustani went on to build a literary legacy that he envisioned as part of modernising Arab society and a propellor for its progress. This legacy included newspapers, lexicons and literary translations. In all these endeavours, translation was the primary tool that was deployed for the production of texts.

This chapter presents al-Bustani as a translator. By starting it with the point of release from biblical labour, I reveal how the interruption in al-Bustani's trajectory was overcome through turning to the Bible and to translation as the root and method that anchored his secular endeavours. Al-Bustani's later work, I argue, embodies one of the great paradoxes of modernity, in how he decided to base his secular thinking on religious thought. The secular inversion, as I show, represses the extent to which the modernity he advocated for was based on religious assumptions. Considered as one of the great secular scholars of nineteenth century Beirut, al-Bustani is often celebrated for his anti-sectarian pronouncements and is identified by academics as the seminal author for a radical rethinking of Lebanese identity outside the sectarian divide. But his approach to the secular fits with Talal Asad's claim that the discourse of modernity posits the secular as 'the ground from which theological discourse was generated (as a form of false consciousness) and from which it gradually emancipated itself in its march to freedom'.[2] Yet in practice as he argues, religion persisted in public life. This chapter traces the religious roots of al-Bustani's secularism through his work as a translator.

In examining how al-Bustani readjusted concepts like *adab* and *tarikh* within a discourse of modernity as a secularisation that leads to progress, I showcase how these two concepts were given a biblical genealogy as the basis for his participation in their definition. As I argue, translation was for al-Bustani not merely an intellectual activity of the technical kind. Rather for him translation carried an epistemic value; emerging as the very model of knowledge production and social commitment. His investment in translation complicates a reading of local translators as postcolonial tricksters, searching for ways to appropriate Western culture in order to subvert it. Al-Bustani's agency as a translator was turned inwards, towards his own society, and what he laboured to subvert was not the power the missionaries exerted on his culture. Rather, he celebrated the missionary intervention and berated his society for its lethargy in catching up with them.

Upon his death on the 2 May 1883, the team that was assisting al-Bustani in writing the encyclopaedia decided to bury him in it, in the entry on (دائرة المعارف Dairat-el-Ma'arif). As they mention 'We were asked to fix an entry on the deceased under the keyword "Da'irat al-Ma'arif" because the B volume had been completed during his lifetime, God rest his soul. So we decided to copy it (*naqlaha*) or translate it (*tarjamataha*) from his eulogy in al-Muqtataf'.[3]

Significantly this entry valorises translation as the single most important contribution of the deceased, alongside his lexicons. As the entry summarises, after he left his employment as a teacher in the school of Ayn Waraqa, the deceased began to work as a translator for the English military power that defeated Ibrahim Pasha and drove him out of the Levant. Then he went into employment with the American missionaries as a teacher and translator, then worked as a dragoman for the American consulate in Beirut, in conjunction with his work as a translator, educator and preacher. He began working on translating the Bible with Eli Smith, but left the work unfinished to embark on his lexical projects. His legacy was remembered for how 'he included many colloquial words [in his dictionary] that could be of use to foreigners learning Arabic . . . Between 1843 and 1866, he spent much time in translation and writing'. In addition to his several authorial achievements in lexicography and journalism, the entry goes on to mention his work in 'translating *Pilgrim's Progress, The History of the Reformation, Salvation History, the Bible, and Robinson Crusoe*'.[4]

This chapter explores the Bible as it shapes the legacy of Butrus al-Bustani. By making direct references to the Bible and the world views that have emanated from it, al-Bustani reformulated the project of Arab modernity embodied by the *nahda* by asserting that a rupture was needed with the Arabo-Islamic tradition to interpolate Western knowledge for modern speakers of Arabic. As he repeatedly suggested, translation 'compresses time', and brings Arabs up to speed with European civilisation.[5] Al-Bustani therefore sought a synchronisation with the West that would align knowledge temporally and identify it with modernity. The Eurocentric axis of this desired synchronicity rested on two temporal points of origin: one is the moment of creation, which he traced back to Genesis, and the second is the moment of truth, which he situated in the nativity of Christ. Through structuring Arabic linguistic and literary history around those two temporalities, al-Bustani replaced the stable force that kept the

Arabic language in orbit around the Qur'an with an alternative narrative that emphasised the role of translation in enriching Islamicate culture across time.

The shift in the temporal axis of Arabic permeates all of al-Bustani's works, and its impact was at its most ambitious in his two lexical projects, his *Muhit al-Muhit*, a two volume dictionary that was written in the classical style typical of Arabic lexicons, and his *Da'irat al-Ma'arif*, an enclyopedia that is largely comprised of translating English, French and Italian modern encyclopaedias in an aggregate that deliberately synchronises Arabic civilisation with a Western standard of knowledge. Prior to embarking on these laborious texts, al-Bustani wrote a schematic literary history in his famous lecture 'Khutba fi Adab al-'arab' (Speech on the Culture of the Arabs). This short lecture, which he later published with the American press in 1859 – six years before the SBV was published, and two years after he resigned from his position as Bible translator[6] – presents his assumptions as well as the narrative that would later frame his cataloguing of Arabic language and literature within the lexicons. From the outset, al-Bustani introduced the Bible as a principal text in the construction of an alternative history of the Arabic language and asserted the role of translation in the production of valuable knowledge.

Al-Bustani desired to establish contemporaneity with the West, which his translations aimed to achieve through their textual signposts and contexts of enunciation. His worldview made no room for the untranslatable, and whenever he encountered it, he cut it out. In his *Khutba* he demanded that words be deleted from the copious Arabic lexicon, and in his translations of *Robinson Crusoe* and *The Pilgrim's Progress*,[7] he left out whole passages that might have offended his readers. These deletions served his ambitions for contemporaneity. For the symbolic potency of this ambition, he has been acknowledged as the *mu'allim*, the teacher whose body of work centred around the dissemination and popularisation of knowledge. Whether in his lexicons, newspapers, translations, grammars, or the short-lived school that he founded in 1863, al-Bustani's pedagogical commitment was fundamentally translational – with lessons from biblical translation providing the framing assumptions and the tools for knowledge production and dissemination.

For al-Bustani, translation carried an epistemic value that exceeded the derivative mechanical creativity of the translator between words and sentences, to emerge as a paradigmatic method for synchronisation, structuring the intellectual vocation and defining its objectives and processes. Yet his work as a translator remains generally unremarked upon in the scholarship. Rather the prism of politics dominates the reading of al-Bustani, with the events of 1860 and the sectarian descent into civil war understood as markers of a transformation in his relationship to the West and the beginning of colonialism. Intervening in current debates about the legacy of al-Bustani, Peter Hill points out his bourgeois positioning. As he argues, al-Bustani addressed the 'leaders of the people', particularly in his broadside periodical *Nafir Suriyya*. While he agrees with others that al-Bustani,

> 'certainly seeks to transcend sectarianism in the name of a greater "general interest."'[8] This transcendence was to be undertaken by 'leaders or notables [while] the commoners – the remainder of the people – are a "silent tool," incapable of independent action and knowledge of their own interests; they do not even deserve Blame'.[9]

While the economic sensibility is important, this understanding of the secular, which governs much of current writing on al-Bustani and the *nahda*, remains unnuanced. Depicting him as a postcolonial subject *avant la letter*, Jeffrey Sacks reads his post-1860 projects as attempts to discursively entangle himself with 'the Ottoman political and social order and "civilizing mission" rather than to the missionaries or the Europeans'.[10] This perspective is shared by Ussama Makdisi, who suggests that al-Bustani spoke the missionary's discourse only to subvert it. Unlike his American patrons, but through discursive means and styles he learned from them, al-Bustani secularised the lessons of his conversion to the Protestant faith and contended that 'the moral and scientific gap that existed between the "civilised" Westerners and the Arabs did not portend a struggle between 'Christianity' and 'Mohammedanism' in which one must vanquish the other'.[11] Makdisi's understanding of the secular is different from its use by Eli Smith, who saw that al-Bustani's secular pursuits would find better expression in the literary sphere than in the church. Makdisi's notion of the secular emphasised al-Bustani's 'vision of modern coexistence based on a secular equality of religions and cultures',[12] which fundamentally questions,

> The conceit of progress envisioned in missionary history and in the broader narrative of American and Western impact on the Middle East, which have routinely viewed liberalism, modernity, and toleration as flowing obviously and automatically from West to East and from America to a stagnant Arab world. Al-Bustani's ecumenism, in reality, was neither indigenous nor foreign, neither American nor Arab: rather it was a synthesis of elements from all of these.[13]

Yet this is a synthesis that was sought through translating Western texts into Arabic, responding to the arrival of the American missionaries through declaring to his countrymen that 'culture is standing on your doors from all sides, knocking, requesting entry' into the heart of the Syro-Lebanese and Ottoman nations.[14] Even in the story of As'ad al-Shidyaq, as al-Bustani wrote it, Makdisi downplays how its author faithfully copied large sections from the *Missionary Herald* into Arabic. The political prism misses the entangled textualities that translation constructs, and misses an opportunity to explore the paradoxes of a contemporaneity based on the transfer of Western knowledge and interests. In his *Khutba*, al-Bustani split hairs as he tried to distinguish between acts of *naql*, or copying, and *tarjama*, the new concept of translation that became popular with his writings, and even as he recollected classical Arabic texts, he did so through the textual prism of Western Orientalism and through the historical moments when Arabs translated from the Greeks.

With the dominance of the political prism, *Nafir Suriyya* and *Khutba* have proved the most popular texts for scholarly pursuit, yet we cannot rely on them too much, and must not forget, as Hala Auji cautions, that these are ephemeral texts not intended by the author to constitute monumental works.[15] Those two texts incidentally do not feature in the list of his works published in his encyclopaedia under the entry *Da'irat al-Ma'arif.*[16] This ephemerality is appropriate to the temporality of politics, a realm of negotiations that relies more on rhetorical dexterity than discursive longevity. The cursory scholarly readings of texts that al-Bustani considered among his masterpieces has not adequately attended to the centrality of translation in his ouevre. His encyclopaedia, the dictionary *Muhit*, his Bible translation, the newspapers and his translation of *Robinson Crusoe* are his most important contributions. With the exception of *Muhit*, and some portions of the encyclopaedia and the newspapers, these texts are faithful translations from Western originals. Even in those portions that were not translated, the structural reliance on translation for epistemic production is clear. Organised around translation, Arabic no longer only pivots around qur'anic influence but derives from the biblical worldview a competitive new centre for a new ideology of language more suitable for al-Bustani's ideas of modernity.

Al-Bustani typified an era that cultivated its cultural specificities and ideological aspirations within a context that was acutely aware of the superiority of Western modes of production. His cultural contributions were produced through a double consciousness of a contemporaneous Western Other, and an othering of the past Islamo-Arabic self. As Stephen Sheehi proposes, this double consciousness was not unique to al-Bustani. In the changing material conditions of knowledge production, this double consciousness and the tools for its expression were a shared feature, and were not specific to an individual author or school of thought, but constituted 'an autogenetic response' to historical materialist conditions, 'that swept across the regions associated with the *nahda*, as well as shared its dynamics with many other places in the world, including the West, but crucially also the modernities of Southwest Asia and North Africa'.[17] The translation of the Bible specifically embodied those material transformations in knowledge production, synchronising worlds and languages. Inasmuch as this was a shared feature, al-Bustani also cultivated individual difference, brought about by the unique geographical location that he occupied. Unlike other modernists and *nahdawis*, he emphasised the Syro-Arabic inflections of Levantine history through etymological sedimentations. These sediments became his witness for the enduring presence of Arabic-speaking Christians throughout the region's history. Butrus Abu Manneh points out that al-Bustani's political imagination was a precursor to more explicit definitions of political identity in the region. As he writes: 'al-Bustani led the way culturally to Arabism, politically to

Ottomanism, and inevitably to Syrian nationalism'.[18] This way was forged through translation and under its influence.

As one of the earliest examples of his work as a translator, the Bible became the prism for subsequent entanglements in al-Bustani's career, particularly in how it evolved into a modern foundational source text for thinking about Arabic as a lingua franca, as well as a local tongue, for a burgeoning Syro-Lebanese nation in an increasingly globalised world. As a synchronic text, the Bible was the site for the creation of the conditions for imagining contemporaneity through constructing metaphors of kinship ties between the world's vernaculars. This synchronicity criss-crossed with the Levantine genesis of the Bible to align deep history with the wide-reaching cartographies of modern, multilingual Bible production. These are exemplary coordinates for a text to mediate the paradoxical desires of achieving a universalism that is so particular, as only a Levantine Arabic Bible can boast.

This rethinking and repositioning of the Bible in relation to Arabic required a new vocabulary. Not only was the new Bible expected to display fresh thinking around the transmission of Greek and Hebrew concepts into a modern form of Arabic, but the very concept of translation had to be replaced and reconstituted to capture the literary power the Bible would yield over Arabic. As early as 1859, al-Bustani cleft *naql* from *tarjama*, synonymous words for translation, with the former the more popular term in the pre-nahda centuries. 'As long as the Arabs are content with *naql wa taqlid* (borrowing and imitation) one has no hope for their progress in the arts and sciences',[19] and yet in the same speech he celebrates the ruler of Egypt, Mohammad Ali Pasha, who supported education and 'graduated many esteemed students and diligent scholars, who have become famous due to their writings and numerous translations (*tarjama*)'.[20] While one was a conduit for progress, the other was a cheap imitation, dull in its impact on Arabic. *Naql* was closer to plagiarism and consumption, a copy that inspires no new knowledge,[21] whereas *tarjama* embodied the translatability that would secure Syria as contemporaneous with Western modernity and honour it as the national site for the production of modern culture. Through *tarjama*, Syria became the location for the exploration of translatability's possibility to function as a framework and method for knowledge production, in order to occupy the position of 'a bridge between Asia and Africa, a melting pot of cultures and civilisations'.[22] Al-Bustani capitalised on his location and aligned with the missionaries on the potency of the Bible to adjust historical inequalities in Ottoman-Arab culture.

For al-Bustani, in the beginning was *tarjama* – before any act of literary creation could take place. *Tarjama* emerged as an epistemic concept capable of shifting the foundations of Arabic in order to create the conditions for what Jens Hanssen describes as 'a transconfessional contract where all of Syria's religious communities were equal before Ottoman law, everyone felt included but also knew their place'.[23] Politically, he advocated for an inclusive, non-sectarian, notion of *watan*, as a homeland that exceeds sectarian belonging and requires co-existence as the basis of its political organisation. Epistemologically, however, this politics was discursively produced within a Christian worldview of translatability and *tarjama*, a discourse that emanates from equating the copy and the original, as a believer does with the Bible, irrespective of whichever language (or quality) the text appears in.

He suggests in his lecture that translation was the cardinal tool that helped lift the Arabs out of their ignorance in the desert and into the literary and scientific glories of their dynasties in Baghdad and Basra. He correspondingly dates the decline of Arabic civilisation, and the fall back into ignorance, to the cessation of translation activity and the hubris of becoming insular to the pursuit of knowledge in the world.[24] He writes to admonish and to transform his society, to usher it back into civilisation and modernity. He wants his Arab audience to submit itself to the pursuit of knowledge, to

> Yield, awaken, become aware, open your eyes and roll up your sleeves. Here is culture (*al-adab*) standing in all directions at your door asking to be let into your magnificent mountains and your valleys, plains, and deserts. Forget your prejudice, partisanship and personal motivations and extend a handshake to this old friend that is coming to you after a long exile.[25]

This lyrical wish for a reawakening motivates the condensed historical plot that he presents in the lecture through his construction of a teleology that instrumentalises translation seriously, as a method for knowledge acquisition. His narrative is epochal and begins with the *jahilis*, those pre-Islamic desert dwellers that were:

> mostly illiterate, while the knowledge (*'ulum*) that made them proud was the science (*'ilm*) of their own tongue and the grammar of their language and the composition of poetry and prose. Together with this, they had knowledge about the rising and setting of the stars and the movement of the constellation, and the rain as much as they could apprehend through careful attention and the length of experience. They satisfied a life need, and were not looking to acquire truth (*ta'allum al-haqayiq*).[26]

The acquisition of truth is al-Bustani's measure for assessing the values dormant in different epochs. This truth is acquired through disinterested knowledge and not through the cunning of human need. The Arabs had taken a long time to reach that state, for even though Islam greatly improved their chances of knowledge acquisition, their widespread illiteracy culminated in Amr bin al-'As burning the great library of Alexandria under orders from the *khalifa* Omar bin al-Khattab. The Umayyads were not any better at appreciating knowledge and were kept busy consolidating their authority over the vast domains of the Empire. It was only with the Abbasids, and particularly those *khalifas* that encouraged translation, that disinterested knowledge flourished. The Abbasid translators saved the Empire from its persistent ignorance, quite literally in the case of the first Abbasid *khalifa* he mentions, Abu Ja'afar al-Mansur, a man who had a chronic ailment in his stomach until the Christian Georgius bin Yakhtishu' al-Nisabawi succeeded in curing him, 'so the Arabs became indebted through this employment to the Greek doctor Yakhtishu' who introduced them to the noble discipline of medicine'.[27]

Al-Bustani goes on to enumerate all the *khalifas* that supported translation as the best way to acquire the knowledge of the Greeks, naming Harun al-Rashid, Abdallah al-Ma'mun and al-Mustansir as model rulers that invested greatly in 'the transfer of knowledge from Greek, Syriac, and Persian to Arabic through translation and *iqtibas*, quotation'. Even so, he states that the Arabs 'are not simply imitators as some have been claiming. For we find that they invented and added a great many things to those disciplines (*'ulum*) they translated from foreign languages'.[28] Al-Bustani is unabashedly only concerned with the entanglements with the West, *al-'alam al-gharbi*, the *Franks* and the lands of Europe, as the main sources for knowledge transfer between Arabic and other languages. He could have attended to Persian, and its entanglements with Arabic through translation, thereby opening up the concept of knowledge universally and in all directions, but he preferred a Euro-skewed lens. In focusing solely on Europe, he underscored the epoch (the Renaissance) that saw Europeans translating into Latin from Arabic sources. So, to translate for a new *nahda*, al-Bustani argued that through translation, Western knowledge would return to its true home among the Arabs. Al-Bustani understands knowledge as a relay, switching hands back and forth in the race towards progress. By thus imagining the relationship with the West as a cooperation for the sake of improving and developing knowledge, al-Bustani casts this relation within this congenial set up, and defends the presence of Western missionaries, both the Protestants and the Catholics, in his native land: 'Their example and tireless efforts [in the improvement of knowledge] through their schools and printing houses are apparent and are refuted only by those who are ungrateful and who are motivated by strife and prejudice'.[29]

In his view of knowledge, al-Bustani is conditioned by his work as a Bible translator. What he learned through working on the Christian scripture is that translation serves as a conduit for the truth which can travel unimpeded from Western languages when done well; so unimpeded that one can assert that truth disseminates in *sola scriptura*, by the book alone – requiring only a good translation to reach an unprecedented readership while carrying its original integrity, and a reading habit that can adjust and mend faulty education through the powerful meeting between an individual and a book. He took this perspective with him to his ideas about science and the necessity of providing readers with adequate texts by translating from European tongues. In his understanding of science, al-Bustani separated knowledge from the language with which it is produced. That which he calls *haqayiq*, the facts, can thus be discussed separately from *al-kalimat*, the words that al-Bustani complains have too many *mutaradifat*, or synonyms in Arabic. One can translate his nuance in Saussurian terms and state that for al-Bustani the signified was separated from the signifier. For him the plethora of signifiers that distinguished Arabic from other languages weakened the language and kept its speakers away from the acquisition of knowledge. A thing that has 'a surplus of names lacks in value'.[30] Thus he called for a reduction of the words contained in the Arabic lexicon, and rhetorically exclaimed that modern life does not require 500 words for 'lion' nor does it require one to name each organ of a camel with many synonyms. Arabic grammar was to be similarly reduced in its rules and its simplified syntax, for one cannot possibly expect the people of this age to 'busy themselves with attaining the useful arts'.[31] So he called for a new grammar book that could simplify the attainment of the language and make it possible to learn it 'in about a year, especially for its native speakers, who have shown how intelligent they are in acquiring foreign languages in such a duration of time'.[32]

In these calls to simplify the language and purify it of useless terms, al-Bustani was propagating a linguistic ideology that was typical of other global locations where missionaries worked and studied the local languages. Framing their work within a narrative of Babylonian sin and translational salvation, the missionaries, as Joseph Errington has shown, pushed towards linguistic purity as the paradigm for Protestant missionary efforts worldwide. Supplying the discipline of comparative philology with its earliest scholars, the missionaries set a linguistic agenda that sought purity and simplification in their quest for salvation. So great was their influence that the entire discipline of philology in the nineteenth century developed out of the concerted attempts to reason 'against the grain of history to excavate original, pure, grammatical forms'.[33] As Errington shows, these models panned out differently in different colonial locations. What was common to colonial philologists was that 'language policies abroad were indirectly shaped by ideologies of language and national identity in Europe'.[34] Errington focuses on Malay and Swahili, but in Arabic the concept of 'purity' had a different effect. Arabic was not like the oral African languages, for its written form exerted a powerful influence on people's daily lives. Arabic, unlike Sanskrit's decline in use, continued to be the vehicular language of many peoples and lands, and its speakers used it for writing persistently, which kept it prolific and complex. If the search for purity, as it began in the work of William Jones in the last years of the eighteenth century,[35] enabled comparative philology to assert a cultural affinity between European languages and the Indian continent, al-Bustani's methods attended to Arabic's specificities and enriched the concept of purity diachronically. The narrative of divine language made room for the Babylonian tale by also engaging the Muslim belief that Adam spoke all the world's languages

> Without a doubt [Arabic is] one of the most ancient of world languages, and its most wholesome and perfect one. If I am asked to provide evidence, I would have even claimed that it was the language of our great father Adam, in his earthly Eden. At least I can claim that this language, together with its sisters Hebrew and Syriac, is from the branches or the remains of the same revealed (*munzalah*) language of Adam. The evidence is that God has miraculously preserved this language in history for unknown reasons and made it unaffected by the movement of time and the changes in epochs.[36]

This description of the Arabic language included Hebrew and Syriac among the family of sacred tongues. Al-Bustani, like Western philologists of the time, therefore treated the Semitic languages as branches from the same tree. Unlike the Orientalists, however, al-Bustani's narrative tried to accommodate the Muslim myth of the origins of language with some adjustments. As he argued, Arabic, Hebrew and Syriac were the sacred 'daughters' of Adam's original language, a language that predated the destruction of Babel. Yet unlike al-Bustani's quote above, Wild tells us that

> Arabic was Adam's language in Paradise until he disobeyed God. Then God deprived him of Arabic, and he started speaking Syriac, evidently considered a lesser language or a corrupted form of Arabic. When Adam repented, however, God gave the Arabic language back to him.[37]

Al-Bustani did not discount the position of Arabic for the Arabs, rather, he made room for the other Semitic tongues. He inserted the myth of Babel into the story of divine languages, thereby suggesting that Adam spoke a proto-Semitic tongue until the sinful disobedience of the people who, from now on, spoke the three Semitic languages. Al-Bustani's innovative narrative of divine speech put this 'perfect and wholesome' Arabic on a par with Syriac and Hebrew and undermined the treatment of the Arabic language as the sole divine tongue.

Not only did Arabic now share its divine status, but it also carried with it the debris of history. All those words and syntactic structures, its openness to foreign influence and its persistent borrowings from European, Ottoman and Persian tongues have corrupted it. For him, 'the linguistic condition of Arabic is that for many generations many words have entered it and there is no more room for more words to enter'.[38] Too many words in the dictionary had made Arabic too heavy for the speed required for social progress. The lexicon needed new words, and these could find a place once the old words had been cast out and the lexicon was spring cleaned. Keen to break ties with the semantic history of Arabic, al-Bustani sought a language reform that expressly invested in advancing a new type of nation-building that derives a new vocabulary through translation. He thus embarked on a project of slimming down the language and blotting out the Islamicate history of Arabic to reconstruct an alternative history that synchronised Arabic speakers with a global missionary movement that maintains the Bible as its central text.

Situated firmly in the present, al-Bustani looked backwards into the past and forward towards a desired future as he allowed his linguistic thinking to be framed by 'purity'. In his constructive recommendations for language development, language purification entailed the shedding of history, and the letting go of synonymic redundancies. It also meant stripping down the structure and decodifying the language such that the excess of signifiers would not hamper the signifieds with syntactical convolutions. This future language, which he securely fastened to a Christian linguistic perspective, aligned with a teleology of pure origins – rooted in the Bible's languages and places of birth. In proposing this alignment, al-Bustani was not copying the ideas of his missionary friends. Indeed, within the Christian Arabic canon there were precedents that facilitated the purification that al-Bustani sought, as I show below.

Reissuing Jirmanos Farhat's Grammar

Before he embarked on his famous *Khutba*, al-Bustani had already practiced his ideas by reissuing what he considered to be a work of grammatical summary. In 1854, he edited and printed the 450-something pages of
grammar by the Maronite patriarch of Aleppo, Jirmanos Farhat, *Misbah
al-Talib fi Ta'allum al-Qawa'id* (The Student's Lantern in Learning
Grammar). This book puts in practice what al-Bustani theorised about
the simplification of grammar. The book itself promises to teach, in an
efficient and systematic manner, all that one needs to know about Arabic
grammar, and includes a table of contents, an innovation at the time, to
facilitate the reader's navigation.

In the introduction to this book, Farhat claimed that 'Syriac is the
origin and Arabic is derivative . . . and evidence of this is in Abraham,
the Chaldean, who spoke Syriac, and Ismail his son, is the grandfather
of the Arabs; thus Arabs derive from Syriacs'.[39] This is a position that
al-Bustani endorsed and built upon, but he also chose to depart from the
trajectory that it led to in Farhat's work. For Farhat, the derivation of
Arabic from Syriac was an argument that he used to encourage his congre-
gation to excel – for he 'noticed that Christian writers had embarked on
learning the rules of Arabic grammar'. Farhat feared that their faith would
be tried, and they would consider converting to Islam, if they become
too steeped in texts written by Muslim philologists. For him, Christians
must learn from a grammar book that does not take for its evidence the
Muslim sources.[40] He wanted to write an alternative grammar, one that
clearly demarcated the readership as followers of Christ. Rather than
being subjected to Muslim writers who use the Qur'an to explicate grammar, Farhat 'used witnesses from the Holy Writ whenever possible . . .
with the intention that the Christian youth find use without becoming
alienated, and their faith be tried'.[41] Al-Bustani would find this ambition
to reach a Christian audience too narrow. What he did instead was to
continue anchoring Arabic in Christianity, but to expand the audience
beyond Farhat's internal focus on his sect. With his expanded intention,
al-Bustani claimed that his linguistic work was relevant to all speakers of
the language, regardless of their religious belonging. As he stated in the

introduction to another summary he produced, in his dictionary *Muhit al-Muhit*, he intended with this work to reach 'all members of the nation and others who are literate in the Arabic language'.[42] Like his predecessor, he added biblical witnesses to this dictionary to elaborate on certain terms, however unlike Farhat, al-Bustani did not seek to protect his *millet* from Islam's powers of conversion, for in this age, it was the Christian missions that were the proselytisers. So, he introduced a shift in the etymological historiography of Arabic from one where the Arabian Desert functioned as a *terra prima* of the tongue's pure origins, to one where the Levant and its biblical languages were asserted as etymological origins to both exceptional and quotidian Arabic concepts and words.

Arabic Lexicography before Al-Muhit

Al-Bustani's interest in lexicography was motivated by the role this linguistic genre plays in language ideology. More than any scriptural or canonical text, lexicons provide a language with a unified reference point that exceeds the borders of its religious or national belonging. So aware of their power, al-Bustani produced three different lexicons during his lifetime. Two concern us here,

1) the dictionary *Muhit al-Muhit* and
2) the encyclopedia *Da'irat al-Ma'arif.*

His third lexicon, *Qutr al-Muhit*, a summary of the larger dictionary that was produced to appeal to the economic austerity of young students, will not be considered here. In separating the genre into the subgenres of the dictionary and the encyclopaedia, al-Bustani made his most forceful inter-vention into the Arabic lexical tradition. In the classical tradition, lexicons were what Ibn Khaldun called the 'science of language' ('*ilm al-lugha*), a label that matches the grand ambitions of lexical projects to function as the key to unlock the secrets of knowledge.

Arabic lexicons are often thought of as texts that have been governed by conserving the proximity of philology to theology, and indeed they are, even with some important exceptions.[43] What usually passes almost unno-ticed is that Arabic lexicons have also played an important function in delineating the precepts of belonging, by judging which words were pure Arabic, and were therefore permitted entry into the lexicon, and which words will not be recorded and will be left to be forgotten outside the lexicon. Yasir Suleiman calls the authors of this process 'border guards',[44] working to safeguard Arabic from the foreign linguistic influences of the vanquished nations they encountered. In the wake of Arabo-Islamic Empire building, purity flourished as the principal motivation for linguistic projects and became common to the most important linguistic references from the classical period.

Beginning with *Kitab al-'ayn*, but almost unanimously, lexicographers operated with a notion of purity that idolised the dialects of the most misanthropic Bedouin tribes, for carrying, as they believed, the purest speech among the Arabs. Such was their obsession that the tribes caught on and as Ramzi Baalbaki recounts that when 'the *A'rab* realised how much they were sought after by the philologists and grammarians, many of them left the *badiya* (desert) and joined the *Hadira* (settled area; city)',[45] to cash in on the interest in their dialect. So dominant was this method that those Arabic speakers it excluded, particularly those of foreign origin, developed an iconoclastic backlash in the genre of *gharib* (foreign) lexicons, those dozens of compendia that collected words borrowed into Arabic and that can be found on the tongues of the prize Bedouins and even in the Qur'an, the jewel of the Arabic language.[46] The participation of the dominant lexicons in the production of the *terra prima* myth of the desert origins of Arabic became hegemonic, with *gharib* literature serving as no more than a curiosity for the ruling Arabs of the Empire.

Perhaps the defeat of the iconoclasts stemmed from another weapon in the arsenal of the linguists, the so-called *lahn* allegations, which point to solecisms in the speech of an adversary. *Lahn* was attached to the uncouth language-use of foreigners or the lower classes, and the linguists that were especially attentive to its slurs were motivated by a 'puristic approach which regards correctness and *fasaha* to be exclusive to a variety of *'Arabiyya* whose norms are derived from pre-Islamic poetry'.[47] But it was more than that, for it instituted linguists as a class of language police and border guards who could detect what (and who) is to be excluded from elite society, thus occasioning *lahn* as the site of what Suleiman dubbed in a more contemporary context 'Arabic language anxiety'.[48] Then, as now, this anxiety is typical of writers of Arabic, especially in the scholarly class. By submitting to the power of *lahn*, the scholars treated as axiomatic the supremacy of the *terra prima* narrative in legitimating elite distinctions.

The last weapon, and perhaps the most consequential for limiting the lexical genre's capacities to develop beyond its *terra prima* myth of origins, has been the historical perspective that shaped the Arabic lexicons. Until al-Bustani's work, canonical Arabic lexicons nurtured a myth of origins through the careful exclusion of post-Islamic literary sources. The *terra prima* depended on a historiography that also excluded the Imperial expansion from its politics of belonging. Thus, only Jahili and early Islamic poetry together with the Qur'an and the Hadith were permitted in the lexicon, with only a few lexicographers taking exception. This way, the linguists participated in creating an almost filiative notion of who an Arab was based on a historical narrative that excluded the possibility of ever including a text whose author carried the blood of a foreign tribe or lowly class. The linguistic repercussions curtailed what constituted legitimate written Arabic and challenged the 'foreigners' to outperform the Arabs in Arabic writing.

Even with their relentless lists and the copiousness of their lexical legacies, the classical lexicographers undermined the two principal lexicographic criteria they set for themselves: comprehensiveness and systematisation, criteria that ensure that lexicons exert a normative influence on language users. The persistence of the *terra prima* narrative had its historical logic, but it affected their lexical horizons. Choosing the myth of pure origins over alternatives, the lexicographers 'did not keep pace with the linguistic and cultural developments that took place following the epochs of reliable usage, and thus largely ignored the new notions and technical terms that were created in literary and scientific domains'.[49]

By writing two lexicons in two distinct genres, al-Bustani earned his name as a modern innovator in the tradition and secured his legacy as a lexicographer, despite his untimely death when working on the eighth letter of the alphabet, the *dal*, at volume 6 of *Da'irat*.[50] To unpack his contribution to the tradition and the crucial ways that made his departure from his predecessors so conclusive, the next section will read through his lexica: firstly, *Muhit* for how he pivots his dictionary toward translation history in order to shift from the *terra prima* of desert origins and claim that Arab civilisation owes much of its glory to its occupation of the Levant, and secondly, in his encyclopaedia, where he capitalised on the epistemic value of translation in the production of knowledge. Through opening up Arabic to translation, al-Bustani emphasised the wide communicative function of Arabic and the dynamic needs of a society composed of diverse sects and groups of people. Rather than the iconoclasms of the *gharib* type intervention in the lexicon, translation allowed him to entirely shift the myth of origins onto the Levant with its biblical pedigree; and from there, to propose new parameters of knowledge acquisition in Arabic.

Al-Bustani's Subtle Alterations to the Classical Lexicon

Upon its publication in 1870, the *Muhit* was instantly hailed a success. Al-Bustani's innovative addition, bolstered by his translation of the Bible (1865), is a legitimating certificate of know-how. The Bible also allowed him to boast methodological training in Western philology, which was undergoing revolutionary developments at the time, most notably in the field of etymology, which was an important tool for Western comparative philologists. *Muhit*'s ambition to become the standard lexicon used by all readers of Arabic was particularly implicated in a wider national project of civilisation. The classical genre of the Arabic lexicon functioned as the main literary form that al-Bustani used to disseminate a Syro-Christian national myth of origins in the modern literary consciousness. The inclusion of the Bible in the Arabic lexicon shifted the textual source of linguistic science in a style continuous with the tradition of Arabic lexicography, to facilitate *Muhit*'s mediation of an emerging Christian nationalism.

Christian nationalism emerges in the subtle ruptures the author made with his predecessors, most notably in his inclusion of the Bible as a main lexical source alongside the canonical Muslim sources. This inclusion was pioneering in several ways. Its most radical contribution was the introduction of a shift in the etymological historiography of Arabic from one where the Arabian desert functioned as a *terra prima* of pure origins, to one where the Levant and its biblical languages were asserted as etymological origins to key and mundane Arabic concepts and words. Through a philological reading of al-Bustani's lexicon, a narrative of ideological embeddedness emerges from this dictionary, one in which belonging to a Christian minority provides a unique opportunity to contribute to thinking about Arabic in the *nahda*.

His discursive assertions widened the geographical history of the classical lexicons. By widening the origins of Arabic, al-Bustani eluded any confrontation with the *terra prima* narrative, and instead suggested that it was not the entire story. He included religious Christian words, sometimes introducing such words for the first time and other times adjusting how such words have been defined in classical lexicons (written by Muslims). His dictionary performed in the genre of classical lexicon, al-Bustani relied not only on al-Fayruzabadi and *al-Sihah* as was advertised in *al-Jinan* (1870) and he translated from Georg Wilhelm Freytag's *Arabic-Latin Lexicon*.[51] By insiting on curating which words make it into the lexicon, al-Bustani made a break with his predecessors, but couched this break less as a confrontation and more within a teleological progression of history.

Al-Bustani actualised this reshuffling of the place of tradition in thinking modern Arabic through a process of temporal sedimentation that deploys a classical method of *iqtibas* and quotation in his composition of his work. Indeed, like its predecessors, *Muhit* is in large part composed of quotations from a number of earlier lexicons. Compiling the definitions of predecessors was a typical way of writing new lexicons. But al-Bustani uses this method to control the traditional dominance of a certain lexicographic approach to Arabic, by layering on top of it his own innovations and coinages.

Take the concept of *masih*, Christ. In defining this word, al-Bustani sedimented the Muslim definition by introducing his own definition under this same lexeme. In his definition, al-Bustani cited material from *al-Qamus al-Muhit* by the fourteenth- century lexicographer Majdeddin Mohammad bin Ya'qub al-Fayruzabadi (d. 1414). Along with Ibn Manzur's *Lisan al-Arab* this specific lexicon was especially popular in the *nahda*, in the Levant and elsewhere. While he had used other lexicographers for other words, in this instance al-Bustani chose al-Fayruzabadi's – a peculiar choice considering that there were less foolhardy alternatives. Al-Fayruzabadi's definition was a summary of what the *Lisan* presented, a summary where religious tolerance, and efforts to include a definition that is acceptable to Christians, were omitted and discarded. This produced an abstruse definition, typical of the level of religious intolerance and ignorance with which Christian concepts were treated. Al-Bustani's selection retained the highly ambiguous construction without even venturing an interpretation. I translate literally what al-Bustani quoted

> Issa, Peace be Upon him, for his blessedness, and I mentioned fifty derivations in my commentary on *Mashariq al-Anwar* and others. The anti-Christ, for his gloom, or he is [morphologically] like a knife, a piece of silver, sweat, believer, as well as the smooth coin, and anointed with something like oil, blessing, bad news, a frequent traveller, and a frequent copulator (*kathir al-jima'*).

Then al-Bustani added his own meaning, which was more orthodox to Christianity. And his definition continued like this

> *Al-masih* is also the title of the Lord Jesus. In Hebrew it is *mashih*, in Syriac *mshiha*, and in Greek *khristós*, and they mean *mamsuh* (anointed). He was thus called because he was anointed (*masah*) by God as priest, prophet and king. In ancient times it was the custom to anoint priests and kings with oil. And the Antichrist is mentioned [under a different root], and it is said that he is *masih* (smooth?) like a knife; and the Franks called him *antikrayst*, and it means *did al-masih* (against Christ) . . . and the *masihi* (Christian) is the one who belongs to *al-masihiyya* (Christianity).[52]

By including his predecessor's definition, alongside the Christian definition, in both its Frankish and Arabic understandings, al-Bustani seemingly followed the formal conventions of the genre and preserved what came before him, even though al-Fayruzabadi's definition was disrespectful to the person of Christ. Al-Bustani could have cited less controversial definitions for the same word in other lexicons, as he did with other words. By choosing al-Fayruzabadi, al-Bustani selected a lexicon that would be described by al-Bustani's contemporary, Ahmad Faris al-Shidyaq, as a highly dogmatic work. For al-Shidyaq, *al-Qamus* received acclaim because of al-Fayruzabadi's religious credentials and not because of his linguistic acumen.[53] Al-Shidyaq's thorough critique of this medieval lexicon in *al-Jasus 'ala al-Qamus* (Spying on the Qamus) documented the heavy reliance of al-Fayruzabadi on Islamic dogma in both its scriptural and more popular varieties.[54]

As the most Islamic of all the pre-modern lexicographers, al-Fayruzabadi strikes an odd figure in al-Bustani's modern lexicon, particularly because of his hostile views towards Christianity. So, with al-Fayruzabadi as his main authority on the concept of Christ, al-Bustani had chosen the one Arabic lexicon that showed a good measure of intolerance towards minorities. Coupling this religious intolerance with more normative Christian definitions, al-Bustani stratified the lexicon into competing religious narratives that have been transhistorically elaborated – and struggled to prevail – in historically contingent contexts. Al-Bustani mediated the competition through sedimenting al-Fayruzabadi: keeping his definition visible but layering it with a new definition that better served the changing times. So in *al-masih*, the semantic range of three religious worldviews competed under the same conceptual sign:

1. The pre-Quranic world of biblical Syriac and Hebrew that is part of Levantine antiquity
2. A thirteenth century chauvinistic Islamic worldview that was confident of its discursive power but that grossly misrepresented Christianity and
3. A Frankish worldview that was developing in the nineteenth century, and that, through the use of the term, conjured the medieval era and its confrontation with Islam.

The consequences of this competitive confrontation were not the inversion of the religious hegemony over the lexicon; rather, al-Bustani's strategy favoured the dynamics of religious power, only it subverted the hegemonic Islamic worldview to make room for Christianity.

This sedimentation practice involved a spatial rearrangement of the temporal logic of Arabic lexicography. As Jens Hanssen argued, al-Bustani was driven by a tormented need to reorder the space after the events of 1860.[55] In the *Muhit*, this reordering was alphabetically concerned with exploring the bibleland in its lexical sedimentations. Al-Bustani's strategy resulted in revealing the competition in religious narratives that vied for representation and authority over the precepts of acceptable language. We may call this a secularisation of the linguistic space, in the sense that it broke down the monopoly of Islam over the lexicon, but this secularity remained competitively governed, and sectarian, in its widening of the historical narrative.

Al-Bustani's Etymologies Compete for *terra prima*

After using the *Muhit* for many years, I continue to find new words that recollect Syriac, Hebrew or Greek etymologies. Such words are often biblical, but many times they are mundane Arabic words that do not have a particular religious flavour. Such is al-Bustani's definition of the word *taqlid* (tradition), which he claims was originally Latin. Religious words such as *kahin* (priest), he claims to be either Hebrew or Syriac, and *'amad* (baptise) is of Syriac origin. Current scholarship has shown some of these words, such as *kahin*, to be originally Arabic rather than loaned.[56] Al-Bustani's use of the Syriac treatise in his etymologies in *Muhit* is a continuation of what his predecessor Jirmanos Farhat firmly believed, but its success depended upon the rise of etymology in Western philology, particularly the latter's search for linguistic origins and the project of categorising the world's languages into linguistic families.[57]

Adopting Western thinking around the Semitic languages, al-Bustani broke with centuries of lexicographic dogma when he emphasised the foreignness of some keywords.[58] By revealing Arabic to be layered on the foreign, al-Bustani makes implicit the centrality of translation in the generation of neologisms. Words such as *suriyya* (Syria), *karaz* (to preach), *masihi* (Christian) and *Adhar* (March) came into Arabic through other tongues and through cross cultural contact. They were arabised: translated and domesticated, until they became native to Arabic. As words typical of a Christian worldview, they had stayed largely outside of the Arabic lexicon even though Arabs understood them, and one can find them in various classical texts written by major Muslim authors.[59] In *Muhit*, they are either mentioned for the first time (as in the case of *karaz*) or corrected according to the tenants of Christian faith. Even mundane words such as *kursi* (chair) were allocated a Syriac etymological root. With al-Bustani, Syriac and Hebrew (but also Greek and Latin) show their sediments in the lexicon. This geographical widening of the roots of Arabic deployed the translational sensibility between languages to assert an alternative founding myth that augments the monolithic submission to the prominence of the Arabian Desert in the *terra prima* narrative.

Firmly anchored in the polyphonic movement across languages, and accounting for translation in the process of meaning generation, al-Bustani's attention to etymology foregrounded the extent to which contact with Arabic was central to the elaboration of its concepts. What distinguishes his gesture from the *gharib* genre of lexicographers is his claim that the Arabs were only civilised when they came into contact with the Levant and its sophisticated culture, including its own holy languages. This alternative origin myth galvanised a feeling of civilisational superiority, if not in language, then most certainly in history.

The new sense of national pride, which he liked to nurture, becomes apparent in what he did with the concept of 'nation'. In his dictionary, al-Bustani replaced *umma* with *watan* as a political concept. This replacement cordoned off the geography he referred to through separating the glorious past of Arabic from the Arabs. Through semantically equating *umma* with ignorance, the nation of the Arabs was equated with backwardness, while some of the basic tenets of Islamic thought were claimed to be originally biblical. Building on earlier lexicons, al-Bustani expanded the definition of *watan* to also include 'the home of man and his residence, whether he was born there or not'. Then he quoted a false Hadith which had earlier been popularised by the Egyptian Rifa'a Rafi' al-Tahtawi in his book *Manahij al-Albab fi Mabahij al-Adab al-'Asriyya* (1869), which says that 'the love of nation (*watan*) is part of faith'. This was a methodological precedent in Arabic lexicology and shows that al-Bustani was less interested in adhering to the classical dictums of the discipline than to perform them stylistically at the level of form.[60] For his *watan* to effectively take root and undermine the earlier Arabic concept of *umma*, al-Bustani invented a new definition for *umma* that was not previously there. In his entry, al-Bustani wrote 'the *ummi* is he who does not write . . . it is said that it refers to the *umma* of the Arabs, for they did not write or read, so it was borrowed to refer to all those who cannot write or read'. This definition replaced *Lisan*'s expansive definition that stressed the relations to *umm*, or mother. In *Lisan*, we find that 'the word comes from being made of his mother's world (*jabalathu ummuhu*), that is because writing is acquired, and so *ummi* refers to how the man is born from his mother (*ummuhu*), and the writers from the Arab tribes of Ta'if took [writing] from a man from Hira'. Whereas for *Lisan*, *ummi* was to be distinguished from *umma*, which he defined simply as 'people', *Muhit* widened the definition of *umma* to include illiteracy. Indeed, whereas *umma* and *ummi* are related words, al-Bustani's definition stresses the illiteracy of the Arabs. And under the lexeme, *'arab*, he mentioned that for the Turks the word 'refers to negroes, and the French use [this word] in their language to mean a stingy and greedy man'. If the Arabs are illiterate and backward people, their language is less so, but the credit does not go to them. For al-Bustani, even the concept of 'language' had been borrowed into Arabic as he suggested under the entry for *lugha*. The word he claims was borrowed from the Greek *logos* (word, speech). The alphabetical sequence of al-Bustani's attacks on Arab ethnicity and his valorisation of a Syrian civilisational past marginalised the Islamicate master narrative of a pan-Arabic language and civilisation that was originally born in the desert and separated Arabic as a language and civilisation from the illiterate Arab tribes who originally spoke it. Even if al-Bustani correctly identified the foreign origin of a word, he worked under the assumption that Syriac and Greek were sources of linguistic borrowings for Arabic, which sometimes also led him into the wrong etymology. Regardless of the great scientific merit of al-Bustani's work, the displacement of etymological origins was politically significant.

Through overdetermining the etymological argument, he constructed a Syriac/Syrian narrative of origins that rooted Syrian identity in the Arabic language and asserted its difference from other Arab identities. This move effectively shifted the date of civilisational prowess to biblical eras as well as to the moment of contact between the Levant and the conquering Arabs in the sixth century, an event that offset an *Islamicate* civilisation, when Muslim and Christian Arabian troops made up one occupying army that colonised the Levant and built the pillars of a new form of governance that was dominated by Islam. But al-Bustani also makes historical reference to more modern events, thus producing a historical account of an Arabic-speaking Christianity, that teaches civilisation to Desert Arabs.

By decentring the carefully nurtured Arab idealisation of the Arabian Desert myth, which anchored all aspects of classical Arabic philology, al-Bustani sedimented an enduring master narrative by attending to the traces of translation. This facilitated the emergence of Christianity as integral to the history of Arabic and forcefully dislocated the classical pride that Arabic exudes in harking from the desert.[61] In other words, rather than accept remaining within the fold of Islam, which the term Islamicate indicates, the ambition was to break free, and to no longer stand in the shadow of the majority.

Translation as a Method of Knowledge Production

Al-Bustani draws on his invented myth that the Christians of late antiquity civilised the Arabs and taught them writing, to produce for himself a genealogy that justifies his own civilisational impetus. Jeffrey Sacks notes that al-Bustani premised his own contributions on declaring Arabic literature ruined. Sacks offers an explanation of how al-Bustani's literary inheritance is characterised by 'unsettling modes according to which a relation to the past must be cut off and repeatedly marked in order to secure a presentation of literature – even as literature already lies in ruin'.[62] The question needs to shift to the causes of this ruin and to its temporal organisation, and not simply its identification. Al-Bustani marshalled inspiration from the ancient times of myth to draw parallels with modernity: the Christian scholar set out to produce civilisation for the Arabs. 'Knowledge (*adab*) amongst the Arabs these days is in a state of absolute decay (*inhitat kulli*)', writes al-Bustani in his *Khutba*.[63] The time has come to move forward, thanks to the missionaries, for 'we are indebted to the foreigners for what we have [retained of our knowledge], regardless of its origins', and to produce new knowledge.[64] He systematised this new knowledge and catalogued it in his encyclopaedia *Da'irat al-Ma'arif*. In the entry for *insayklubidya* al-Bustani says that he translated the word *da'ira* from the *cycl* component of *encyclopaedia*. This work was inspired by, and partially translated from, *Appleton's Annual Cyclopedia and Register of Important Events*, a general encyclopaedia that saw its first volume published in 1873 in New York, and a French encyclopaedia of Catholic tutelage published between 1839 and 1852 by Ange de Saint-Priest under the title, *Encyclopédie du 19ème siècle, répertoire universel des sciences, des lettres et des arts.*[65] In *Da'irat,* translation is not only of the technical type, where he transmitted an American or French source (and perhaps others) into Arabic, but emerges as an epistemic practice of knowledge production. Translation for him is the transposition of a worldview, a tool for synchronising the world's knowledge according to one synchronic modern temporality. Remarkably, he did not include a separate entry on *tarjama* or any of its cognates in his work but repeatedly scattered the term and its synonyms across his entire corpus. In the encyclopaedia, translation was an overdetermined organising principle, with most entries even carrying synonyms in both English and French, synchronising the terms with European knowledge. Entries that did not receive European synonyms were largely connected to Islam and its history, rendering them untranslatable and provincial in relation to the universal translatability of Western knowledge.

Thinking of translation through the historical lens of synchronisation requires a paradoxical reversal of what al-Bustani was claiming with his etymological interests. Rather than asserting the evident entanglements as the starting point for interrogating how texts and ideas travel, al-Bustani subscribed to a synchronistic approach that kept 'the histories of different peoples concomitantly . . . apart, and presented as separate and singular'.[66] Take the entry on *insayklubidya*, which he defines as a genre that purports to 'the gist of knowledge (*mulakhkhas al-ma'rifa*)', in other words, a type of translation, according to the basic textbooks of most translation studies programmes today.[67] He attests that the genre has a long history that stretches back to the Greeks, but also includes Arabs, European, Persian, Chinese and Japanese works. During its lifetime, the genre was transmitted through translation to Europeans who were much impressed with the Arabic encyclopaedias of Ibn Sina, al-Qazwini and others.

As a gist, the encyclopaedia operates with the assumption that meaning can be essentialised to its basic unit. Pre-nineteenth century Christian Arabic serves us here, with *istikhraj* as its most widely used synonym for translation: what encyclopaedias do is to *extract* the gist from the rich history and practice of knowledge-making. The authority of entries which give the gist derives from their reduction of meaning to its most essential elements, stylised into a format that can either be arranged alphabetically or thematically. The rhetorical register used depends on whether its target audience is the class of professional scholars or the lay public, and this affects whether it has a limited thematic focus, or like *Da'irat al-Ma'arif*, its entries are thematically diverse, and so arranged alphabetically, catering to the ever-increasing literate graduates of the new missionary schools. In both cases, it is a work of dissemination that intends to break out of narrow specialisations to make the gist of knowledge accessible far beyond its individual producers. As Ilham Khuri-Makdisi describes al-Bustani's encyclopedia, the gist comprised

> a weaving of various discourses and sources, and various schools of thoughts, European (or Western) and local, ancient and modern, some already familiar, others perhaps less so, or not at all, to synthesize them all, add, remove, intervene in the texts, and ultimately create something quite unique.[68]

In this process, knowledge is stripped of its authorial roots, favouring the encyclopaedic gist against the careful referencing of the sources being interweaved. Authors, when they are mentioned, are like other entries, their lives translated into succinct biographies – what the Arabs termed *tarjama* or *sira* in their encyclopaedic practices.

This encyclopaedia foregrounded translation as its main feature and signalled this priority through the keywords it provided. By including both English and French synonyms of keywords for many of the entries, readers were expected to move their curiosities beyond a monolingual knowledge base, thereby facilitating their pursuit in European sources and reference books. This feature of *Da'irat al-Ma'arif* prompted the leading German Orientalist Heinrich Fleisher, who reviewed the encyclopaedia for the Oriental studies journal *Zeitschrift Der Deutschen Morgenländischen Gesellschaft*, to recollect Goethe's assertion in the *West–Östlicher Divan* that the 'Orient and Occident dwell separately no more'. Quoting Goethe, Fleischer emphasised the feat of integrating, through translation and synthesis, disparate knowledges into one composite *weltliteratur*, with

Figure 4.1 *Da'irat al-Ma'arif*, entry on Adab.
Source: American University of Beirut.

Europe as its literary arbiter.[69] For al-Bustani, translation from English, French and, according to Fleischer, Italian, enabled the emergence of a more confident Christian narrative, one native to Arabic, that overcame its marginal position through this exchange with powerful producers of knowledge. The Bible was the original *weltliteratur* text that bolstered this narrative, and while al-Bustani excluded metaphysics as a subdiscipline from the encyclopaedia, his focus on elaborating a shared Christian narrative becomes clear in some of the entries.

One such key location is his treatment of the concept of '*tarikh, histoire*, history'. Through proposing a multi-temporal understanding of history as the 'timing of Time', al-Bustani presents a short historiography of history as a discipline that records the passing of time in a way native to people from China and India to Arabs and Christians as well as non-human beings in natural history and archaeology. Despite his awareness of all the

Figure 4.2 *Da'irat al-Ma'arif*, entry on Tarikh.
Source: American University of Beirut.

myriad ways of keeping time, al-Bustani insists that the Levant is 'the general site of history', a history that he ultimately understood through the prism of Genesis and the nativity of Jesus. He writes,

> Sacred history emerges in all history books as the greatest source for human events, all emanate from it and return to it. It is entirely continuous without rupture in the chain of narration: it mentions the first man and . . . then, it mentions how people became dispersed . . . but old history is not just an enumeration of those dispersed nations, rather it was organised with one nation and people coming one after the other . . . until the fall of the old kingdom and the arrival of Christian nomos.[70]

In this teleologically Christian view of history, al-Bustani centres the concept of his faith in a unitary origin point while simultaneously producing a heterotopic world of multiple times and dispersed events. While Muslims may use the event of the immigration of the Prophet Muhammad to Medina as the *chronos* of the Islamic calendar, the Greeks used the Olympics, the Armenians their refusal to join the Chalcedonian Council, the Chinese the occupation of the throne of their emperor, and so on with all the nations of the world that he mentions. Yet it is only in proximity to Genesis that the nations and their separate histories acquire value. In the paradox of acknowledging the multiple temporalities of the world – while insisting on Genesis as the unitary origin of humanity – al-Bustani declares that whatever rests outside Genesis may not even be human and its inclusion in the species is a subject of debate. Thus, he writes about the Indians

> who the sceptics pronounced as not belonging to the human genus, and instead were proclaimed as a separate species that survived mysteriously since profoundly ancient times – which is a violation of the sacred texts. History came and clarified these mythologies and returned these nations, after much deliberation and research, to the true origin.[71]

History, for al-Bustani, is the 'Christian canon that connects the world to its ancient origins, for it is since the nativity of Christ until today filled with events, transformations and amazing accidents that signify the presence of divine grace in the universe'.[72] In accepting the Indians as human against the sceptical notion that they may in fact belong to another species, al-Bustani's Christian generosity reigns him in and we find him emphasising that indeed, typically, it is the dating of the origins practiced by that nation that is wrong, rather than the idea that the Indian nation is non-human.

With the biblical temporalities of Genesis and nativity, al-Bustani synchronised the histories of the world to align within this teleology, and to centre the world around the Christian *chronos*. Framing history within the worldview of a universal Christianity, al-Bustani turned to *adab* as the concept that carries the particular. Al-Bustani presented *adab* without English or French cognates. His entry would have pleased Goethe, for *weltlitteratur* was treated as the mark of the superior tastes of European modernity: 'For the Franks, the meaning of this art is different in their language than what the Arabs call it. For them it is called *literātūr* and is taken from Latin from the meaning of writing and reading'.[73] The term is untranslatable to Arabic, for the Arabs understand *adab* only as 'safeguarding discourse from mistakes',[74] and so they include in it all kinds of grammatical and rhetorical disciplines as well as poetic training, but no reading except from the truncated canon of Islamic faith: juridical sciences, including the Qur'an and the Hadith, 'for there are no disciplinary opening for any other science in the speech of the Arabs',[75] except for much later when they discovered rhymed prose. The Europeans are different. They fling the term open to mean all that is knowledge in the world, but sometimes

> they restrict it to history, grammar, morphology . . . or in an even smaller circle to mean the entertaining sciences (*al-'ulum al-mustazrafa*) only as a synonym. In this definition they come closer in their concept to the Arabs, except that the Arabs use it only for their Arabic sciences, while the Franks call *litratur* all knowledge, Frankish or otherwise. [This encyclopaedia] uses *adab* in the Frankish way, and so we say Greek *adab*, Roman *adab* etc.[76]

The national adjectives that al-Bustani attached to *adab* produce it as the binary opposite of his view of history. If historiography deploys a synchronistic method in its treatment of the multiple temporalities existing in the world, then *adab* is where the singularities of those multiple histories are produced as untranslatables. If the objective of historiography is universal time, *adab* provides multiple temporalities, provincial and without alignment, with one single and important exception. Only enlightened (Christian) Europeans can imagine a concept of *litratur* that is wide enough to include all the texts of the world. Arabs, by contrast, neglected what existed outside their language.[77] In this view of the literary history of Arabs, al-Bustani produced an understanding of the classical Arabic canon as insulated from the influences and movements that were crucial for its evolution. In this way, his own work as a literary translator, whether with the Bible, with the encyclopaedia or with a text like Defoe's *Robinson Crusoe*, emerges as a rupture with the old modes of literary production prior to the *nahda*.

What al-Bustani sought in his commitment to modernise Arabic literature and language was a comparative approach. Through translation, he hoped that Arabs would become more entangled horizontally with a world in tongues, that shares a common history and humanity, dating back to the pre-Babylonian moment of the Genesis of Adam and Eve. His was a project of synchronisation that laboured to forge ties with Europe based on a shared historical narrative that nevertheless asserts for Europe, as well as for his countrymen, the paradigmatic place of the Levant as the *terra prima* of this universal historical narrative to which he subscribed. For this synchronisation to work, al-Bustani loosened the Muslim entanglements that give Arabic its distinctive identity, and revealed how the Bible, and not only the Qur'an, can be engaged as a foundational text for Arabic language and literature. Through translation, al-Bustani positioned himself mainly as a pedagogue, a man whose scholarship is constituted through translational endeavours, and through a commitment to his role as a conduit that popularises and disseminates translatables: those ideas that were coming into being in the West, yoked through aggregations and summaries to the untranslatable literary history of a thousand years of Muslim scholarship.

As his works show, and contrary to what most scholars are willing to admit, al-Bustani's political allegiances cultivate a nuanced performance of the sectarian. Al-Bustani asserted his Christian identity by shifting the historical narratives of Arabic to the biblical legacy of the Levant. His alternate historical imagination foregrounded the political transformations that would transpire in a burgeoning Lebanese nation, built on sectarian competition and contradictory anchors in myths of origin. His calls for co-existence, as we find them in some of his works, do not contradict this reading. They were secular calls, but this secularism was not a renunciation of religion. It was a secularism that compliments Talal Asad's argument about the persistence of the influence of religion in modernity. As Asad writes

The 'secular' should not be thought of as the space which real human life gradually emancipates itself from the controlling power of 'religion' and thus achieves the latter's relocation. It is this assumption that allows us to think of religion as 'infecting' the secular domain or as replicating within it the structure of theological concepts.[78]

This replication, as I have argued, precedes the secular and gives it its foundation. In the work of this foundational Syro-Lebanese writer, modernity relied on translation as a replicating practice. Its relation to the Bible was not merely pragmatic, it was ontological. Recall that in St John 1:1, the Word is translated into flesh. This kind of translatability is one aware of its own paradoxes, which Jacques Derrida captures succinctly with his edict that 'nothing is translatable, and by the same token, nothing is untranslatable'.[79]

By sometimes papering over this paradox, and on other occasions rhetorically turning it to his political advantage, al-Bustani actively produced translation as an epistemic science, one capable of setting the precepts for how knowledge should be produced – albeit by Arabs, and to gain time and achieve this sought-after catching up with the West. This was what he had hoped for himself and was why he was content to occupy the role of the translator who subverts the hegemony of the Muslim establishment over the production of Arabic culture. His reliance on translation furnished his literary and historiographical imagination of a new political community. The Bible gave him the anchoring point and legitimated the power of translation in his eyes. In foregrounding the political future of his imagined community, al-Bustani supplied it with a coherent narrative and historical claim that places the Arab Christians at the centre of civilisational progress.

Notes

1. Letter from Eli Smith to Butrus Al-Bustani Explaining Why He Was Rejected for the Post of Minister at the Local Evangelical Church, March 1855, Eli Smith Papers, Houghton Library, Harvard University, Cambridge, USA. 11 pages, 6.
2. Talal Asad, *Formations of the Secular: Christianity, Islam, Modernity* (Stanford: Stanford University Press, 2003), 192.
3. Butrus al-Bustani, *Da'irat Al-Ma'arif*, vol. 6 (Beirut: al-Matba'ah al-adabiyyah, 1887), 589.
4. Ibid.
5. See his introduction of his translation of Robinson Crusoe. Butrus al-Bustani. *Kitab al-tuhfa al-bustaniyyah fi al-'asfar al-kruziyya, or, The Travels of*

Robinson Crusoe (Beirut: Publisher unnamed, 1861). Also see his entry on Daniel Defoe in the encyclopaedia.

6. Grafton, *The Contested Origins of the 1865 Arabic Bible*, 29–30.

7. Peter Hill, 'Early Translations of English Fiction into Arabic: The Pilgrim's Progress and Robinson Crusoe', *Journal of Semitic Studies* LX, no. 1 (2015): 177–212.

8. Hill, *Utopia and Civilisation in the Arab Nahda*, 101–2.

9. Ibid.

10. Jeffrey Sacks, *Iterations of Loss: Mutilation and Aesthetic Form, al-Shidyaq to Darwish* (New York: Fordham University Press, 2015), 80.

11. Makdisi, *Artillery of Heaven*.

12. Ibid., 181.

13. Ibid., 182.

14. Butrus al-Bustani, 'The Culture of the Arabs Today', trans. Stephen Sheehi, in *The Arab Renaissance: A Bilingual Anthology of the nahda*, ed. Tarek El-Ariss (New York: The Modern Language Association of America, 2018), 3–19, 12.

15. Hala Auji, 'The Implications of Media: A Material Reading of Nineteenth-Century Arabic Broadsides', *Visible Language* 53, no. 1 (2019): 20–49, 44.

16. Albert Hourani, 'Al-Bustani's Encyclopedia', *Journal of Islamic Studies* 1 (1990): 111–19.

17. Sheehi, 'Towards a Critical Theory of Al-Nahdah', 274.

18. Butrus Abu-Manneh, 'The Christians between Ottomanism and Syrian Nationalism: The Ideas of Butrus al-Bustani', *International Journal of Middle East Studies* 11, no. 3 (1980): 287–304, 71.

19. Al-Bustani 'The Culture of the Arabs Today', 7.

20. Ibid., 11.

21. Issa, 'Genealogies and Kinships: Biblia Arabica and Translation in the *Nahda*'.

22. Fruma Zachs, *The Making of a Syrian Identity: Intellectuals and Merchants in Nineteenth Century Beirut*, Social, Economic, and Political Studies of the Middle East and Asia (Leiden: Brill, 2005), 41.

23. Jens Hanssen, Hicham Safieddine trans, and Buṭrus ibn Būlus Bustānī, *The Clarion of Syria: A Patriot's Call against the Civil War of 1860*, ed. Ussama Samir Makdisi, 1st ed. (Oakland: University of California Press, 2019), https://doi.org/10.2307/j.ctvr7fcz9, Chapter 5, 2.

24. It is worth noting that the theory of *inhitat*, or decay and ignorance was itself a periodisation calque that aligned the terminology with Western periodisation, specifically here with the relegation of the pre-Renaissance era to Medieval decadence.

25. Al-Bustani, *Khutba fi Adab Al-Arab*, 39.

26. Ibid., 4.

27. Ibid., 9.

28. Ibid., 14.

29. Ibid., 28.

30. Ibid., 21.

31. Ibid., 24.

32. Ibid.

33. James Joseph Errington, *Linguistics in a Colonial World: A Story of Language, Meaning, and Power* (Malden: Blackwell, 2008), 81.

34. Errington, *Linguistics in a Colonial World*, 126.

35. Thomas R. Trautmann, *Aryans and British India* (Berkeley: University of California Press, 1997).

36. Al-Bustani, 'Khutbah Fi Adab Al-'Arab'.

37. Stefan Wild, 'Arabic Avant La Lettre Divine Prophetic and Heroic Arabic', in *Approaches to Arabic Linguistics: Presented to Kees Versteegh on the Occasion of His Sixtieth Birthday*, ed. C. H. M. Versteegh, E. Ditters and H. Motzki (Leiden: Brill, 2007), 189–208.

38. Al-Bustani, 'Khutbah Fi Adab Al-'Arab', 24.

39. Jirmanus Farhat and Butrus Al-Bustani, *Kitab Misbah Al-Talib Fi Bahth al-Matalib: Mutawwal fi al-Sarf w al-Nahu w al-Qawafi* (Beirut: Publisher Unknown, AUB Special Collections, 1854, 3).

40. Hilary Kilpatrick, 'The Arabic Culture of Christians in Syria in the 16th and 17th Centuries'.

41. Farhat and Al-Bustani, *Kitab Misbah Al-Talib fi Bahth al-Matalib*.

42. Butrus al-Bustani, *Muhit Al-Muhit* (Beirut: Publisher Unknown, 1870).

43. John A. Haywood, *Arabic Lexicography: Its History, and Its Place in the General History of Lexicography* (Leiden: Brill, 1965); Ramzi Ba'labakki, *The Arabic Lexicographical Tradition: From the 2nd/8th to the 12th/18th Century* (Leiden: Brill, 2014).

44. Suleiman, *The Arabic Language and National Identity*, 22.

45. Ba'labakki, *The Arabic Lexicographical Tradition*, 18.

46. On the *gharib* genre: Ibid., 63–99.

47. Ibid.

48. Yasir Suleiman, 'Arab(Ic) Language Anxiety: Tracing a "Condition"', *'Arabiyya: Journal of the American Association of Teachers of Arabic* 47 (2014): 57–81.

49. Ba'labakki, *The Arabic Lexicographical Tradition*, 409.

50. Albert Hourani reads too quickly when he claims that al-Bustani discontinued the encyclopaedia on the eighteenth letter 'ayn. In fact, it was Sulayman al-Bustani who inherited the project upon the death of Salim al-Bustani, Butrus's son, who died two years after the death of his father and could not see the project to completion. Later on, the project would be continued and turned into a copious encyclopaedia by Fouad Ifram al-Bustani, the famous scholar and president of the Lebanese University for many years. See Albert Hourani, 'Al-Bustani's Encyclopedia'.

51. Yusuf Quzma al-Khoury, *Rajul sabiq li 'asrih: Al-mu'allim Butrus al-Bustani (1819–1883)* (Beirut: Bisan, 1995), 89.

52. Al-Bustani, *Muhit Al-Muhit*.

53. Strotmann seems to agree with al-Shidyaq. She identifies such polemics and argues that al-Fayruzabadi's linguistics covered his ulterior religious motives. As she writes: 'Although it is not unfounded to say that Al-Firūzābādi was much more educated in *lugha* than in legal matters, it is noteworthy that *al-Qari'* uses *lugha* to discredit the scholar rather than criticising his legal abilities. This also shows that some of the critique levelled against al-Firūzābādi's Qāmūs may have been motivated by dispute in fields other than lexicography'. Vivian Strotmann, *Majd Al-Dīn al-Fīrūzābādī (1329–1415): A Polymath on the Eve of the Early Modern Period* (Leiden: Brill, 2016), 159.

54. Al-Shidyaq, *Al-Jasus 'ala l-Qamus*.

55. Jens Hanssen, *Fin de Siècle Beirut: The Making of an Ottoman Provincial Capital* (Oxford: Clarendon Press, 2005), 20.

56. Martin R. Zammit, *A Comparative Lexical Study of Qur'ānic Arabic* (Leiden: Brill, 2002), 37.

57. Biblical scholars and philologists made astounding discoveries of ancient manuscripts that contested the divine genesis of human language, especially after groundbreaking work in Sanskrit studies revealed it to be a more ancient language than Hebrew. This discovery radically challenged the myth of creation advanced by the Book of Genesis. In some philological circles, Adam's birthplace and burial ground was purported to be in India, and

some archaeologists even went on excursions to find proof for this theory. Scholarship covering various parts of the impact of this shift in philological sensibility and its continued anchoring in biblical studies has proliferated in recent years. see Rachel Beckles Willson, *Orientalism and Musical Mission: Palestine and the West* (Cambridge: Cambridge University Press, 2013); Thomas R. Trautmann, *Aryans and British India*; Suzanne Marchand, *German Orientalism in the Age of Empire: Religion, Race and Scholarship* (Cambridge: Cambridge University Press, 2009); Benes, *In Babel's Shadow*; Maurice Olender, *The Languages of Paradise: Race, Religion, and Philology in the Nineteenth Century* (Cambridge, MA: Harvard University Press, 1992).

58. Al-Shidyaq, *Al-Wasitah ila ma'rifat ahwal Malta wa kashf al-mukhabba' 'an funun 'Urubba.*

59. I ran keyword searches on the classical corpus of books supplied by al-waraq. net. These words were largely absent from the classical corpus.

60. This concept and the hadith were originally mentioned in al-Tahtawi, which could be the reason why al-Bustani was emboldened to use them.

61. For a study about the origins of this myth, see Jaroslav Stetkevytch, *The Zephyrs of Najd: The Poetics of Nostalgia in The Classical Arabic Nasib* (Chicago: University of Chicago Press, 1993).

62. Sacks, *Iterations of Loss*, 42.

63. Al-Bustani, 'Khutba Fi Adab al-'Arab', 32.

64. Ibid., 30.

65. See also Fleischer who mentions an unnamed Italian source. Heinrich Fleischer, 'Bistâni's Encyclopedie arabe', *Zeitschrift Der Deutschen Morgenländischen Gesellschaft* 34, no. 3 (1880): 579–82.

66. Helge Jordheim, 'Synchronizing the World: Synchronism as Historical Practice, Then and Now', *History of the Present* 7 no. 1 (Spring 2017): 59–95, 64.

67. See for example the first chapter on 'gist translation' in the translation textbook series, *Thinking Translation,* published by Routledge since 2002, which provides a practical approach to teaching translation from many languages into English. See for example James Dickens, Sandor Hervey and Ian Higgins. *Thinking Arabic Translation.* (London: Routledge, 2016).

68. Ilham Khuri Makdisi argues this in a forthcoming article. 'Worlds in Motion: Al-Bustani's Arabic Encyclopedia (Da'irat al-Ma'arif) and the Global Production of Knowledge in the Late Ottoman Levant and Egypt (1870s–1900s)'. I thank her for letting me use unfinished work.

69. Fleischer, 'Bistâni's Encyclopedie arabe'.

70. Al-Bustani, 'Tarikh, Histoire, History', in *Da'irat Al-Ma'arif* (Beirut: al-Matba'ah al-Adabiyyah, 1887), 11.

71. Ibid.

72. Ibid.

73. Al-Bustani, 'Adab', in *Da'irat Al-Ma'arif* (Beirut: al-Matba'ah al-Adabiyyah, 1887), 655.

74. Ibid.

75. Ibid.

76. Ibid.

77. More recently Kilito argues that the classical author al-Jahiz was the first to articulate this position. See Abdel Fattah Kilito and Wail Hassan, *Thou Shalt Not Speak My Language* (New York: Syracuse University Press, 2008). For a nuanced and thorough revision of Kilito's opinion on al-Jahiz, Anna Ziajka Stanton argues in her forthcoming monograph on Arabic translations into English that al-Jahiz was governed by a modality that separated *lafz* (form) from *ma'na* (meaning), and that he meant that *lafz* as a material expression of Arabic poetry's literariness was untranslatable. I thank Anna for allowing me to borrow from her her forthcoming monograph *The Worlding of Arabic Literature: Language, Affect, and the Ethics of Translatability* (New York: Fordham University Press, 2023).

78. Asad, *Formations of the Secular*, 256.

79. Jacques Derrida, 'What is a "Relevant" Translation', in *The Translation Studies Reader*, ed. Lawrence Venuti (New York: Routledge, 2004), 423–46.

5

Ahmad Faris Al-Shidyaq's Bible as Literature

Recounting the scene of the Last Supper, St John writes in 13:4, that upon finishing the meal, Jesus 'riseth from supper, and laid aside his garments; and took a towel and girded himself'. When Ahmad Faris al-Shidyaq sat down to translate those words into Arabic, he chuckled to himself, took note, and later commented on the verse in a polemical manuscript entitled *Mumahakat al-ta'wil fi Munaqadat al-Injil* (Squabbles and Disputations over Gospel Interpretations, 1851). He was still in the employment of the British SPCK, working with the Chair of Oriental Studies at Cambridge Rev. Samuel Lee (1783–1852) on translating the Bible, when he began to circulate this manuscript amongst a trusted group of friends. In it, al-Shidyaq ridicules the narrative produced in the Bible. He writes

> John recounts that after the supper, Issa [Jesus] took off his clothes and tied a towel around his waist to wash the feet of his disciples. This implies that, at the time, Issa was drunk; that he did not know what he was doing, for the washing of feet does not require getting naked.[1]

This was the first book al-Shidyaq circulated that was not on commission from the missionaries. Keeping it in manuscript and never printing it, al-Shidyaq controlled its circulation. Nevertheless, with this small book, al-Shidyaq sets the framework through which he would define his literary vocation.

Literature as he contended was irreverent; not even the Bible was too divine for its whimsical exploits. His is what Emily Apter would have characterised as a 'dispossessive stance' that cast the Bible 'as an unownable estate, a literature over which no one exerts propriety prerogative and which lends itself to a critical turn that puts the problem of property possession front and center'.[2] Dispossessing the Bible through carnal acts of reading, al-Shidyaq recuperates the literary as a critical possibility that questions the precepts of capitalist relations of production in the scholarly and authorial professions. Through working towards a new conception of *adab*, al-Shidyaq wrestled with the modalities of alienated labour as a Bible translator. Through metaphors of literary consumption, he reconciled his labour with the whims and desires of the authorial self and evolved a notion of *adab* that emanates in concrete and intimate ways from the body and its activities.

Adab provided al-Shidyaq with the space to wrestle with the modalities of alienated labour as a Bible translator. While in Cambridge translating the Bible, al-Shidyaq did not only write a biblical critique, but he also embarked on *al-Saq 'ala al-Saq* (Leg over Leg, 1855), his magnum opus and the book by which he is most remembered today. Although he did not know Hebrew or Greek, and even though his knowledge of Syriac was hardly used in his work, he depended on Bible translation for his living. This income was much better than what al-Bustani was making with the Americans. Nevertheless, al-Shidyaq laboured to break away from his translational skills and establish himself as a writer, *mu'allif*, or a creator of literary texts. As he wrote his way out of the translational mould of his early employment with the missionaries, al-Shidyaq produced *adab* as the locus for a theory of language. Unlike al-Bustani, who found in translation an epistemic value, al-Shidyaq focused on *adab* as the process of meaning generation to contend that the creation of new knowledge is native to all languages. When he made arguments about translation, he suggested that its overdetermination as a tool for knowledge production in his time was blocking the creative path and limiting originality. Through metaphors of literary consumption, he reconciled his labour as a translator with the whims and desires of the authorial self and evolved a notion of *adab* that emanates in concrete and intimate ways from the body and its activities.

Adab and the Carnal Consumption of the Bible

Al-Shidyaq derived *adab* from *ma'duba*, a delectable feast, and not from its more conventional understanding as a concept for 'good manners', with its antonym in *qillit adab* or 'impoliteness'. Conceived as a feast, al-Shidyaq devoured the Bible through irreverent, carnal acts of writing. Like other writers in the *nahda*, he showed a relentless interest in the question of religion. His writings on religion as well as his multiple conversions effectively elide any easy categorisation of his religious belonging. His views were idiosyncratically at odds with more dogmatic treatments of religion that we find in the *nahda*. His immense textual corpus reveals that he was well versed in religion, and that he spent an entire lifetime subverting religious authority through his literary schemes. Through literature he constructed an alternative ethics from which to counter the monolithic interpretation of scripture. This literary feast occurred mostly during sleepless nights. Unable to sleep because of the miseries of his translation labour, al-Shidyaq used to leave his insomniac bed to write. The nights' quiet allowed him to confront his thoughts and search for a new conception of *adab* that he could inhabit, and that could provide him with ways to confront and subdue the scriptural force of the Bible. He marshalled the insomniac hour as a critical distance from contemporary fashions of thinking around Arabic in the nineteenth century. While his contemporaries allowed themselves to be inspired by the metaphor of *nahda* and awakening, al-Shidyaq's insomnia desynchronised itself from the temporal metaphor of *nahda*, and its consequent master narratives, from the imagination of the modern self to its propositions about *adab* as it expresses national desire. Sleeplessly writing the literary feast, al-Shidyaq's pen 'smack[s] its lips'[3] at the Bible (and the Qur'an).

    This chapter explores the somatic tropes of feasting and insomnia, to trace al-Shidyaq's approach to scripture. I appropriate Frank Kermode's concepts of the 'carnal' and the 'spiritual' to parse through the extent that al-Shidyaq's *adab* emanates from the somatic, and not from the disciplining of the body that anchored the typical *nahdawi* understanding of *adab*'s function as a vessel for national desire. For Kermode, the carnal and the spiritual are hermeneutic functions, with the 'literary' being identified with the spiritual success of overcoming the carnal. Preferring the spiritual to the carnal, Kermode writes that 'carnal readings are all the same. Spiritual readings are all different. Speculation thrives; we each want to say something different about the text'.[4] For Kermode, a spiritual reading overcomes the flesh of the text and allows it to interact with the abstracted meanings we hold within us. Thus, a spiritual reading yields different interpretations, while the carnal reading consumes the text without savouring its complexities. Kermode's interests in the reception of texts as diverse as the Bible and the dime-store novel can be expanded and appropriated to also thinking about writing and about the structures of meaning authors provide, which guide the process of how readers make sense of texts. For writers, spiritual and carnal acts of intertextual influence need not stand in binary opposition to one another. Rather, they turn into tools in the service of the authorial gesture. This gesture, as al-Shidyaq's notion of *adab* posits, is an embodied one, whereby the bodily flesh is not separated from the mental energies of abstraction.

In his theory of the beginnings and evolution of language, which he proposes in *Sirr al-Layal fil Qalb wal Ibdal*, al-Shidyaq argues that linguistic construction is like building a house. The builder must first 'cut (*qaṭʿ*) that with which to build a house from stone or wood, etc'.[5] Then after cutting what one needs one gathers (*jamaʿ*) the material, 'for gathering is not devoid of cutting'.[6] In this imaginative process of cutting and gathering phonemes and words to make meaning, the language-user forges meaning out of existing sound material. We have no access to the *tabula rasa* where the mimicking of the natural world through language was initiated. But there is evidence that humans have built on the lexicon throughout the generations by deriving metaphors from the natural world. In his interest in beginnings, al-Shidyaq described the move from natural sounds to meaning-making as involving two types of processes: 'A tale of sound (*hikayat sawt*), or a tale of an attribute (*hikayat sifa*)'.[7] As tales, those processes have narrators. The narrator is the language-user who creates meaning based on what is available to them in the material world. He illustrates the 'tale of a sound' through the word *busa*, where the word emulates the phonetic sound made by puckered lips planting a *kiss*. For the 'tale of an attribute', al-Shidyaq recounts the story of the word *hadhaba*, or 'to be polite'. He reports that the linguists are all in agreement that the word comes originally from the act of pruning a tree, which is another proof that 'the spiritual or immaterial issues (*al-umur al-maʿnawiyya aw al-ʿaqliyya*) are taken from material things (*ashyaʾ hissiyya*)'.[8] If words are tales of sound or attributes, then they are phonetic metaphors for lived experience. The sociologist Ahmad Beydoun remarked that al-Shidyaq's linguistic contribution can be termed 'the science of phonetic tropes', where the sign phonetically tropes a referent, a process that for Beydoun emphasises human agency, contrary to the norms of structuralist linguistics.[9] The emphasis on agency here is key, if we are to understand al-Shidyaq's theory of embodied language.

For al-Shidyaq, then, meaning is generated by human agents and is not given a priori to human need. By collecting his findings in a semantic lexicon, al-Shidyaq claims that in the beginning there were only a few words. however, as the needs of man multiplied and he manufactured more tools, he evolved new words to fit his context. This is universal to all languages, even though Arabic maintains the strongest links to the history of its semantic development. With these insights about the evolution of language, al-Shidyaq provides us with the historical depth that we need to appropriate Kermode's notions of the carnal and the spiritual. To deploy the carnal and the spiritual to talk about writing means to theorise how meaning is generated through carnal metaphors of lived experience and how it subsequently accumulates and acquires more abstract semantics to connote spiritual meaning. In his acts of feasting on scripture, al-Shidyaq develops a literary process that is opposite to what Frank Kermode imagined as the *raison d'etre* of classical texts. His is a stance that rejects the interpretation of classical texts, and he would instead have agreed with Susan Sontag that 'interpretation is a radical strategy for conserving an old text, which is thought too precious to repudiate, by revamping it'.[10] Confronted with the spiritual authority of scripture, al-Shidyaq subverted the need to interpret the Bible, and instead of working through the carnal to reach some spiritual biblical plane, he broke the scriptural in the Bible, by snapping it out of its spiritual aura and serving it as a textual meal in an elaborate literary feast.

Al-Shidyaq's construction of the concept of *adab* depended on the somatic to carve out for literature a space without purpose, against the *nahda*'s attempts to assimilate it in the civilisational deployments of *adab*. I contrast his notion of *adab* with his disdain for translation to show how he celebrated *adab* as a native modality of the imagination against the *nahda*'s inflation of the role translation plays in the development of knowledge in

Arabic. Through a close reading of al-Shidyaq's carnal reception of the Bible during bouts of excessive wakefulness and insomnia, I show how he dismantles the *nahdawi* claim that the Bible was a moderniser of Arabic. Instead of modernising Arabic, the Bible was forcefully digested into al-Shidyaq's Arabo-centric notion of world literature. Rather than entering into communion with an imagined Christian community, al-Shidyaq cannot seem to sleep, and in his wakefulness, he embarks on long projects of reading and writing.

Insomnia works against the metaphors of awakening that his contemporaries were circulating. Unlike wakefulness, insomnia interrupts the night's sleep without posing as a salubrious moment of rejuvenation. Rather insomnia obsesses about itself and its inability to assimilate into the synchronised temporal cycles of society. In the throes of its intensity, al-Shidyaq carnally tears at scripture, quotes from it with irreverence and mirth, critically rejects its moral authority, and questions its relevance for his modern context.

As he was acutely aware, *Adab* is not only the root for politeness (*mu'addab*), but also for feasting (*ma'duba*). Al-Shidyaq defines the politeness of *adab* through the latter derivation, framing it through the metaphor of table manners, which allows him to cultivate a relationship to the carnal that produces an alternative to the politicised parameters of *nahdawi* literature with its didactics of national desire. The patronage institutions that supported the *nahdawi* authors and their *adab* demanded spiritual legitimacy, which it could expect from its dependents based on its ability to coerce material authority on its subjects. Al-Shidyaq's literary gesture emerges from demystifying the centrality of the spiritual/material binary that institutions put in motion for their assertion of power. In other words, by exposing the carnal power of the institution, literature becomes the practice by which to break free of its hold, and into an individuated form of spiritual cohesion.

Al-Saq as Carnal Feast, Tradition as Sumptuous Dish

Al-Saq is al-Shidyaq's clearest assertion of the metabolic power of the literary to destabilise the binaries of institutional power. The title of the book parodies the Qur'an's 'Surat al-Qiyamah' (The Sura of Resurrection, Q. 75). Verse 29 contains the phrase '*wa-iltaffat al-saq bil-saq*' to describe the mangled bodies on the Day of Judgment, which Tarif Khalidi's Qur'an translation renders as 'and leg is entwined with leg'.[11] Al-Shidyaq changed a mere preposition (*over* replaced *with*), to rearrange the legs, and parody the apocalyptic contours of the qur'anic verse into the literary postures of polite society, anticipating, in the title, the playful sexual undercurrent that run through the rest of *al-Saq*. The title exceeds the qur'anic subversion however to also subvert the missionary institutions then ascendant in Beirut. It satirises a now-forgotten text that was circulating among the American missionaries in Beirut in the late 1840s.[12] Found in the personal papers of Eli Smith, who notes that this text is a 'striking peculiarity of [the Muslim] religion', a tiny scrap of paper is said to have been found tucked into the *tarbush* of an Egyptian soldier who died in battle near al-Hosn, in Syria. It contained an erotic quotation that puns on the Qur'an's 'Surat al-Qiyamah'. The scrap quotes verses 29–32 from this *sura*, and then follows these lines with a rhyming invocation

> And leg is entwined with leg, to your Lord that Day is the rounding up,[13] and if a woman comes to you, uncover her right ankle and it will show your love and lover, your motivation and inspiration; and then pull it toward you and say, 'I give my face to the light of my Lord, the creator of land and sky, as a Hanafi Muslim . . .'[14]

The text, which could possibly be a *hijab*, or amulet – perhaps to increase the chances of its bearer in love – produced a scandal in Beirut that originated with the French consul, who seems to have acquired it from one of his soldiers. The missionaries had it transcribed by their secretary Nasif al-Yaziji, who also corrected the colloquial Arabic in the text to make it conform to the conventions of standard written Arabic. Could it be that the scandalous airs that surrounded this text were the writing prompt al-Shidyaq needed for his magnum opus? Or is it mere coincidence that Chapter 20 in book 4 concludes with a quotation of the same qur'anic verses in a parody that parallels the amulet?

Humphrey Davies translates these lines thus:

> any who wishes to bless [al-Firyaq] or curse him shall, when 'leg is intertwined with leg' and it is said, 'unto thy Lord that day shall be the

driving,' receive his wages. As for [the reader] who prays for the restoration of [al-Firyaq's] marriage before he breathes his last, I guarantee he'll invite you to a banquet around and upon whose table will be set out, in proper order, everything this book mentions that the appetite may *stimulate* or the eye *captivate*, be it presented on couch or on dinner *plate*.[15]

Inviting analogies with a local scandal that was of no consequence beyond the small circle of foreigners and their assistants, and simultaneously punning on a qur'anic verse, al-Shidyaq challenges the dominant discourse on literature that was flourishing in the *nahda*, by also subverting the idea that literature must serve a purpose. The only purpose he expresses for *al-Saq* is that the main character resolves his marital strife with his wife. He deploys the carnal against the promise of spiritual betterment that scripture and literature exercise on people. For well-wishing readers, he promises the feast of everything in the book: of the book itself as the feast. The literary, as he underscores many times in the book, is the feast, whether it serves spiritual texts or carnal ones, while manners only matter for food rather than for literature.

Visiting the Druze emir, the effective ruler of Mount Lebanon until the 1850s, al-Shidyaq manifested the literary subversion of the carnal. By rejecting the bounties that come by allowing oneself to be co-opted by power, the poem he composed bolstered his will to overcome his subservience to the emir. Invited by his brother, who was the emir's secretary, al-Shidyaq stays long enough to find Druze customs and table manners intolerant. They were too carnal at the dinner table:

Such rumbling and mumbling and teeth-gnashing and lip-smacking was to be heard you would have thought they were wild beasts at a carcass. They are like animals taking huge bites, burying their front teeth in the food, stripping off the meat down to the bone, sucking out the marrow, licking their lips and smacking them, polishing off their dessert, licking the plates with their tongues, and throwing half-eaten food down on the table, all the while seated on the ground with their legs crossed under them at their ease ... When the Fariyaq ate with them, he'd get up hungry from the table and his guts would rise against him, so that till late at night to sleep he'd be unable.[16]

The sight of such carnal frenzy over food led him to insomnia. In its séance, he composes an ode of satirical verse that he shared with his brother. The brother agrees with him about the uncouthness of the Druze, but he also tries to gently defend them by saying:

> These people are endowed with pride and chivalry, courage and gallantry, and though ill-mannered at board (*sayyi'u al-adab 'ala al-ta'am*), they're well-mannered with deed and word (*muta'addibun fil fi'l wal kalam*) . . . The Fariyaq however, could appreciate no manners (*adab*) but those of the dining table (*ma'duba*).[17]

The ode becomes popular, and he angers the prince, but fearing the writer's sharp tongue, the prince decides to contain his evil by inviting him to an extraordinary banquet, where al-Fariyaq is forced to compose lines of poetry on the food displayed. He does this, witty as he is, but he swears to 'never again tie his forelock to any great man's skirts',[18] particularly those great men that demand he becomes court poet. In this episode where food and feasting become the occasion for literary license, the distinctions of *adab* are occasioned through insomnia which allows the author to work through, and appropriate, the carnal. As a somatic condition, insomnia facilitates the overcoming of the carnal and with it the institutional manipulation of its use.

He dreamt it once,

> Behold the Fariyaq, seated on a chair, in front of him a table bearing a large number of books, among them, for all the scraps of paper they contained, not a scrap of food, in his fingers a long pen, and in his hands a pot containing ink as black as tar.[19]

In this digestive dream about tradition, al-Shidyaq makes a metaphoric leap from food to books. The canon is turned scrumptious in order to support a reading diet that is digested through intertextual writing.

His reading habits differed from those of other *nahdawis* who were more interested in periodisation and rupture. As they deployed the *nahda* as the metaphor for their literary pursuits, al-Shidyaq offers a complex notion of rupture that locates it in the somatic and generational, but questions its centrality to the epochal view of history. The *nahda*'s semantics of rupture and periodisation as a method of canonisation kept al-Shidyaq up at night, and he would painstakingly dismantle this sense of rupture in his work on *adab* and associated concepts in language and literature.

In this circadian approach to writing, al-Shidyaq discovered a way to engage tradition by overcoming the *nahda*'s theological dismissals and celebrations of past cultural expression, by in fact staying awake to engage his predecessors in reading and writing. Al-Shidyaq's insomnia unlocked for him other metaphors, of linguistic secrets, and the night's slower rhythms of uninterrupted thinking. These metaphors becam his portals to reflection on Arabic. In his linguistic treatise, *Sirr al-Layal fil Qalb wal Ibdal*, he writes:

> The ancients may have worked in this honourable language, but in its love I fell passionately, and loved in it truly, and slaved away loyally, I flowered until withering and many a night I spent reflecting, my gaze focusing, its hidden ways discovering; and nothing could distract, no goal, private or public could me side-track. It was my solace from loneliness, and my succour during sadness, and my pleasure in gloom, and my happiness against dolefulness.[20]

In the secret of the night, Arabic anthropomorphs to become his companion, and his most trusted interlocutor. Nocturnal activity frames his disciplinary engagement with the language, and as the book progresses, al-Shidyaq underscores that meaning is generated by intending human agents and is not given a priori to human need, and nor is it arbitrary as Saussure would later suggest. His handling of scripture applied this theory, and the overarching critical question he posed was: what do societies need of the past in order to formulate adequate ethical worlds in the present? This is a question that radically rejects the theological edict, which demands that people follow scripture dogmatically and therefore disregard their contingent historical moment and its peculiar needs.

Al-Shidyaq's approach to scripture does not intend upon a clear rupture as was typical of how the *nahdawis* treated the canonical books that they disdained. Al-Shidyaq took pride in his work as a Bible translator and often wrote in praise of the modesty of faith. Yet this pride was produced by his linguistic experiments and his commitment to the literary. This pride stoked his carnal sampling of the Bible and works of scripture, to distance the moral views of these texts from legitimate authority in the contemporary world. This is best captured by his paradoxical treatment of the Bible and of the scriptural genre generally.

Al-Shidyaq quoted the Bible in ways that disarticulated the authority of missionaries as pedagogical agents, teachers of local scholars, like himself, from the technologies and languages that mattered in modernity, and rejected the missionary treatment of the Bible as a non-textual genre. He engaged scripture for literary ends that far exceeded the dictates of modernity and its paradoxical relationship to faith. To borrow a phrase from Michael Allan, al-Shidyaq's biblical intertextuality 'entextualised', scripture, that is reframed its discursive power,[21] as literature, by displacing veneration and proposing a way of reading them that engenders more than exegetical epiphanies.

Al-Shidyaq's intertextuality displayed his intimate mastery of the contents of classical Arabic texts. His background as the son of a scribe provided him with an early familiarity with the Arabic canon. His schooling started at a young age by apprenticing with his father and two older brothers. The breakthrough in his career came with his contact with British and American missionaries, where he produced less memorable works. Two foundational texts stand out from this period: *The Book of Common Prayer* (1848) that he worked on with George Badger in Malta, and the translation of the Bible with Rev. Samuel Lee in Cambridge (1857).[22]

His early career with British and American missionaries and his concurrent study with Muslim *'ulama* in Egypt provided him with a comprehensive knowledge in various theological traditions.[23] Rather than revere his tutors, al-Shidyaq evaluated his acquired knowledge by constantly subjecting religion's established truths to the authority of literature. Having left London and his employment as a translator, before his translation of the Bible was sent to the press, al-Shidyaq did not wait for his Bible translation to come out before beginning to publish texts that were critical of Christianity. Such works included his unique literary magnum opus, *al-Saq*, and the manuscript he began circulating before he left Cambridge, *Mumahakat*. This text was written when al-Shidyaq was employed by the British missionaries and worked with Lee, on translating the Bible.

Before the published translation of the Bible was printed, al-Shidyaq circulated this text, an anti-Bible polemic in manuscript form.[24] As Nadia al-Bagdadi argued, this little book was a prelude to his work in *al-Saq* in that it allowed him to sever himself off from the dictates of religious decorum and into the creative force of literary production.[25] This manuscript, which was first printed a century after it began to circulate, was a highly controversial text to write for a translator of the Bible.

By keeping it as a manuscript, the author effectively limited the circulation of the text. As al-Bagdadi contends in regards to his strategies of publication, the forms of repression that were practiced in his own society stipulated that *Mumahakat* existed solely in manuscript form, for it was a society that had little tolerance for the critique of foundational texts.[26] Briefly put, he wrote a book with such a polemical title to express his wariness of any misunderstanding that would place him on the side of the pious, and kept it in manuscript to control its readership and avert any censorship that might have halted its dissemination.

Mumahakat was the earliest book al-Shidyaq published without commission from the missionaries. It was a prelude to *al-Saq*, in terms of legitimising his literary autonomy, but exceeded his need for an independent intellectual space, to provide insight on the nature of narrative form. In *Mumahakat*, al-Shidyaq focuses on two main problems with the gospels. Firstly, he points out that eyewitnesses did not write the gospels. And secondly, through an exhaustive intertextual rearrangement of the Holy Book, al-Shidyaq aligns extensive biblical quotes according to their contradictions to show us that the gospels dispute one another. He points to the impossibility for two authors to deliver an identical narrative. This is the main reason behind the contradiction: because more than one author wrote the gospels. This was a radical pronouncement in Arab circles, yet the radicality was hemmed in by its scarce manuscript circulation at a time when industrial printing had begun to dominate the book market.

The style of this manuscript conformed to what al-Shidyaq later defined as the act of literary creativity. In his definition of what he calls 'the productive imagination' (*al-mukhayyila l-muntija*), al-Shidyaq argues that literary creation stems from the writer's ability to *select* elements from reality. In his own words, from an article in his newspaper, *al-Jawa'ib*, he writes:

> The productive imagination adds to the innovation and pensiveness of memory so we can either observe distant things a little closer, or we can distinguish between things and create them. This has led to the thought that the productive imagination invents the origins of things even though all it does is to arrange and organize things. Man has no perceptions (*tasawwurat*) of his own; he only creates according to particular methods (*kayfiyyat makhsusa*).[27]

The productive imagination must therefore process existing material in new directions. This imaginative process re-arranges the elements that make up an object and intervenes in memory in order to strengthen its discerning capacity, for both readers and creators. The act of literary creation lies in distinguishing the contours of objects. The author assembles certain existing elements in novel ways to sharpen the critical capacities of memory. Al-Shidyaq termed this rearrangement *method* (*kayfiya*). *Mumahakat* is an example of this method of re-arrangement and assemblage. By unveiling the relationship between the author and the narratives of the gospels, al-Shidyaq effectively rejected Revelation as the author of scripture, whilst also providing an insight into narrative form.

By assembling the gospels according to their contradictions, this manuscript makes the Bible divulge its nature as a composite of dissimilar books that blatantly oppose one another on key events. In his introduction to the *Mumahakat*, he presents a close reading of Matthew, the gospel most known among literate Arabic readers,[28] against the grain of the other three gospels. He writes:

> Let it be known that Christian claims [which state that] these books between their hands were revealed, are empty falsifications and that the author of this gospel [Matthew] was not an eyewitness. Rather he recklessly imitated some narrators of his era, where he was one among them . . . Did they know that these four gospels were going to be collected in one book to enlighten people on the important events in Issa's

[Jesus] life? . . . As we mentioned, those writers were not eyewitnesses; these are divergent narratives on Issa, that spread throughout the land, and each [of the apostles] copied what he received from the mouths of storytellers in his land.[29]

Positing a rhetorical question about the collation of the gospels that became an essential part of the New Testament, al-Shidyaq begins by creating a gap between the evangelists' writing and the time of emergence of the Bible as scripture. He historicises the limits of what the apostles could foresee as the impact of their writing. When they recorded the oral tales circulating during their lifetime, did they know that their work was going to be promoted as divine Revelation upon the institutionalisation of Christianity? He rhetorically lets the historical context hang unanswered, and then moves into source textual critique of the gospels. As he lists his evidence of contradictions in the four gospels in point form, al-Shidyaq does not express any view on Jesus himself. Instead, he suggests that by presenting such contradictory accounts of the life of Jesus, the evangelists implicitly attacked his person, and rendered him into a less than divine figure.

After a short introduction, the rest of *Mumahakat* – which can also be described as a long list of quotations with feeble attempts at synthesis – has a startlingly quiet authorial presence. Paradoxically, al-Shidyaq's frugal presence in the text sobers the polemics of the critique by providing very little analysis and contenting himself with assembling a collage of quotations. With minimal interventions in those lists, al-Shidyaq directs the reader's gaze to a method of critique but does not himself provide cogent analysis that could bind this text into theoretical coherence. By rarely intervening to analyse what he has quoted, al-Shidyaq invites his readers to come to their own critical judgments about the contradictions in the gospels. In general, he maintains the quotes in a state of interpretive vacuum,[30] best captured by his alternative title for this book, *No Interpretation on the Bible*! (*La ta'wil 'ala al-Injil*).[31]

His translation of the Bible provided him with the necessary fodder for an attack on the interpretive stances of religious institutions. Even though he proudly speaks of himself as also a Bible translator, he was more motivated to flaunt his skill and his profound knowledge of the classics than he was to ascribe to the piety one may associate with such labours. I have spoken at length about his translation in Chapter Two and have been loath to conflate that work with the actual location the Bible came to occupy in his literary career. Reading him otherwise threatens to obscure the significance of writing and circulating *Mumahakat* while he was still in the employ of the BSPCK as a Bible translator.

Mumahakat indexed the distance that al-Shidyaq constructs in relation to the dictates of religious institutions. Less than five years later, he decided to write what we might classify today as an 'autofictional' work, *al-Saq*, a book that shows clear inspiration in the multitude of genres that are grouped in the Bible. *Al-Saq* was the first independently authored text that he published in print. In a way, the book was a fitting sequel to the anti-Bible manuscript. It follows the technique of assemblage deployed in the *Mumahakat* and contains a more explicit attack on the Bible and on Christian institutions. Finally, in this book, the author pondered the change from manuscript to print as it impacts on the production of ideas.

Al-Shidyaq was cognisant of the relationship between technology and the proliferation of meaning. Even when he began to operate, and eventually own a printing press, he continued to rely on book copying as a way to acquire books for his copious collection. As he mentions in his travelogue, he copied many books and portions of texts when he visited European libraries.[32] As Geoffrey Roper describes him, 'al-Shidyaq was always surrounded by books and built up a large collection of his own'.[33] Having spent his youth working the press in Malta and later operating his own press, al-Shidyaq often commented on the shifting materiality of the book and the radical consequences for the emergence of a new reading public. He constantly alerted his readers to this changing materiality as it transformed the relationship that connected the author to his readers. He wrote in *al-Saq*, 'as you can see I've now made (that is to say written not printed or bound) this book and placed it before you'.[34] Unlike the Protestant publishers who capitalised on this shift and included it in a larger narrative of salvation, al-Shidyaq critiqued its shortcomings, even as he full heartedly embraced its possibilities. By fleshing out the materiality of book making in the industrial age, he distanced himself from the totality of the chain of production. He only wrote the book, (made it, like one prepares a dish) and thus his responsibility was mediated through an industrial form of knowledge production that he did not control. Purposefully exposing the materiality of the book-making process, al-Shidyaq reveals the dependency of meaning on the materiality of language.

The Bible's Relevance to Modern life

Through intertextuality, al-Shidyaq uncovers the dissonance between the Bible and reality, to deliver another blow to the church and its use of the Bible as a text that stipulates ethical positions in the world. The first mention of the Bible comes at the end of the first quarter of *al-Saq*. The Bible in this instance frames a reflection on the state of the homeland that he has abandoned, and its erupting civil violence from the 1840s onward.[35] He writes:

> Should the Emir of the Mountain, once he's grown old and wrapping himself up in his clothes is no longer enough to keep him warm, be permitted to cosy up to a beautiful virgin girl, i.e., warm himself with her and heat himself with the warmth of her body, like King David? When he makes war on the Druze and God grants him victory over them, is he permitted to slay their married women and their children and leave their virgins alive for the stud bulls among his troops to debauch, the way Moses did to the people of Midian, as stated in Numbers chapter 33? ... If the religion of the Christians makes lawful the slaying of men, women, and children and the debauching of virgins ... why did the first abrogate the second and declare its laws null and void? In fact, though, the Christian religion is built on high moral values and its aim from beginning to end is to maintain peace among men.[36]

If David and Moses are entitled to their voracious violence by virtue of their position as prophets, the prince of the mountains does not partake in the immunity and his acts will not be rewarded by a Christian religion founded on the best of morals. The rhetorical play with Christian moral goodness reveals how the world lacks such values. By deploying a typical rhetorical technique of contrast, al-Shidyaq withholds any solid example from the Bible to reveal it to be a text of moral strength.

By drawing parallels of violence between the acts of prophets and ordinary mortals, al-Shidyaq demands of the reader, as he did with *Mumahakat*, to come to her own conclusions about Christian ethics. In *Mumahakat*, the gospels are mirrored against one another, while in *al-Saq*, the Bible is mirrored against the historical realities of Syro-Lebanese violence that erupted between the Maronites and the Druze in 1841. The congruence of biblical violence with the social context of Syro-Lebanon topples the legitimacy of the Bible as an ethical foundation for the modern world. Al-Shidyaq's rhetorical comparisons position a humanist commitment as the basis on which to judge political actions. Those women, children and men whose integrity was violated by lascivious old men in the course of war, challenge the biblical as well as the church's sanction on violence. Having rendered the Bible into a literary anthology of varying narrative quality in *Mumahakat*, his critique in *al-Saq* is directed against the institutional deployment of the Bible to sanction murder, rape and the abandonment of political and ethical responsibility.

Al-Shidyaq never forgave the church for the event that would lead him to a life in exile for sanctioning the murder of his older brother As'ad. *Al-Saq* is his revenge; here is literature grinding and digesting scripture. From its opening pages, *al-Saq* frames itself as a dismantling of this hypocrisy. The first volume is especially dedicated to attacking the clergy and their hypocritical approach to power. In the opening chapter of the very first section, as the author imagines who his critics might be, we encounter a paragraph full of different men of the church all of them 'clamoring and havering, mooing and snorting, raging and roaring, shouting and shrieking fuming and venting, ventilating, and hyperventilating, yelling and gasping, praying and spittle-spraying'[37] about this book that they shall attack because it is about 'beauty and beautiful women'.[38] They will fault it as obscene even though all they speak about are

> things quivering, things rounded, things tightened, things huge . . . the vulva mighty, the vulva long of clitoris, the buttocks, the vulva's inner chamber and space, the wide wet one and the bulgy one . . . the women's sexual parts in general, the bulge, the sprayer, the fleshy vagina, [which

Humphrey Davies translates as] the bizarrely spelled, the shrunken, the gripper, the nock.[39]

On and on he goes until he enumerates ninety-nine attributes of the vagina in Arabic, before he moves on to a shorter list of penis synonyms, performing subversion by overkill, drowning the hypocritical discourse of those he repeatedly accused of *rakaka*, and being 'lame of speech' with his obsessive mastery of the Arabic lexicon and its excess synonyms.

As the narrative meanders along its crooked path, Book One dedicates entire chapters for the subversion of the local church of his youth, to end the book in grief over his brother, As'ad, the first Arab convert to Protestantism, who died in incarceration in the cellar of the Maronite patriarchy in Qannubin, where he was forced 'to taste every form of humiliation, degradation, misery and distress ... [because] he was at odds with you over matters that call for neither punishment nor reproach'.[40] This incident forced the author to flee with the help of the American and British missionaries to Egypt, in his own words 'the Fariyaq has now escaped your *lands*, and slipped through your *hands*. He's blown a raspberry in all your *faces*, and at your threats his pulse no longer *races*'.[41] His triumph is *al-Saq* and its purpose, as he announces in the beginning of Book Two, is the inverse of the myth of Sisyphus. Unlike the Greek hero's absurd toil, al-Shidyaq pronounces his book as 'a boulder of [precious] material [rolled] down from the topmost peaks of my thoughts to the lowest bottom of men's hearts'. The purpose of this boulder-rolling-text is that at its speed, its author will only learn that 'all that passes before him is beyond his comprehension and moves too fast for his discernment'.[42]

Apprehending the church and its objects at a slower speed is only attempted to 'test the reader's endurance',[43] for there is no nourishment to be obtained from the church and its agents and objects besides a bread so dry that,

[A]fter they have baked it in thin layers, they expose it to the sun for several days in rows until it dries and gets so hard that if one were to take a loaf in each hand and strike them against each other, the din would panic all the rats in the monastery.

As places of Christian reflection and scholastic dedication to the divine, the monasteries that we encounter in the text are intellectually bereft, their academic life even more impoverished than the meagre portions of lentil soup that they serve daily.[44]

The Christian clergy are so ignorant that they have never heard of the most basic of reference books, *al-Qamus al-Muhit* by Majd al-Din Muhammad bin Ya'qub al-Fayruzabadi's (1328–1414).[45] This had been by far the most popular lexicon since its publication in the fourteenth century, and was assumed to be a mainstay of any institution's library.[46] So powerful was its status that its title became synonymous with *dictionary*. It thus becomes hilarious when the monk he meets in a wayside monastery in Mount Lebanon one night mistakenly hears him ask for *jamus*, buffalo, while the other monk hears *kabus*, nightmare, even though both of them are 'zealous in religion' and supposedly well-read in the scripture and other basic texts.[47] Their illiteracy and punishing corporal rituals make their company 'harder on the sleeper than a nightmare'.[48]

Figure 5.1 *Al-Jawa'ib*, first year of publication. Source: Shirin Abou Shaqra.

With food as a metaphor for intellectual nourishment, al-Shidyaq allo-
cates the nocturnal hours for its production. Temporally, al-Shidyaq takes
insomniac recourse against any need to revise the literary histories being
published in the *nahda*, by al-Bustani, al-Tahtawi and others. Instead, he
carves out his turf, choosing not literary history, but literary composition.
This desire to compose encouraged him to focus on literary genre. He
writes *al-Saq* as a catalogue of various genres and enacts a spatial rupture
(for genre is a spatial category vs periodisation, a temporal category) that
distinguishes his work from the selection of canonical books that he keeps.

With his Bible version published two years after *al-Saq*, al-Shidyaq
deliberately taunted the sedate demeanour of a Bible translator. The Bible,
as *al-Saq* polemically advanced, was no longer capable of offering solutions to the conundrums of modern life. As a Bible translator, al-Shidyaq
was an alienated labourer. To drive the point home with Karl Marx, the
Bible was external to him, it did not

> belong to his essential being, that in his work he does not affirm himself
> but denies himself, does not feel content but unhappy, does not develop
> freely his physical and mental energy but mortifies his body and ruins
> his mind. The worker feels therefore outside his work, and in his work
> he feels outside himself.[49]

From then on, al-Shidyaq developed a disdain for translation as a pale
imitation of original composition and wrote against its overdetermined
position in Arab *nahda* culture.

The paradox is that he continued to translate as part of his daily work
as a journalist and man of letters until the end of his days. His newspaper
al-Jawa'ib (the Circulars) even carried on its masthead for the first three
years of its life that it 'was published weekly and is translated from Turkish
and Frankish languages'. Yet, he rejected the role translation played in
increasing 'inequality between the Ottomans and Europeans and restricting
the ability of the Ottoman government to act on the international political
arena'. Translation, as he wrote in a short article in *al-Jawa'ib*, did not
alleviate 'the suffering of the residents of Istanbul, and does not lighten
the load of effort, tiredness and costs on anyone'.[50] Rather it enabled the
nonreciprocal penetration of European ideas into the world of Arabs.

Devaluing Translation

In a lengthy reflective essay entitled 'Fi Usul al-Siyasah wa Ghayriha' (On the Principle of Politics and Other Things), about the need for a change in political structures in the Ottoman domains, he demanded new conceptions of politics that were not dependent on translation. In this article, he clearly argued against the over-valuation of translation in the process of civilising society. He wrote,

> He who presumes that the path towards civilisation (*tamaddun*) comes by learning foreign languages like French, is greatly misguided. Learning those languages is the greatest deterrent to learning crafts (*sana'i'*). Such a man turns away from doing something with his own hands, for he believes that crafts are beneath him, and it is more appropriate for him to be a translator.[51]

For al-Shidyaq, translation was the kind of alienated labour that interfered with learning, especially because it was becoming more widespread than local creations of original texts. Al-Shidyaq was addressing what he perceived to be an ailing political structure incapable of addressing the needs of all its citizens. He dismissed translation for increasing the inequality between the Ottoman ruling class and the Europeans and restricting the ability of the Ottoman government to act on the international political arena. Therefore, new political thought was needed which would transform the internal relations within Ottoman society by finding a new political language that was not simply translated from the West:

> All European countries realised that adjustment in politics is what brings glory to the kingdom. And here we must search in this word, adjustment (*ta'dil*), which contains the most difficult concepts of civilisation (*tamaddun*). If we think of *tamaddun* in terms of the abundance of goods, crafts and the expansion of trade, then we have no disagreement. However, once we come to adjustment of politics (*ta'dil al-siyasah*), reaching our objectives becomes difficult, especially because some strong states can attack and humiliate weak states, and perhaps even occupy a part of land.[52]

With the threat of colonialism so clearly manifest in his diagnosis, the need for churning local political adjustment was urgent. *Ta'dil* shares its root with the Arabic concept of justice, *'adl*, which I have here translated as adjustment. It suggests a particular conception of politics that proposes in the text a non-synchronous translation of the concept of democracy. By choosing not to borrow the term into Arabic, as al-Tahtawi did before him,[53] al-Shidyaq sought to protect the right for the local elite to generate knowledge products and cultural capital.[54] *Dimuqratiyya* had become the standard term, and embodies how translation, in his age, was more like a free trade agreement that guaranteed the Western access to mobility without reciprocation.[55] Al-Shidyaq was against such unequal trade relations, and blamed the scholars in his homeland for wasting their time in trivial pursuits. Unlike Europeans, whose superior scientific capabilities were realised in many inventions, Eastern scholars found it 'more beneficial [to find] twenty possibilities for the declension of compound adjectives'.[56] The solution to this as he imagined it lay in improving the people's education and access to the tools of making knowledge.

In a literary world economy, *adab* was akin to local goods, emanating from local conditions and produced through local craftsmanship. If it were to translate into function, then it shall manifest in material transformations to society. Writing about the fame of the Phoenicians and their reputation for making glass, al-Shidyaq chided the Beiruti intellectuals congregated around the Syrian Scientific Society, headed by Butrus al-Bustani, for advocating a 'knowledge without labour, which is like a tree without fruit'. Writing his article in *al-Jawa'ib*, seven years after Ernest Renan's famous expedition to the Levant in search of Phoenician ruins, al-Shidyaq criticised this surge of interest displayed among his countrymen.[57] He saw in their translative efforts of French interest in bygone ancestors an opportunity to wax lyrical about a glory that is forgotten and erased from living memory. Rather, as he argued, a nutritious relationship with the French would be that the local scholars 'correspond with scientific societies in Paris and London requesting assistance . . . to even send an emissary on their behalf to these cities to expand their horizon'.[58] Thus his attack on translation did not amount to a wholesale dismissal, but was subjugated to local needs and relevance to one's context.

Overcoming the anxieties of alienation, al-Shidyaq exploits its insomniac consequences to arrange feasting séances with the canon and the digestion of its nutrients in a new literary dish. Replacing stupor and awakening with insomnia, al-Shidyaq forged a temporal space for critique and cultivated *adab* as discourteous, functioning to unhinge the foundations that allow institutions to deploy intellectual, economic and political capital to disenfranchise people. His understanding of the concept was a radical alternative to al-Bustani's civilising take on *adab*. Instead, through his carnal and spiritual techniques, al-Shidyaq anchored literature in somatic acts of reading, as concrete as they are different from the metaphoric cultivation of *adab* for the sake of imagining communities.

Notes

1. I acquired the xeroxed manuscript version based on the version that used to be in Baghdad's Waqf Library. The manuscript is not in his handwriting and is clearly a copy by an unnamed scribe. In this copy the lexeme Issa is used and not Yasu', for the name of Jesus. I have written about this version in an encyclopaedia entry, 'Mumahakat al-ta'wil fi munaqadat al-Injil', in *Encyclopedia of Christian–Muslim Relations 1500–1900*. General ed. David Thomas (Leiden: Brill, 2022), http://dx.doi.org/10.1163/2451-9537_cmrii_COM_31295. Ahmad Faris Shidyaq, *Mumahakat al-Ta'wil fi munaqadat al-Injil* (Amman: Dar Wa'il lil-nashr, 1851).
2. Apter, *Against World Literature*.
3. Al-Shidyaq, *Leg over Leg*, vol. 2, 9.
4. Kermode, *The Genesis of Secrecy: On the Interpretation of Narrative* (Cambridge, MA: Harvard University Press, 1979), 9.
5. Ahmad Faris al-Shidyaq, *Sirr al-layal fi al-qalb wal-'ibdal: Al-muqaddimah wa mukhtarat* (Beirut: Dar al-Gharb al-'Islami, 1868), 130.
6. Ibid., 132.
7. Ibid., 132.
8. Ibid., 142.
9. 'Aḥmad Beydoun, *Kalamun: Min mufradat al-lughah 'ila murakkabat al-thaqafah* (Beirut: Dar al-Jadid, 1997), 60–1.
10. Susan Sontag, *Against Interpretation and Other Essays* (New York: Picador, 1966), 21.

11. Tarif Khalidi, *The Qur'an: A New Translation* (London: Penguin Classics, 2008).

12. Waltaffat al-saq scrap, undated, Eli Smith Arabic Papers, ABC 50, Houghton Library, Harvard University Press, Cambridge, USA.

13. Up to here, the scrap is verbatim from the Qur'an. I use Khalidi's translation for this part. See Tarif Khalidi, *The Qur'an*.

14. 'Waltaffat al-saq scrap'.

15. Aḥmad Faris al-Shidyaq, *Leg over Leg*, vol. 4, 426.

16. Aḥmad Faris al-Shidyaq, *Leg over Leg*, vol. 1, 111.

17. Ibid., 113.

18. Ibid., 115.

19. Ahmad Faris al-Shidyaq, *Leg over Leg*, vol. 3, 178.

20. فإن يكن المتقدمون قد اشتغلوا بهذه اللغة الشريفة، فإني قد عشقتها عشقا، وكلفت بها حقا، حتى صرت لها رقا، فأزهرت لها ذبالي وسهرت فيها الليالي؛ معملا فيها النظر، باحثا عما خفي واستتر، وخفا وجهر؛ فلم يشغلني عنها هم، ولم يصدقني أرب خص أو عم؛ فكانت أنسي عند الوحشة، وسلواني عند الحزن؛ وصفوي عند الكدر، وسروري عند الشجن al-Shidyaq, *Sirr al-Layal*, 112.

21. Allan, *In the Shadow of World Literature*.

22. Al-Shidyaq finished working on the translation in 1850, yet with the death of Samuel Lee, his supervisor and editor in 1852, the publication of the Bible was delayed. The work was finally published in 1857 in London by the British Society for the Promotion of Christian Knowledge.

23. For his biography. Mohammad Hadi al-Matwi, *Ahmad Faris al-Shidyaq (1801–1887): Hayatuhu wa atharuhu fi al-nahda al-'arabiyyah al-haditha*, vol. 2 (Beirut: Dar al-Gharb al-Islami, 1989), 2.

24. This text remained in manuscript form until it was printed in 2003. Al-Shidyaq, *Mumahakat al-ta'wil fi munaqadat al-injil*.

25. Nadia Al-Bagdadi, 'The Cultural Function of Fiction: From the Bible to Libertine Literature. Historical Criticism and Social Critique in Aḥmad Fāris al-Šidyāq', *Arabica* 46, no. 3 (1999): 375–401, https://doi.org/10.2307/4057546.

26. Nadia Al-Bagdadi, 'Print, Script, and the Limits of Free-Thinking in Arabic Letters of the 19th Century: The Case of Al-Shidyaq', *Al-Abhath* 48–9 (January 2000): 99–122.

27. Ahmad Faris al-Shidyaq, 'Fi al-khayal wat-takhayyul (On Imagination and Imagining)', in *Kanz al-ragha'ib fi muntakhabat al-Jawa'ib*, ed. Salim Faris al-Shidyaq (unknown,1881) 10–13, AUB Special Collections, 12.

28. In al-Khoury's catalogue, one notices that a sizable number of biblical quotations in Arabic texts come from the gospel of Matthew. See Boulos al-Khoury, *Al-Kitab al-muqaddas fi nususih al-'arabiyyah al-qadimah* (Jounieh: Al-Maktabah al-bulisiyyah, 2012).

29. Al-Shidyaq, *Mumahakat al-ta'wil fi munaqdat al-injil*, 14–21.

30. When biblical stories are no longer material for interpretation, the Bible itself becomes a book of legends, for its stories and moral authority are at such historical remove that interpretation becomes necessary for the vitality of the text's claims to truth.

31. Al-Matwi, *Ahmad Faris al-Shidyaq*, 215.

32. Al-Shidyaq, *Al-Wasitah ila ma'rifat 'ahwal Malta wa kashf al-mukhabba' 'an funun Urubba*.

33. Roper, 'Ahmad Faris Al-Shidyāq and the Libraries of Europe and the Ottoman Empire', 234.

34. Ahmad Faris al-Shidyaq, *Leg over Leg*, vol. 4, 409. See also his description of how he almost lost the opportunity to correct the proofs of *Saq* in the same volume, 408.

35. Traboulsi, *A History of Modern Lebanon*; Ussama Makdisi, *The Culture of Sectarianism: Community, History, and Violence in Nineteenth-Century Ottoman Lebanon* (Oakland: California Digital Library, 2003).

36. Al-Shidyaq, *Leg over Leg*, vol. 1, 289.

37. Ibid., 39.

38. Ibid.

39. Ibid., 41–52.

40. Ibid., 297.

41. Ibid.

42. Al-Shidyaq, *Leg over Leg*, vol. 2, 9–11.

43. Al-Shidyaq, *Leg over Leg*, vol. 1, 175.

44. Ibid., 178.

45. Ibid., 178–9.

46. Strotmann, *Majd Al-Dīn al-Fīrūzābādī*.

47. Al-Shidyaq, *Leg over Leg*, vol. 1, 179.

48. Al-Shidyaq, *Leg over Leg*, vol. 2, 181.

49. Karl Marx, *Economic and Philosophical Manuscripts of 1844*, trans Martin Milligan (New York: Prometheus Books,) 74.

50. Ahmad Faris al-Shidyaq, 'Satan'aqid jam'iyyah 'ilmiyya fi majlis al-ma'arif al-'umumiyya lil-Tarjama', *Al-Jawa'ib*, 9 July 1869.

51. Ahmad Faris al-Shidyaq, 'Fi Usul al-Siyasah w Ghayruha', in *Ahmad Faris Al-Shidyaq*, ed. Fawwaz Traboulsi and Aziz Azme (London: Riad el-Rayyes Books, 1995), 262–84, 270.

52. Ibid., 274–5.

53. I thank Peter Hill for sharing with me his notes on al-Tahtawi's concept of democracy.

54. Rana Issa, 'Al-Ta'dil 'Ind al-Shidyaq: Al-Siyasah w Afkaruha fi Zaman al-Isti'mar', *Al-Jumhuriya*, 2016, http://aljumhuriya.net/34672.

55. See for example the stipulations of the *Balta Liman* trade agreement of 1838, where taxes on British goods imported to the Ottoman Empire were noticeably reduced while Ottoman products to Britain were levied as before, without any change. In this way, British products gained competitive advantage over Ottoman craftsmanship which undermined local production. See Akram Khater, *Sources in the History of the Modern Middle East*, 2nd ed. (Boston: Wadsworth, 2011), 48–9; Geyikdagi, *Foreign Investment in the Ottoman Empire*.

56. Quoted in Rasheed El-Enany, *Arab Representations of the Occident: East West Encounters in Arabic Fiction* (London: Routledge, 2006), 22.

57. Ernest Renan, *Mission de Phénicie* (Paris: Impr. impériale, 1864).

58. Ahmad Faris al-Shidyaq, 'Yurwa fi al-Tawarikh al-Qadima', *Al-Jawa'ib*, 5 May 1868.

Conclusion: In the Beginning was Translation

I remember the days of old;
I meditate on all that you have done;
I ponder the work of your hands.
Psalm 143:5

When the Bible began to proliferate in vernacular translations around the world of ancient antiquity, it was not language that the churches cared for, but the capacity of the church and its adherents to interpret the Bible within accepted creeds. Nevertheless, biblical translation has been at the root of many of the schisms that would befall the ancient, as well as the modern churches, and that ultimately caused the creation of various sects within Christianity. Until the nineteenth century, the place of translation in the history of Christian churches has been an internal matter, of relevance only to the Christian nation. With the advent of nineteenth-century colonial rule, this history gained importance, particularly because European colonialism provided opportunities for Protestant and Catholic missionaries to spread newly-translated vernacular Bibles around the world. These Bibles, as I have shown through studying the Arabic case, rose to prominence as key modern texts that were part of a sweeping moment of language synchronisation around the world, constructing kinship ties with languages that previously had little to do with one another.

With the American ability to produce cheap Bible editions, translations became available on the book market and had an impact beyond the ready audience of local Christians who were the immediate target buyers for these objects. This impact has led to a dominant narrative that the Bible modernised Arabic language and literature and caused its revitalisation and its *nahda*. I have argued in this book for the necessity of more nuance, if we are to better understand what the concept of 'modernity' entailed when applied to Arabic and to Bibles. I have instead claimed that the standardisation that Arabic underwent in the modern Arabic Bibles departed in style and glossary from the tradition of Biblia Arabica that includes hundreds of translations of the Bible into Arabic. This departure led to a concomitant change in the conceptualisation of grammar and lexicon, how we conceive of these as sciences that can be taught to children and adults. I also argued that these are sciences that exert much political force in enabling certain master narratives to permeate the structure of language and how it is taught. Their discursive force reflects a historical reality of heightened sectarian sentiment, and of local groups vying for control over public discourse and its arenas. The question of sectarianism that became foregrounded in the nineteenth century is clearly reflected in how the different translations distinguished themselves from one another. Despite ongoing debates about how best to translate the Bible, I have argued that if by 'modernising language' we mean modernising the writing style, then the Bible had the adverse impact – it took recourse to a style that was considered classical, and had been morphologically stable for more than a millennium. Rather than promoting dialectical writing in Arabic, and choosing to continue with centuries of colloquial writing, the new Bible and its local translators obliterated any memory that such a style had been historically prevalent.

Rather than writing style, the innovation came at the level of concepts. In the Smith Bustani Van Dyck version, lexemes that are key to a Christian worldview were chosen based on their absence from the Qur'an. The Jesuits distinguished their Bible by suggesting a difference between Protestant interpretations of the Bible and their own translation of scripture, also at the level of the concept. With the Shidyaq Lee version, one encounters an alternative possibility. This Bible deployed a glossary of terms that are shared with the Qur'an, a selection that reflects al-Shidyaq's notorious irreverence towards dominant ideologies like sectarianism and evangelism. This choice was one of the reasons his Bible never gained traction. By contrast, the successful Bible versions invented a Christian glossary of theological terms, an invention that mediated the emergence of Christian identity as a political and national construct under the negligent governance policies of the Ottomans vis-à-vis religious minorities since the seventeenth century.

In this book, I chose a mode of storytelling that is biographical. I have written a narrative that follows the life cycle of the Bible's inception, production and proliferation. This mode has allowed me to reconcile stories that are otherwise kept separate, and to reveal entanglements that are not always explored in tandem. Writing about the missionaries in the first two chapters is a very different experience and mindset from delving into the complex textual worlds of al-Bustani and al-Shidyaq in the last two chapters. The Bible's life cycle allowed me to reorient the gaze back to the early beginnings of those two complex Syro-Lebanese thinkers, lexicographers, journalists and translators. Whereas the missionaries were a powerful group that owned the means of production for a new way of making and marketing books, as well as thinking about Arabic language and literature, these local authors seized the opportunities provided to them to cultivate a new vision of Arabic and of the societies that speak it.

These local scholars attached much importance to language, an interest that was staged as a response and intervention in modernity. They struggled to achieve the most *fasih* of Arabic expressions; except that they interpreted this *fasaha* in ways that mediated their own political and ideological visions. For Ahmad Faris al-Shidyaq, language was a tool of expression that was infinitely more than the sum of its parts, and for him *fusha* kept the gates locked in the face of those he considered pretenders to writing. Butrus al-Bustani by contrast, represented minority expression as the necessary first step to secularise and invent a nation. For him mastering *fusha* enacted a transference of the symbols of rule, a *translatio studii* that signals for the majority the rising star of Christian influence. The missionary foreigners were uninterested in those larger ideological questions about Arabic. What they cared for was the production of a vehicular Bible that would have an audience that they estimated at forty million heathens. As they commoditised the Bible, the American missionaries sought in *fusha* a capacity to travel beyond the narrow confines of the Levant and its peculiar dialect to everywhere Arabic was spoken back then, all the way from Calcutta to Morocco.

By using the *fusha* standard in the *nahda* Bible translations, the local translators began to question the precepts of what constitutes good Arabic, and how one can teach it, as well as write in it. For the first time in Arabic, Christian authors produced discourses about Arabic language and literature, covering many of its structural disciplines such as lexicography, grammar or history. They wrote for general audiences and expected Muslims to pay attention to them and to respect their opinions about the language. This is the point in the story where Christian identity becomes less stable, at the point where it bifurcates into the two distinct legacies of al-Bustani and al-Shidyaq, foundational figures that Lebanese literature is proud to inherit. Whereas al-Bustani promoted a Christian narrative in his most important literary works, al-Shidyaq bracketed the Christian narrative in favour of an audacious literary license. On one end of the spectrum presided al-Bustani, who sought to turn the study of Arabic language and literature into a vehicle for imagining a new nation, where Christians would be admitted into the echelons of the elite, not only in scholarly circles, but also in political and economic spheres. In radical opposition we find al-Shidyaq, whose solitary example in the *nahda* reveals that the master narratives of this epoch, with its enthrallment with Europe and its civilisation, and its strong nationalist desires, were not the only Arabic proposals for modernity. Unlike al-Bustani, al-Shidyaq laboured to preserve the space for critique and became its progenitor for future generations of Arabic writers. Amongst the inheritors of the legacy, we can include writers as diverse as Farah Antun and Gibran Khalil Gibran, Marun Abbud, Hoda Barakat and Elias Khoury, and film makers, artists and curators like Shirin Abou Chakra, Emily Jacir and Rasha Salti. However on a systemic level, it was al-Bustani's project that prevailed in the dominant discourses about modernity, just as his Bible work would triumph over al-Shidyaq's, and his dictionary became more famous than the abstruse style that we encounter in al-Shidyaq's linguistic treatises. As for the missionaries, they became a fixture of the Beiruti landscape, founding a university, several schools and hospitals. Nevertheless their connection to the region remains contentious: viewed with suspicion for their links with imperialism as well as welcomed for the salubrious effects they brought into being in the history of modern culture and society in the Levant. However, it did not take long for those missionaries to abandon Arabic as their vehicular language. As Shafik Jeha and Marwa Elshakry have shown, it was the Lewis Affair of 1882 that ushered in a new era of language politics, which eventually succeeded in weakening the links between Arabic and the production of academic knowledge.[1]

The Bible did not so much impact the Arabic language. Rather, its lasting influence came from its translators. In this book I have explored more thoroughly their arguments about what a future for the Arabic language might be. I have sought to recollect the beginnings of the careers of those Syrian men from Christian backgrounds who shaped the *nahda*, attending to the Bible as their first professional endeavour. In so doing, I have pondered how the Bible became the gateway for intellectual labour in Arab modernity and how it was used by these local scholars to advance a career that only tangentially had anything to do with the evangelists and their mission, even if at times the local scholars wanted nothing more than to become on par with Europe.

Note

1. Shafiq Jeha, *Darwin and the Crisis of 1882 in the Medical Department*; Marwa Elshakry, *Reading Darwin in Arabic, 1860–1950*.

Bibliography

Bibles

Biblia Sacra Arabica Sacræ Congregationis de Propaganda Fide jessu edita ad usum ecclesiarum orientalium. Rome: 1671.

The Smith Bustani Van Dyck Bible. Beirut: Syrian Mission Press, 1860, 1865.

The Shidyaq Lee Bible. London: William Watts, 1857.

The Jesuit Bible. Beirut: The Jesuit Press, 1871–7.

The King James Bible.

The International Bible Version.

Accordance Bible Corpus Software.

Le Nouveua Testament Syriaque: La Peshitta: Interlinéaire Syriaque Arabe, edited by Paul Feghali. (Antelias: Centre d'Études et de Recherches Orientales, 2010).

Archival Sources

Bible Society Archives, University of Cambridge, UK.

Eli Smith Personal Papers, ABC 50–60. Houghton Library, Harvard University, Cambridge, USA.

Society for the Propagation of Christian Knowledge Archive. Bodleian Library, University of Oxford, UK.

Syria Mission Archive and Special Collection. Near East School of Theology, Beirut, Lebanon.

American University of Beirut Special Collection.

Bibliothèque Orientale Rare Books Collection.

Syria Mission Records. Presbyterian Historical Society, Philadelphia, USA.

The Private papers of Ahmad Faris al-Shidyaq, courtesy of Fawwaz Traboulsi and Hala Bazri.

Works Cited

'Mediterranean: Malta', *The Missionary Herald*, 23 January 1832.

Abu-Manneh, Butrus, 'The Christians between Ottomanism and Syrian Nationalism: The Ideas of Butrus al-Bustani', *International Journal of Middle East Studies* 11, no. 3 (1980): 287–304.

Al-Bagdadi, Nadia, 'The Cultural Function of Fiction: From the Bible to Libertine Literature. Historical Criticism and Social Critique in Aḥmad Fāris al-Šidyāq', *Arabica* 46, no. 3 (1999): 375–401.

Al-Bagdadi, Nadia, 'Print, Script, and the Limits of Free-Thinking in Arabic Letters of the 19th Century: The Case of Al-Shidyaq', *Al-Abhath* 48–9 (January 2000): 99–122.

Al-Bustani, Butrus et al., *Al-Jam'iyyah al-Suriyyah lil 'ulum wal funun* (Beirut: Dar al-hamra', 1848).

Al-Bustani, Butrus et al., 'The Culture of the Arabs Today', trans. Stephen Sheehi, in *The Arab Renaissance: A Bilingual Anthology of the Nahda*, edited by Tarek El-Ariss (New York: The Modern Language Association of America, 2018), pp. 3–19.

Al-Bustani, Butrus et al., *Da'irat Al-Ma'arif* (Beirut: al-Matba'ah al-Adabiyyah, 1887).

Al-Bustani, Butrus et al., *Khutba Fi Adab al-'arab* (Beirut: AUB Archives and Special Collections, 1859).

Al-Bustani, Butrus et al., *Kitab al-tuhfa al-bustaniyyah fi al-asfar al-Kruziyya* (Beirut: Publisher unnamed, 1861).

Al-Bustani, Butrus et al., *Muhit Al-Muhit* (Beirut: Publisher Unknown, 1870).

Al-Hamawi, Yaqut ibn-Abdullah al-Rumi, *Kitab Mu'jam al-Buldan*, edited by Mohammad Ahmad Khalifa Al-Suwaydi, 1226, *alwaraq.net*, http://www.alwaraq.net/Core/waraq/coverpage?bookid=94&option=1.

Al-Khoury, Boulos, *Al-kitab al-muqaddas fi nususih al-'arabiyyah al-qadimah* (Jounieh: Al-Maktaba al-Bulisiyyah, 2012).

Al-Khoury, Yusuf Quzma, *Rajul Sabiq Li 'Asrih: Al-Mu'allim Butrus al-Bustani (1819–1883)* (Beirut: Bisan, 1995).

Allan, Michael, *In the Shadow of World Literature: Sites of Reading in Colonial Egypt* (Princeton: Princeton University Press, 2016).

Al-Ma'any al-Jami', https://www.almaany.com/.

Al-Matwi, Mohammad Hadi, *Ahmad Faris al-Shidyaq (1801–1887): Hayatuhu wa atharuhu fi al-nahda al-'Arabiyyah al-haditha* (Beirut: Dar al-Gharb al-Islami, 1989).

Al-Shidyaq, Ahmad Faris, 'The Travelogues of Ahmad Faris al-Shidyaq', trans. Rana Issa and Suneela Mubayi, *A Public Space* 27 (2019): 36–57.

Al-Shidyaq, Ahmad Faris, 'Fi al-khayal wal-takhayyul', in *Kanz al-ragha'ib fi muntakhabat al-Jawa'ib*, edited by Salim Faris al-Shidyaq (Beirut: 1881. AUB Special Collections, Beirut, Lebanon).

Al-Shidyaq, Ahmad Faris, 'Fi usul al-siyasah wa ghayruha', in *Ahmad Faris Al-Shidyaq*, edited by Traboulsi and Aziz Azme (London: Riad el-Rayyes Books, 1995), pp. 262–84.

Al-Shidyaq, Ahmad Faris, 'Satan'aqid Jam'iyyah 'ilmiyya fi majlis al-ma'arif al-'umumiyya Lil tarjama', in *Al-Jawa'ib*, 9 July 1869.

Al-Shidyaq, Ahmad Faris, 'Yurwa fi al-tawarikh al-qadima', *Al-Jawa'ib*, 5 May 1868.

Al-Shidyaq, Ahmad Faris, *Al-Jasus 'ala l-Qamus* (Qustantiniyah: al-Jawa'ib, 1882).

Al-Shidyaq, Ahmad Faris, *Al-Wasitah Ila Ma'rifat Ahwal Malta Wa Kashf al-Mukhabba' 'an Funun Urubba* (Beirut: Kutub, 1866, 2002).

Al-Shidyaq, Ahmad Faris, *Sirr al-layal fil-qalb wal'ibdal: Al-Muqaddimah wa mukhtarat* (Beirut: Dar al-Gharb al-'Islami, 1868, 2003).

Al-Shidyaq, Ahmad Faris, *Mumahakat al-ta'wil fi munaqadat l-Injil* (Amman: Dar Wa'il li l-nashr, 1851, 2006).

Al-Shidyaq, Ahmad Faris, *Leg over Leg or The Turtle in the Tree: Concerning the Fāriyāq, What Manner of Creature Might He Be*, trans. Humphrey Davies (New York: New York University Press, 2013).

American Bible Society, *Annual Report of the American Bible Society*, vol. 4 (New York: American Bible Society, 1871).

Anderson, Rufus, *History of the Missions of the American Board of Commissioners for Foreign Missions, to the Oriental Churches* (Boston: Congregational Publishing Society, 1872).

Antonius, George, *The Arab Awakening: The Story of the Arab National Movement* (Beirut: Librairie du Liban, 1969).

Appadurai, Arjun, *The Social Life of Things: Commodities in Cultural Perspective* (Cambridge: Cambridge University Press, 1986).

Apter, Emily S., *The Translation Zone: A New Comparative Literature* (Princeton: Princeton University Press, 2006).

Apter, Emily S., 'Taskography: Translation as Genre of Literary Labor', *PMLA* 122, no. 5 (October 2007): 1403–15.

Apter, Emily S., *Against World Literature: On the Politics of Untranslatability* (New York: Verso, 2013).

Asad, Tala, *Formations of the Secular: Christianity, Islam, Modernity* (Stanford: Stanford University Press, 2003).

Auji, Hala, 'The Implications of Media: A Material Reading of Nineteenth-Century Arabic Broadsides', *Visible Language* 53, no. 1 (2019): 20–49.

Auji, Hala, *Printing Arab Modernity: Book Culture and the American Press in Nineteenth Century Beirut* (Leiden: Brill, 2016).

Azmeh, Aziz, *Al-'ilmaniyyah min manzur mukhtalif* (Beirut: Markaz dirasat al-wihdah al-'arabiyyah, 1998).

Ba'labakki, Ramzi, *The Arabic Lexicographical Tradition: From the 2nd/8th to the 12th/18th Century* (Leiden: Brill, 2014).

Balserak, Jon, *Divinity Compromised: A Study of Divine Accommodation in the Thought of John Calvin* (Dordrecht: Springer, 2006).

Benes, Tuska, *In Babel's Shadow: Language, Philology, and the Nation in Nineteenth Century Germany* (Detroit: Wayne State University Press, 2008).

Benjamin, Walter, 'The Task of the Translator: An Introduction to the Translation of Baudelaire's Tableaux Parisiens', in *Illuminations* (London: Pimlico, 1999), pp. 70–82.

Beydoun, Ahmad, *Kalamun: Min mufradat al-lughah 'ila murakkabat al-thaqafah* (Beirut: Dar Al-Jadid, 1997).

Beydoun, Ahmad, *Ma'ani al-Mabani: Fi Ahwal al-Lughah wa A'mal al-Muthaqqafin* (Beirut: Dar Annahar, 2006).

Bhabha, Homi K., *The Location of Culture* (London: Routledge, 1994).

Binay, Sara and Stefan Leder eds., *Translating the Bible into Arabic: Historical, Text-Critical, and Literary Aspects* (Beirut: Ergon Verlag, 2012).

Birdal, Mehmet Sinan, *The Holy Roman Empire and the Ottomans: From Global Imperial Power to Absolutist States* (London: I. B. Tauris, 2014).

Blau, Joshua, 'Are "Judaeo-Arabic" and "Christian Arabic" Misnomers Indeed?', *Jerusalem Studies in Arabic and Islam* 24 (2000): 49–57.

Blau, Joshua, 'The Status and Linguistic Structure of Middle Arabic', *Jerusalem Studies in Arabic and Islam* 23 (1999): 221–7.

Blau, Joshua, *A Grammar of Christian Arabic: Based Mainly on South-Palestinian Texts from the First Millennium* (Louvain: Secretariat du Corpus SCO, 1966).

Blau, Joshua, *Studies in Middle Arabic and Its Judaeo-Arabic Variety* (Jerusalem: Magnes Press, 1988).

Bourdieu, Pierre, *Outline of a Theory of Practice*, trans. Richard Nice (Cambridge: Cambridge University Press, 1977).

Buchanan, Claudius, *Christian Researches in Asia, with Notice of the Translation of the Scriptures into the Oriental Languages* (New York: Largin & Thompson, 1812).

Cachia, Pierre, 'Translations and Adaptations 1834–1914', in *Modern Arabic Literature*, edited by M. M. Badawi (Cambridge: Cambridge University Press, 1992), pp. 23–35.

Calvin, John, 'Preface to Olivétan's New Testament (1534)', https://www.moner gism.com/preface-oliv%C3%A9tans-new-testament.

Calvin, John, *Institutes of the Christian Religion: Translated from the Original Latin and Collated with the Author's Last Edition in French*, trans. John Allen (Philadelphia: Presbyterian Board of Publication, 1813).

Canton, William A., *History of the British and Foreign Bible Society* (London: John Murray, 1910).

Cantwell Smith, Wilfred, 'The Study of Religion and the Study of the Bible', in *Rethinking Scripture: Essays from a Comparative Perspective*, edited by Miriam Levering (New York: State University of New York Press, 1989), pp. 18–28.

Cantwell Smith, Wilfred, *What Is Scripture? A Comparative Approach* (Minneapolis: Fortress Press, 1993).

Carter, Michael G., *Sībawayhi's Principles: Arabic Grammar and Law in Early Islamic Thought* (Atlanta: Lockwood Press, 2016).

Coakley, J. F., 'Homan Hallock, Punchcutter', *Journal of the American Printing History Association* 45.23, no. 1 (January 2003): 18–40.

Cohen, David and J. Cantineau, *Dictionnaire des racines sémitiques ou attestées dans les langues sémitiques* (Paris: Mouton, 1976).

Copperson, M. and S. Somekh, 'Translation', in *Encyclopaedia of Arabic Literature*, edited by Julie Scott Meisami and Paul Starkey (New York: Routledge, 1998).

Damrosch, David, *What Is World Literature?* (Princeton: Princeton University Press, 2003).

Deringil, Selim, *Conversion and Apostasy in the Late Ottoman Empire* (Cambridge: Cambridge University Press, 2012).

Derrida, Jacques, 'What is a "Relevant" Translation', in *The Translation Studies Reader*, edited by Lawrence Venuti (New York: Routledge, 2004), pp. 423–46.

Dickens, James, Sandor Hervey and Ian Higgins, *Thinking Arabic Translation* (London: Routledge, 2016).

Dogan, Mehmet Ali and Heather Sharkey (eds), *American Missionaries and the Middle East: Foundational Encounters* (Salt Lake City: University of Utah Press, 2011).

Dogan, Mehmet Ali, 'American Board of Commissioners for Foreign Missions (ABCF) and "Nominal Christians": Elias Riggs (1810–1901) and American Missionary Activities in the Ottoman Empire', PhD Diss. University of Utah, 2013.

Doss, Madiha and Humphrey Davies, *Al-'amiyyah al-misriyyah al-maktubah: 1401–2019* (Cairo: Al-Hay'ah al-Misriyyah al-'ammah li al-Kitab, 2013).

El-Ariss, Tarek, *The Arab Renaissance: A Bilingual Anthology of the Nahda* (New York: The Modern Language Association of America, 2018).

El-Ariss, Tarek, *Trials of Arab Modernity: Literary Affect and the New Political* (New York: Fordham Press, 2013).

El-Cheikh, Nadia Maria, Bilāl Urfah'lī, and Lina Choueiri (eds), *One Hundred and Fifty* (Beirut: American University of Beirut Press, 2016).

El-Enany, Rasheed, *Arab Representations of the Occident: East West Encounters in Arabic Fiction* (London: Routledge, 2006).

Elshakry, Marwa, *Reading Darwin in Arabic, 1860–1950* (Chicago: University of Chicago Press, 2013).

Elshakry, Marwa, 'The Gospel of Science and American Evangelism in Late Ottoman Beirut', *Past and Present* 196, no. 1 (August 2007): 173–214.

Errington, James Joseph, *Linguistics in a Colonial World: A Story of Language, Meaning, and Power* (Malden: Blackwell, 2008).

Fabian, Johannes, *Language and Colonial Power: The Appropriation of Swahili in the Former Belgian Congo, 1880–1938* (Cambridge: Cambridge University Press, 1986).

Farhat, Jirmanus and Butrus Al-Bustani, *Kitab misbah Al-talib fi bahth al-matalib: mutawwal fi al-sarf w al-nahu wal-qawafi* (Beirut: Publisher unknown, 1854).

Farhat, Jirmanus, *Ahkam al-i'rab fi lughah al-a'rab*, edited by Rochaid de Dahdah (Marseille: Imprimerie Carnaud, 1849).

Féghali, Paul, *Al-Muhit al-jami' fi al-kitab al-muqaddas wal-sharq al-qadim* (Beirut: Pauline Bookstore, 2009).

Feingold, Mordechai, 'Learning Arabic in Early Modern England', in *The Teaching and Learning of Arabic in Early Modern Europe*, edited by

Jan Loop, Alistair Hamilton and Charles Burnett (Leiden: Brill, 2017), pp. 33–55.

Feldtkeller, Andreas and Uta Zeuge-Buberl, *Networks of Knowledge. Epistemic Entanglement initiated by American Protestant Missionary Presence in 19th century Syria* (Stuttgart: Franz Steiner Verlag, 2019).

Fleischer, Heinrich, 'Bistâni's Encyclopedie arabe', *Zeitschrift Der Deutschen Morgenländischen Gesellschaft* 34, no. 3 (1880): 579–82.

Foucault, Michel, 'Governmentality', in *The Foucault Effect: Studies in Governmentality*, edited by Graham Burchell, Corin Gordon and Peter Miller (Chicago: University of Chicago Press, 1991), pp. 87–104.

Frenkel, Yehoshu'a, 'Baybars and the Sacred Geography of Bilād Al-Sham: A Chapter in the Islamization of Syria's Landscape', *Jerusalem Studies in Arabic and Islam* 25 (2001): 153–70.

Genette, Gerard, *Paratexts: Thresholds of Interpretation*, trans Jane E. Lewin (Cambridge: Cambridge University Press, 1997).

Geyikdagi, V Necla, *Foreign Investment in the Ottoman Empire: International Trade and Relations 1854–1914* (London: I. B. Tauris, 2011).

Ghobrial, John-Paul 'The Life and Hard Times of Solomon Negri: An Arabic Teacher in Early Modern Europe', in *The Teaching and Learning of Arabic in Early Modern Europe*, edited by Jan Loop, Alistair Hamilton and Charles Burnett (Leiden: Brill, 2017), pp. 310–31.

Glass, Dagmar, *Malta, Beirut, Leipzig and Beirut Again: Eli Smith, the American Syria Mission and the Spread of Arabic Typography* (Beirut: Orient-Institut der Deutschen Morgenländischen Gesellschaft, 1998).

GlossGA – Glossarium Græco-Arabicum', http://telota.bbaw.de/glossga/. Accessed 1 October 2019.

Graf, Georg, *Die Christiche Arabische Literature bis Frankischen Zeit* (Freiburg: Herder Forlag, 1905).

Grafton, David D., *The Contested Origins of the 1865 Arabic Bible: Contributions to the Nineteenth Century Nahda* (Leiden: Brill, 2016).

Grand'Henry, Jacques, 'Christian Middle Arabic', in *Encyclopaedia of Arabic Language and Linguistics,* edited by Rudolf de Jong and Lutz Edzard (Leiden: Brill Online, 2014).

Griffith, Sidney, 'The Gospel in Arabic: An Inquiry into Its Appearance in the First Abbasid Century', *Oriens Christianus* 69 (1985): 125–67.

Griffith, Sidney, *The Bible in Arabic: The Scriptures of the "People of the Book" in the Language of Islam* (Princeton: Princeton University Press, 2013).

Hafez, Sabry, *The Genesis of Arabic Narrative Discourse: A Study in the Sociology of Modern Arab Literature* (London: Saqi Books, 1993).

Hall, David (ed.), *A History of the Book in America* (Chapel Hill: University of North Carolina Press, 2000–10).

Hall, Isaac, 'The Arabic Bible of Drs. Eli Smith and Cornelius V. A. Van Dyck', *Journal of the American Oriental Society* 11 (1885): 276–86.

Hanna, Nelly, 'Language Registers: What Did They Signify', in *Ottoman Egypt and the Emergence of the Modern World: 1500–1800* (Cairo: American University of Cairo, 2014).

Hanssen Jens and Max Weiss, *Arabic Thought beyond the Liberal Age: Towards an Intellectual History of the Nahda* (Cambridge: Cambridge University Press, 2016).

Hanssen, Jens and Hicham Safieddine trans, and Buṭrus ibn Būlus Bustānī, *The Clarion of Syria: A Patriot's Call against the Civil War of 1860*, edited by Ussama Makdisi (Oakland: University of California Press, 2019).

Hanssen, Jens, *Fin de Siècle Beirut: The Making of an Ottoman Provincial Capital* (Oxford: Clarendon Press, 2005).

Hary, Benjamin and Martin Wein, 'Religiolinguistics: On Jewish-, Christian-, and Muslim-Defined Languages', *International Journal of the Sociology of Language* 220 (March 2013): 85–108.

Haywood, John A., *Arabic Lexicography: Its History, and Its Place in the General History of Lexicography* (Leiden: Brill, 1965).

Henrich, Sarah and James Boyce, 'Martin Luther – Translations of Two Prefaces on Islam: Preface to the Libellus de Ritu et Moribus Turcorum (1530), and Preface to Bibliander's Edition of the Qur'an (1543)', *Word and World* 16, no. 2 (Spring 1996): 250–66.

Heyberger, Bernard, *Les chrétiens du Proche-Orient au temps de la Réforme catholique Syrie, Liban, Palestine, XVIIe–XVIIIe siècles* (Rome: École française de Rome, 1994).

Hill, Peter, 'Early Translations of English Fiction into Arabic: The Pilgrim's Progress and Robinson Crusoe', *Journal of Semitic Studies* LX, no. 1 (2015): 177–212.

Hill, Peter, *Utopia and Civilisation in the Arab Nahda* (Cambridge: Cambridge University Press, 2020).

Hjälm, Miriam L., *Christian Arabic Versions of Daniel: A Comparative Study of Early MSS and Translation Techniques in MSS Sinai Ar. 1 and 2* (Leiden: Brill, 2016).

Hodgson, Marshall G. S., *The Venture of Islam: Conscience and History in a World Civilization* (Chicago: University of Chicago Press, 1974).

Homsi, Hala, 'Translations that Islamicise the Bible and is Being Disseminated Regionally ... and the Lebanese who is on the Lookout', *Lebanese Forces*, accessed 17 Oct 2019. https://www.lebanese-forces. com/2012/05/30/216691/.

Hourani, Albert, *Arabic Thought in the Liberal Age, 1798–1939* (Cambridge: Cambridge University Press, 1984).

Hourani, Albert, 'Al-Bustani's Encyclopedia', *Journal of Islamic Studies* 1 (1990): 111–19.

Hourani, Albert, 'Ottoman Reform and the Politics of Notables', in *The Modern Middle East: A Reader*, edited by Albert Hourani, Philip Khoury and Mary C. Wilson (London: I. B. Tauris, 2009), pp. 83–110.

Howsam, Leslie, *Cheap Bibles: Nineteenth-Century Publishing and the British and Foreign Bible Society* (Cambridge: Cambridge University Press, 1991).

Hussain, Taha, *Mustaqbal al-thaqafa fi Misr* (Cairo: Hindawi, 1938, 2014).

Hutchison, William R., *Errand to the World: American Protestant Thought and Foreign Missions* (Chicago: University of Chicago Press, 1987).

Ibn Jinni, Abi Fath al-Uthman, *Al-Khasa'is*, edited by Mohammad Ali Al-Najjar, 4th ed. (Cairo: Al-Hay'ah al-masriyyah al'amah li al-kitab, 1039, 2018).

Ibn Manzur, Jamal al-Din Muhammad ibn Mukarram, *Lisan al-'arab* (Beirut: Sader, 1290/2010).

Ibn Sina, 'Al-Qanun Fi al-Tibb', edited by Mohammad Ahmad Khalifa Al-Suwaydi (Al-waraq.net, 2003), http://www.alwaraq.net/Core/waraq/ coverpage?bookid=94&option=1.

Ignatius, David, 'The American University of Beirut Deserves Our Help', *The Washington Post*, 11 June 2020, https://www.washingtonpost.com/ opinions/2020/06/10/american-university-beirut-deserves-our-aid/. Accessed 17 March 2021.

Issa, Rana, 'Al-Shidyaq-Lee Version (1857): An Example of a Non-Synchronous Nineteenth-Century Arabic Bible', in *Senses of Scripture, Treasures of Tradition: The Bible in Arabic among Jews, Christians and Muslims*, edited by Miriam L. Hjalm (Leiden: Brill, 2017), pp. 305–26.

Issa, Rana, 'Al-ta'dil 'ind al-Shidyaq: Al-siyasah wa afkaruha fi zaman al-isti'mar', *Al-Jumhuriya*, 2016, http://aljumhuriya.net/34672.

Issa, Rana, 'Genealogies and Kinships: Biblia Arabica and Translation in the Nahda', in *In the Shoes of the Other: Interdisciplinary Essays in Translation Studies from Cairo*, edited by Samia Mehrez (Al Kotob Khan, 2019), 201–10.

Issa, Rana, 'Missionary Philology and the Invention of Bibleland' in *The Jerusalem Code*, edited by Ragnhild Zorgati and Anna Bohlin (Berlin: De Gruyter, 2021), pp. 309–27.

Issa, Rana, 'Mumahakat al-Ta'wil fi Munaqadat al-Injil', in *Encyclopedia of Christian–Muslim Relations 1500–1900*, edited by David Thomas (Leiden: Brill, 2022). http://dx.doi.org/10.1163/2451-9537_cmrii_COM_31295

Issa, Rana (ed.), *Yubil 150 Sana 'ala Al-Tarjama al-Bayrutiyya al-Injiliyya Lil Kitab al-Muqaddas: Ahamiyyatuh al-Tarikhiyya w al-Ijtima'iyya w al-Lahutiyya* (Beirut: Near East School of Theology, 2018).

Jacquemond, Richard, 'Towards an Economy and Poetics of Translation from and Into Arabic', in *Cultural Encounters in Translation from Arabic*, edited by Said Faiq (Clevedon: Multilingual Matters, 2004), pp. 117–27.

Jeffery, Arthur, *The Foreign Vocabulary of the Qur'ān* (Baroda: Oriental Institute, 1938).

Jeha, Shafiq, *Darwin and the Crisis of 1882 in the Medical Department* (in Arabic) (Beirut: American University Press, 1991).

Jeha, Shafiq, *Tarikh al-ta'lim wal-madaris fi Bishmizzin: 1850–1951* (Beirut: Beirut International Book Capital, 2009).

Jessup, H. H., *Fifty-Three Years in Syria* (New York: Fleming H. Revell Co., 1910).

Jinbachian, Manuel, 'Introduction: The Septuagint to the Vernaculars', in *A History of Bible Translation*, edited by Philip A. Noss (Roma: Edizioni di storia e letteratura, 2007), 29–57.

Jordheim, Helge, 'Against Periodization (Koselleck's Theory of Multiple Temporalities)', *History and Theory* 51 (May 2012): 151–71.

Jordheim, Helge, 'Introduction: Multiple Times and the Work of Synchronization', *History and Theory* 53, no. 4 (2014): 498–518.

Jordheim, Helge, 'Synchronizing the World: Synchronism as Historical Practice, Then and Now', *History of the Present* 7 no. 1 (Spring 2017): 59–95.

Jusdanis, Gregory, *The Necessary Nation* (Princeton: Princeton University Press, 2001).

Kachouh, Hikmat, 'The Arabic Versions of the Gospels: A Case Study of John

1.1 and 1.18', in *The Bible in Arab Christianity*, edited by David Thomas (Leiden: Brill, 2007), pp. 9–36.

Kachouh, Hikmat, *The Arabic Versions of the Gospels: The Manuscripts and their Families* (Berlin: De Gruyter, 2012).

Kam Wah Mak, George, *Protestant Bible Translation and Mandarin as the National Language of China* (Leiden: Brill, 2017).

Kassir, Samir, *Beirut*, trans. M. B. DeBevoise (Berkeley: University of California Press, 2010).

Keane, Webb, *Christian Moderns: Freedom and Fetish in the Mission Encounter* (Berkeley: University of California Press, 2007).

Kermode, Frank, *The Genesis of Secrecy: On the Interpretation of Narrative* (Cambridge, MA: Harvard University Press, 1979), 9.

Khalaf, Ghassan, *Lubnan fil-kitab al-muqaddas* (Mansuriyeh: Dar al-Manhal lil Hayat, 1985).

Khalaf, Ghassan, *Adwa' 'ala tarjamat al-Bustani Van Dyck (Al'ahd al-jadid)* (Beirut: Jam'iyat al-kitab almuqaddas, 2009).

Khalidi, Tarif, *The Qur'an: A New Translation* (London: Penguin Classics, 2008).

Khater, Akram (ed.), *Sources in the History of the Modern Middle East* (Boston: Wadsworth, 2011), pp. 48–9.

Kilpatrick, Hilary, 'The Arabic Culture of Christians in Syria in the 16th and 17th Centuries', in *Contacts and Interaction: Proceedings of the 27th Congress of the Union Européenne des Arabisants et Islamisants Helsinki 2014* (Leuven: Peeters, 2017), pp. 221–31.

King, Jonas, 'Remarks on Asaad Shidiak', *Missionary Herald*, March 1827, Hathi Trust.

Kirkhusmo Pharo, Lars, *Concepts of Conversion: The Politics of Missionary Scriptural Translations* (Berlin: De Gruyter, 2017).

Kling, David W., 'The New Divinity and the Origins of the American Board of Commissioners for Foreign Missions', in *North American Foreign Missions, 1810–1914: Theology, Theory, and Policy*, edited by Wilbert R. Shenk (Grand Rapids: William B. Eerdmans, 2004), pp. 11–38.

Konstantinou, Miltiadis, 'Bible Translation and National Identity: the Greek Case', *International Journal for the Study of the Christian Church* 12, no. 2 (August 2012): 176–86.

Koselleck, Reinhart, *Futures Past: On the Semantics of Historical Time* (Cambridge, MA: MIT Press, 1985).

Lane, Edward William, *Arabic-English Lexicon* (Cambridge: The Islamic Texts Society, 1984).

Lehmann, Paul, 'The Reformers' Use of the Bible', *Theology Today* 3, no. 3 (1946–47): 328–44.

Lentin, Jerome, 'Middle Arabic', in *Encyclopaedia of Arabic Language and Linguistics,* edited by Rudolf de Jong and Lutz Edzard (Leiden: Brill Online, 2012).

Luther, Martin, 'An Open Letter on Translating', (15 September 1530), 4. http://www.blackmask.com. Accessed 5 May 2021.

Makdisi, Ussama, *Artillery of Heaven: American Missionaries and the Failed Conversion of the Middle East* (Ithaca: Cornell University Press, 2008).

Makdisi, Ussama, *The Culture of Sectarianism: Community, History, and Violence in Nineteenth-Century Ottoman Lebanon* (Oakland: California Digital Library, 2003).

Marchand, Suzanne, *German Orientalism in the Age of Empire: Religion, Race and Scholarship* (Cambridge: Cambridge University Press, 2009).

Marx, Karl, *Capital*, trans. Samuel Moore and Edward Alvling (London: Wordsworth Classics, 2013).

Marx, Karl, *Economic and Philosophical Manuscripts of 1844*, trans. Martin Milligan (New York: Prometheus Books, 1988).

Mashaqqah, Mikha 'il, 'Kashf al- 'awham 'amman mazzaqathu al-siham', in *Kashf al-mughalatat al-sufastiyyah raddan 'ala aa 'ansharuh hadithan 'ahad khadamat al-brotstantiyah did ba'd al-asfar al-'Ilahiyyah*, edited by Yusuf Van Ham (Beirut: Jesuit Press, 1870).

Masters, Bruce, *Christians and Jews in the Ottoman Arab World: The Roots of Sectarianism* (Cambridge: Cambridge University Press, 2001).

Mauss, Marcel, *The Gift: Expanded Edition*, trans. Jane I. Guyer and Bill Maurer (Chicago: Hau Books, 2016).

McKee, Elsie, 'Praying for the Dead or for the King? Prayers of Intercession in the Roman Catholic and Reformed Traditions', in *International Congress for Calvin Research* (Philadelphia: Westminster Theological Seminary, forthcoming).

McKenzie, Donald F., *Bibliography and the Sociology of Texts* (Cambridge: Cambridge University Press, 1999).

Metzger, Bruce and Bart E. Ehrman, *The Text of the New Testament: Its Transmission, Corruption, and Restoration* (Oxford: Oxford University Press, 1964).

Millet, Olivier, *Calvin et la dynamique de la parole: Étude de rhétorique Réformée* (Paris: Slatkine, 1992).

Mitchell, Timothy, *Colonising Egypt* (Berkeley: University of California Press, 1988).

Moreh, Shmuel, *Studies in Modern Arabic Prose and Poetry* (Leiden: Brill, 1988).

Moretti, Franco, *Atlas of the European Novel, 1800–1900* (London: Verso, 1999).

Mullett, Michael A., *The Catholic Reformation* (London: Routledge, 1999).

Negri, Salomon, 'An Extract of Several Letters Relating to the Great Charity', SPCK Collection Oxford, May 1725, Oxford Bodleian Library Archive, Oxford University, UK, 6.

Nida, Eugene A., *Fascinated by Languages* (Amsterdam: J. Benjamins, 2003).

Olender, Maurice, *The Languages of Paradise: Race, Religion, and Philology in the Nineteenth Century* (Cambridge, MA: Harvard University Press, 1992).

Orne, John, 'The Arabic Press of Beirut, Syria', *Bibliotheca Sacra* 51, no. 202 (1894).

Owen, John, *The History and Origin and First Ten Years of the British and Foreign Bible Society* (London: Tilling and Hughes, 1816).

Patel, Abdulrazzak, *The Arab Nahdah: The Making of the Intellectual and Humanist Movement* (Edinburgh: Edinburgh University Press, 2013).

Philipp, Thomas, 'Bilad Al-Sham in the Modern Period: Integration into the Ottoman Empire and New Relations with Europe', *Arabica* 51, no. 4 (Oct 2004): 401–18.

Pollock, James W., 'Catalogue of Manuscripts of the Library of the near East School of Theology', *The Theological Review* 4, no. 1–2 (1981).

Pollock, Sheldon, 'Future Philology? The Fate of a Soft Science in a Hard Word', *Critical Inquiry* 35 (Summer 2009): 931–61.

Porson, Richard, *Letters to Archedeacon Travis: In Answer to His Defence of the Three Heavenly Witnesses, I John v 7* (London: T. & G. Egerton, 1790).

Powell, Arvil, 'The Legacy of Henry Martyn to the Study of India's Muslims and Islam in the Nineteenth Century', Henry Martyn Centre, Cambridge University, https://www.cccw.cam.ac.uk/wp-content/uploads/2017/07/Powell-Dr-Avril.pdf. Accessed 28 September 2019.

Presbyterian Church in the U.S.A. Board of Foreign Missions and Beirut American Mission Press Syria, 'Illustrated Catalogue and Price List of Publications of the American Mission Press', Beirut, 1896.

Qaddura, Wahid, *Bidayat al-tiba'ah al-'Arabiyyah fi Istambul wa Bilad al-Sham* (Riyadh: Matba'at al-Malik Fahd, 1993).

Ranke, Leopold von, *History of the Reformation in Germany*, trans. Sarah Austin (London: Longman, Green, Brown, and Longmans, 1845).

Rashkow, Ilona N., 'The Renaissance', in *The Blackwell Companion to the Bible and Culture*, edited by John F. A. Sawyer (Oxford: Blackwell Publishing, 2012), pp. 54–68.

Renan, Ernest, *Mission de Phénicie* (Paris: Impr. Impériale, 1864).

Retsö, Jan, 'Arabs and Arabic In the Age of the Prophet', in *The Qur'ān in Context: Historical and Literary Investigations into the Qur'ānic Milieu*, edited by Angelika Neuwirth, Nicolai Sinai and Michael Marx (Leiden: Brill, 2011), pp. 281–92.

Roper, Geoffrey, 'Ahmad Faris al-Shidyaq and the Libraries of Europe and the Ottoman Empire', *Libraries and Culture* 33, no. 3 (Summer 1998): 233–48.

Roper, Geoffrey, 'Arabic Printing in Malta 1825–1845: Its History and Its Place in the Development of Print Culture in the Arab Middle East', PhD Diss. Durham University, 1988.

Rosenthal, Franz, *The Classical Heritage in Islam* (Berkeley: University of California Press, 1975).

Sacks, Jeffrey, *Iterations of Loss: Mutilation and Aesthetic Form, al-Shidyaq to Darwish* (New York: Fordham University Press, 2015).

St Jerome, 'Letter to Pammachius', in *The Translation Studies Reader*, edited by Lawrence Venuti (London: Routledge, 2012), pp. 21–30.

Sajdi, Dana, *The Barber of Damascus: Nouveau Literacy in the Eighteenth-Century Ottoman Levant* (Stanford: Stanford University Press, 2013).

Salibi, Kamal and Yusuf Quzma Khuri (eds), *The Missionary Herald: Reports from Ottoman Syria, 1819–1870*, 5 vols. (Amman: Royal Institute for Inter-Faith Studies, 1995).

Salibi, Kamal, *A House of Many Mansions: The History of Lebanon Reconsidered* (Berkeley: University of California Press, 1988).

Salibi, Kamal, *Al-Mawarinah: Surah tarikhiyyah* (Beirut: Dar Nelson, 2011).

Samir, Khalil Samir, 'Nahu mustalahat masihiyyah arabiyyah mu'asirah muwah-hadah', in *Nahu mustalahat lahutiyyah masihiyyah 'arabiyyah muwahha-dah* (Ghazir: Manshurat Ikriliyyat al-batriyarkiyah al-maruniyyah, 2005), pp. 11–18.

Schodde, George H., 'The Targums', *The Old Testament Student* 8, no. 7 (1889): 262–6.

Scott, David, *Conscripts of Modernity: The Tragedy of Colonial Enlightenment* (Durham, NC: Duke University Press, 2004).

Selim, Samah, *Popular Fiction, Translation and the Nahda in Egypt* (Cham: Springer International Publishing, 2019).

Sharabi, Hisham, *Al-Muthaqqafun al-'arab wa al-Gharb* (Beirut: Dar Nilson, 1970).

Sharkey, Heather, 'Sudanese Arabic Bibles and the Politics of Translation', *The Bible Translator* 62, no. 1 (January 2011): 30–6.

Sharkey, Heather, *A History of Muslims, Christians, and Jews in the Middle East* (Cambridge: Cambridge University Press, 2017).

Sharkey, Heather, *American Evangelical in Egypt: Missionary Encounters in an Age of Empire* (Princeton: Princeton University Press, 2008).

Shea, Nina, 'Bibles That Translate "The Father" as "Allah,"' *Hudson Institute*, 14 February 2012, https://www.hudson.org/research/8737-bibles-that-trans late-the-father-as-allah-.

Sheehi, Stephen, 'Towards a Critical Theory of Al-Naḥḍah: Epistemology, Ideology and Capital', *Journal of Arabic Literature* 43, no. 2–3 (2012): 269–98.

Skarsaune, Oskar, 'From the Reform Councils to the Counter-Reformation—the Council as Interpreter of Scripture', in *Hebrew Bible/Old Testament: The History of Its Interpretation*, edited by Magne Sæbø (Göttingen: Vandenhoeck & Ruprecht, 1996), pp. 319–28.

Smith, Eli and Josiah Conder, and H. G. O. Dwight, *Missionary Researches in Armenia: Including a Journey through Asia Minor, and into Georgia and Persia, with a Visit to the Nestorian and Chaldean Christians of Oormiah and Salmas* (London: G. Wightmann, 1834).

Somekh, Sasson, 'Arabic Bibles in the Modern Age: Linguistic and Stylistic Issues', in *The Professorship of Semitic Languages at Uppsala University 400 Years*, edited by Bo Isaksson, Mats Eskhult, and Gail Ramsay (Uppsala: Uppsala Universitet, 2005), pp. 191–8.

Somekh, Sasson, 'Biblical Echoes in Modern Arabic Literature', *Journal of Arabic Literature* 26, nos. 1/2 (st 1995): 186–200.

Sontag, Susan, *Against Interpretation and Other Essays* (New York: Picador, 1966).

Stanton, Anna Ziajka, *The Worlding of Arabic Literature: Language, Affect, and the Ethics of Translatability* (New York: Fordham University Press, Forthcoming 2023).

Stetkevytch, Jaroslav, *The Zephyrs of Najd: The Poetics of Nostalgia in The Classical Arabic Nasib* (Chicago: University of Chicago Press, 1993).

Stierle, Karlheinz, 'Translatio Studii and Renaissance: From Vertical to Horizontal Translation', in *The Translatability of Cultures: Figurations of the Space Between*, edited by Sanford Budick and Wolfgang Iser (Stanford: Stanford University Press, 1996), pp. 55–67.

Strauss, Johann, 'Langue(s) sacrées et recherche de langue sacrée(s) dans l'Empire ottoman au XiXe siècle', in *Hiéroglossie: Moyen âge latin, monde arabo-persan*, edited by Jean-Noel Robert, (Tibet: Collège de France, 2019), pp. 115–52.

Strotmann, Vivian, *Majd Al-Dīn al-Fīrūzābādī (1329–1415): A Polymath on the Eve of the Early Modern Period* (Leiden: Brill, 2016).

Suleiman, Yasir, 'Arab(Ic) Language Anxiety: Tracing a "Condition,"' *'Arabiyya: Journal of the American Association of Teachers of Arabic* 47 (2014): 57–81.

Suleiman, Yasir, *The Arabic Language and National Identity: A Study in Ideology* (Washington: Georgetown University Press, 2003).

Tageldin, Shaden M., *Disarming Words: Empire and the Seductions of Translation in Egypt* (Berkeley: University of California Press, 2011).

Tamari, Steve, 'Arab National Consciousness in Seventeenth and Eighteenth Century Syria', in *Syria and Bilad Al-Sham under Ottoman Rule*, edited by Peter Sluglett and Stefan Weber (Leiden: Brill, 2010), pp. 309–21.

The Doha Historical Dictionary of the Arabic Language. https://www.dohadic tionary.org/dictionary/%D8%B1%D8%AC%D9%85. Accessed 9 August 2020.

The Missionary Herald, 1839. Vol. 35.

The Missionary Herald, 1847. Vol. 43.

Thomson, William, *The Land and the Book; or, Biblical Illustrations Drawn from the Manners and Customs, the Scenes and Scenery of the Holy Land* (New York: Harper, 1880).

Tibawi, A. L., *American Interests in Syria, 1800–1901: A Study of Educational, Literary and Religious Work* (Oxford: Clarendon, 1966).

Traboulsi, Fawwaz, *A History of Modern Lebanon* (London: Pluto Press, 2012).

Trautmann, Thomas R., *Aryans and British India* (Berkeley: University of California Press, 1997.

Turner, James, *Philology: The Forgotten Origins of the Modern Humanities* (Princeton: Princeton University Press, 2014).

United Bible Societies, 'Key Facts about Bible Access', https://www.unitedbi blesocieties.org/key-facts-bible-access/. Accessed May 20, 2020.

Vagelpohl, Uwe, 'The 'abbasid Translation Movement in Context: Contemporary Voices on Translation', in *Abbasid Studies II*, edited John Nawas (Leuven: Uitgeverij Peeters, 2010).

Van Dyck, Cornelius and Eli Smith, 'Brief Documentary History of the Translations of the Scriptures into the Arabic Language' (Beirut: Syria Mission Press, 1900).

Van Dyck, Cornelius, ''Irtida' al-siham 'ala al-yasu'i Van Ham, 2nd Response', 24 December 1872, Near East School of Theology Special Collections, Beirut, Lebanon.

Van Dyck, Cornelius, ''Irtida' al-siham 'ala al-yasu'i Van Ham, 4th Response', *Al-Nashra Al-Usbu'iyyah*, 7 January 1873, Near East School of Theology Special Collections, Beirut, Lebanon.

Van Dyck, Cornelius, ''Irtida' al-siham 'ala al-yasu'i Van Ham, 6th Response', 7 January 1873, 14.

Van Ham, Yusuf, *Kashf al-mughalatat al-sufastiyyah raddan 'ala aa 'ansharuh hadithan 'ahad khadamat al-brotstantiyah did ba'd al-asfar al-'Ilahiyyah* (Beirut: Jesuit Press, 1870).

Van Ham, Yusuf, *Kashf al-tala'ub wal-tahrif (fi mass ba'd 'ayat al-kitab al-sharif)* (Beirut: Jesuit Press, 1872).

Venuti, Lawrence, *The Translator's Invisibility: A History of Translation* (London: Routledge, 1995).

Versteegh, Kees, 'Religion as a Linguistic Variable in Christian Greek, Latin and Arabic', in *Philologists in the World: A Festschrift in Honour of Gunvor Mejdell*, edited by Rana Issa and Nora Eggen (Oslo: Novus Forlag, 2017), pp. 57–88.

Versteegh, Kees, *The Arabic Language* (Edinburgh: Edinburgh University Press, 1997).

Vollandt, Ronny, 'Some Historiographical Remarks on Medieval and Early-Modern Scholarship of Biblical Versions in Arabic: A Status Quo', *Intellectual History of the Islamicate World* 1 (2013): 25–42.

Vollandt, Ronny, *Arabic Versions of the Pentateuch: A Comparative Study of Jewish, Christian, and Muslim Sources* (Leiden: Brill, 2015).

Von Lüpke, Johannes, 'Luther's Use of Language', in *The Oxford Handbook of Martin Luther's Theology*, edited by Robert Kolb, Irene Dingel and L'Ubomir Batka (Oxford: Oxford University Press, 2014), pp. 143–55.

Walbiner, Carsten-Michael, 'Macarius Ibn Al-Za'im and the Beginnings of an

Orthodox Church Historiography in Bilād al-Shām', in *Le role des historiens orthodoxes dans l'historiographie* (Balamand: Universite de Balamand, 2010), pp. 11–29.

Weber, Max, *Economy and Society: An Outline of Interpretive Sociology* (Berkeley: University of California Press, 1978).

Weber, Max, *The Protestant Ethic and the Spirit of Capitalism*, trans. Talcott Parsons (London: Routledge, 1992).

Werner, Michael and Benedicte Zimmermann, 'Beyond: Comparison: Histoire Croisée and the Challenge of Reflexivity', *History and Theory* 45, no.1 (February 2006): 30–50.

Wild, Stefan, 'Arabic Avant La Lettre Divine Prophetic and Heroic Arabic', in *Approaches to Arabic Linguistics: Presented to Kees Versteegh on the Occasion of His Sixtieth Birthday*, edited by C. H. M. Versteegh, E. Ditters, and H. Motzki (Leiden: Brill, 2007), pp. 189–208.

Willson, Rachel Beckles, *Orientalism and Musical Mission: Palestine and the West* (Cambridge: Cambridge University Press, 2013).

Yucesoy, Hayrettin, 'Translation as Self-Consciousness: Ancient Sciences, Antediluvian Wisdom, and the Abbasid Translation Movement', *Journal of World History* 20, no. 4 (December 2009): 523–57, https://doi.org/10.1353/jwh.0.0084. Accessed 5 November 2020.

Zachs, Fruma, 'Toward a Proto-Nationalist Concept of Syria? Revisiting the American Presbyterian Missionaries in the Nineteenth-Century Levant', *Die Welt Des Islams* 41 no. 2 (2001): 145–73.

Zachs, Fruma, *The Making of a Syrian Identity: Intellectuals and Merchants in Nineteenth Century Beirut, Social, Economic, and Political Studies of the Middle East and Asia* (Leiden: Brill, 2005).

Zammit, Martin, *A Comparative Lexical Study of Qur'ānic Arabic* (Leiden: Brill, 2002).

Zaydan, Jurji, 'Tarjamat Al-Tawrat', *Al-Hilal*, 1893.

Zaydan, Jurji, *Tarikh adab al-lugha al-'arabiyyah* (Cairo: Al-Hindawi, 2012).

Index